USING DIGITAL VIDEO

ARCH C. LUTHER

AP PROFESSIONAL

Boston   San Diego   New York
London   Sydney   Tokyo   Toronto

This book is printed on acid-free paper. ∞

AP PROFESSIONAL
955 Massachusetts Avenue, Cambridge, MA 02139

An Imprint of ACADEMIC PRESS, INC.
A Division of HARCOURT BRACE & COMPANY

United Kingdom Edition published by
ACADEMIC PRESS LIMITED
24–28 Oval Road, London NW1 7DX

Library of Congress Cataloging-in-Publication Data

Luther, Arch C.
    Using digital video / Arch C. Luther
        p.   cm.
    Includes bibliographical references and index.
    ISBN 0-12-460432-3 (pbk. : acid-free paper)
    1. Digital video. I. Title.
QA76.575.L88   1995
778.59--dc20   94-38708
                                                CIP

Printed in the United States of America
94 95 96 97 98 ML 9 8 7 6 5 4 3 2 1

Contents

Preface

Personal computer buyers have become used to the fact that the new computer they just bought likely will be obsolete in six months or at least by then the price will have dropped substantially below what they paid for it. They also realize that new features and capabilities for existing machines will regularly appear through new software. This constant shifting of the ground beneath the feet of PC owners is one reason why personal computers are so exciting and, at the same time, so exasperating.

One recent such movement is the growing mass-market availability of digital motion video for PCs. Now we can see and create television-style video and sound through software on any PC. It has its limitations, but they soon will fade away as the hardware industry catches up with the demands of this new software. Although I used the words "television-style," PC video isn't the same as television because it exists in the environment of the PC *along with everything else the PC could already do.* PC video is a new tool that creates new opportunities for those who embrace it and integrate it effectively into applications.

Unlike television, PC video is so new that the rules for the best ways to use it are not yet fully written. It is different from everything else in the PC, and it is different from other uses of video technology. At the same time, PC video has a price in terms of its required system performance and data storage capabilities. The benefits of using video must be in proportion to the price it exacts. This means that the opportunity is also a challenge.

People who create video applications today are breaking new ground, finding new applications, writing new rules. However, there is already a lot to know about PC video in both technical and nontechnical areas. This book presents that information, for either technical or artistic readers. Its purpose is to give you the background needed so you can effectively move into that elite group who are pioneering PC video, learning where it fits and where it doesn't fit, and writing the guidelines for its use.

Although PC video is being enabled by technological developments, it will not be widely used until it is embraced by the developer community—those people who figure out what computers should be used for and how best to use them. There are developers at many levels, from those who create commercial applications for mass sale to the individuals who create applications for their own use or for use locally in their companies. The thrust of this book is more toward the latter developers than the former. My experience falls in both developer camps, and I also have a lot of technological experience. I have focused this book on the needs of the small developer, who does not care about the technical details except where they are necessary to understand what a product can do. Technical discussions do appear, but believe me, they are things that every PC video user has to know to make sensible decisions about applications. In any case, you do not need a great technical background to read this book.

To help those who are not familiar with the terminology and jargon of the video industry, I have carefully defined every such term the first time I use it. To signify that, I italicize the term at that time. The most important terms are also included in the Glossary at the end of the book. In most cases, the Glossary definition goes a little further than the definition in the text. However, once you see an italicized term, I will expect that you will know what it means when I use it later.

I have always been disturbed by the need to use compound personal pronouns such as he/she to recognize both genders, since the English language doesn't provide a simpler approach. In this book I have adopted an approach that I hope won't disturb anyone. In odd-numbered chapters, the pronouns are male, and in even-numbered chapters they are female. So, if at any point you are upset with my use of personal pronouns, just read on to the next chapter.

The book is organized into 15 chapters, as follows: Chapters 1–4 are introductory and tutorial to acquaint you with the video industry and the technologies. Beginning with Chapter 5 and continuing to Chapter 9, I cover the basic principles of audio and video production and postproduction, which are the processes of acquiring audio and video from original sources. From Chapter 10 up to Chapter 14, I discuss the various techniques and alternatives for creating applications of motion video and audio. Chapter 15 is a look at the future of this industry. That is important because things are changing rapidly and they are likely to move even faster in the future. This chapter will help you keep your feet on the ground as the industry dashes past!

Many hardware and software products are mentioned or described in the book. The purpose of this is to teach how typical products work for specific tasks—it is not to compare products with one another. Video products are changing so rapidly that the book sticks to fundamentals; to keep up to date, you should follow the periodicals mentioned in the Bibliography.

A CD-ROM is included with this book. It contains a large number of data items and software tools for testing and evaluating digital video (and audio) systems. These can be used on Windows or OS/2 PC systems. Instructions for setting up your system to use the CD are given in Appendix C at the back of the book.

The application of motion video and audio on computers has finally come of age. It is now possible to have it on almost any PC, but it is still very much frontier country and the number of new programs being developed is mind boggling. This book will introduce you to all that and help you decide how digital video will become part of your life.

Acknowledgments

Although this book has only one author, it not the work of one person. Many others helped me with input material, discussions, reviews, figures, software packages, and many of the other things that go into a project like this. I'll try to name as many here as possible; if I have left someone out—I'm sorry—it was not intentional. My friends and helpers include Tom Vreeland, Alan Rose, Kayle Luther (my daughter), Wayne Jerves, Les Wilson, Rickey Gold, Jim Wickizer, John Smiley, Barbara Tescher, and especially Helen Larkin (my aunt), who has had to put up with my constant alternation between California and New Jersey.

Thank you all.

1

Introduction

video: electronic reproduction of images

Television is by far the largest and oldest application of video technology, and we often equate video with television. However, the preceding definition embraces many other kinds of video, some of which are covered in this book. Returning to TV, it is a means of mass communication where a centralized source (station) broadcasts video and audio program material to many receivers (viewers). Most TV program material is motion video, where separate images (*frames*) are transmitted often enough that smooth motion is perceived by the viewer. A TV system displays a wide range of colors and provides realistic reproduction of almost any natural scene. Television is a mature technology that has a massive infrastructure in place for both the technology and the programming that supports it.

TV broadcasting uses radio frequency transmission or, in cable TV, receivers are wired directly to the source with cable or optical fiber. A viewer usually can choose from a number of sources—in fact, with cable TV, the number of available sources connected to one cable may reach into the hundreds.

From a viewer's standpoint, each source is called a *channel* and it is accessed through a selector on his TV receiving equipment. However, once a viewer chooses a channel, he can see only whatever that channel is broadcasting at the moment. It is not possible for any viewer to affect the behavior of the video source because TV is a one-to-many *one-way* communication system. The viewer's only means of interacting is to change sources (channels) or to turn off the TV. In spite of being noninteractive, TV has a powerful ability to inform, teach, or entertain.

A subset of the TV business has developed because of the explosive emergence of video recorders (VCR) in the home. An entire industry is devoted to creation, replication, and distribution of pre-recorded TV video on tape for both entertainment and information publishing.

But TV is only one of many possible applications for video technology. For example, video equipment similar to that of TV is often used for surveillance, monitoring, engineering, etc. In most of these cases, each video pickup device (camera) is connected to one or only a few receivers (*monitors*). The purpose is for someone at a remote location to view what is happening at the location of the camera. The camera may be located where it would be impractical for an observer to be physically present or it may be that the output of the camera is recorded for viewing at a later time. Other possibilities are that one viewer can observe several locations or several viewers can observe the same things. Such applications usually depend on motion video capability.

Another large application of video technology is in personal computer (PC) displays. Every PC has a video monitor that dynamically displays the current status and output of the computer. In this case, the video may or may not be motion video. In fact, most computer displays today do not show motion video, but, by the previous definition, they still qualify as video devices. But the video equipment for computer display is totally different from TV equipment—it is digital.

A digital video application that is related to PCs is the video game. These are special-purpose devices designed to provide dynamic video and audio capability at the lowest cost for interactive entertainment use. Because of their low cost, there are more video game machines in use in homes than there are PCs. Another class of video game is designed for use in arcades. Here the need for performance outweighs the need for low cost. Video game machines will not be discussed further in this book.

ANALOG AND DIGITAL

Image reproduction in TV is *analog* (see Figure 1.1). That means the electrical signals for TV are continuously varying: at any time the TV video signal can have minute variations of value as long as the value stays within the available range. This analog nature allows a TV system to reproduce a wide range of colors with very fine gradation or shading wherever needed by the scene in front of the camera. (This will be discussed with much more technical exactness in Chapter 2.) Although the existing systems of TV broadcasting and cable TV work fine, analog systems have many difficulties that limit their performance. These problems are caused by the system introducing small changes into the signals that accumulate as signals are transmitted or processed. The changes may be in the form of small random fluctuations (called *noise*), amplitude changes, or other distortions. However, analog technology was the only thing that existed when

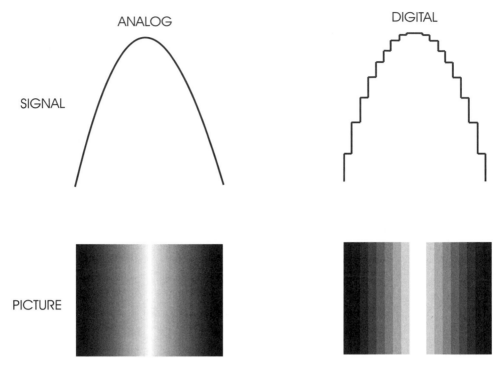

Figure 1.1 Analog and digital signals, shown in electrical form (top) and as a gray-scale image (bottom). (The digital quantizing effect is highly exaggerated.)

TV was originally developed and over the years, the TV industry has found ways to either overcome the analog difficulties or work around the limits they create.

The technology of computers—*digital*—is very different. Properly designed digital systems do not accumulate errors and signals can be processed, stored, or transmitted endlessly without distortions. Digital technology grew up with computers and has been reduced in cost until today it is being applied to many other fields. One of those other fields is video, so today we have digital video technology. It is a competitor with many advantages over analog technology. However, at equal levels of performance, digital video technology is often more expensive— but that is changing. Although the broadcast transmission of TV must remain analog because of the hundreds of millions of receivers in use, digital video technology is now widely used at the source end of TV because of its performance and reliability advantages and because it makes possible many features that are impractical with analog technology. One example of such a feature is the wide use of dynamic transition effects in TV programs, where multiple motion video sources are combined dynamically with sliding, rotating, page turning, or other

Figure 1.2 Some examples of dynamic digital video effects: zoom (top), slide, zoom with rotation, expand (bottom).

effects as shown in Figure 1.2—these are all done digitally. The television industry is even designing a new video broadcast system (HDTV) that will fully exploit digital technology.

WHY DIGITAL VIDEO?

The electrical signals for digital video are *not* continuously varying as in analog technology; rather, they are *quantized*, meaning that only a certain number of signal levels are possible at any time. This is shown highly exaggerated in Figure 1.1. The quantized values are represented as a series of bits, which can have values of only 0 or 1. By using multiple bits to represent each signal value, one may transmit signals having any desired number of levels, so that the quantizing effect shown in Figure 1.1 can be made negligible. The performance advantages of digital technology come because digital systems can be designed to transmit bits exactly, with no loss. The result is that digital video signals are transmitted, stored, or processed repeatedly without any loss of the information contained in the bits. But I am getting ahead of myself—I will discuss this much more in subsequent chapters. The point here is that digital video technology is the wave of the future—not just in computers, but everywhere video technology is used and it will even foster new uses of video that are not practical today.

PERSONAL COMPUTERS

Next to TV, the personal computer is the widest user of video technology. But all video on PCs is digital—that is natural because the PC itself is a digital system. The PC's processor and mass storage system work with video data the same way they handle any other data, so video information can be stored, controlled, or manipulated through software just like everything else in the PC. This offers a degree of capability and flexibility that is impossible in an analog system.

However, most PCs today do not display very realistic digital video. This is because it has been too expensive before now for digital displays to deliver enough colors to reproduce realistic images. The current trend toward super-VGA displays with *high color* or *true color* reproduction is changing all that, and most high-end PCs available today contain the inherent capability to display realistic images and motion video. Because the price–perfomance of PCs continues to improve steadily year-to-year, we can expect that the PC of a few years from now will have even more video capability built-in.

Why Should a PC Have Better Video?

One might say that the blocky graphics and cartoonlike images shown by most PCs are actually good enough for the usual purposes of a PC such as word processing, spreadsheets, or databases. That is true, but it is a shortsighted view that does not see the many new applications for PCs that become possible or the many ways that present applications can be enhanced with better video capabilities. For example, realistic still images are required to display the many photographs contained in an on-line encyclopedia such as the several products that are currently available on CD-ROM. An encyclopedia is just an enhanced database, where data items (records) can include not only text but drawings, photographs, audio, video, or animations. Because each of the data types can be thought of as a medium of communication or storage, such a multitype database is called *multimedia*. Enhanced video capabilities are a necessity for computers to deliver quality multimedia presentations.

Many other CD-ROM products containing images or motion video from historical archives also need better video. Training applications that teach procedures from video sequences need better video. New applications in simulation for training, information, or entertainment purposes need better video. In short, almost all applications that deal with information captured from nature are crying for better video. Up to now, their cries couldn't be answered at a reasonable price, but now that moderately priced good video is available, every PC should have it!

Video Overlay

Hardware has been available for some time to display analog video on a computer screen—this is called *video overlay*. Video applications are created by connecting a computer-controllable videodisc player or a VCR as a video source for the overlay board. This approach is widely used for *computer-based training* (CBT). Although overlay is an easy way to display realistic video on a computer, most of the advantages of digital video technology are lost because the computer cannot store or modify the video—you can play in real time only whatever is recorded on the disc or tape. You also usually require a separate box for the analog source equipment and a separate storage medium. Video overlay is an interim technology that is being replaced by true digital video as rapidly as users can afford to make the change.

In digital video, a board called a video *capture* board is used to convert analog video signals to digital formats, which can be stored on and played from the computer's hard disk. Most video capture boards can also do video overlay, but the use of video overlay as a substitute for digital video is not discussed further in this book.

Digital Motion Video

Digital motion video is created by digitizing video from an analog source such as a video camera or VCR using a video capture board. This is a quick and easy process when you use the proper hardware and software. You play the video source in real time and capture each frame as a digital video image onto the hard disk of your PC. Once you have the video on the hard disk, many tools are available to edit it and integrate it into your applications. However, as you will learn in Chapter 3, digital motion video requires massive amounts of data to display frames fast enough to reproduce the effect of smooth motion. It taxes the capabilities of even the best PCs today and the use of video *compression* to reduce data rates is absolutely mandatory.

But video compression is extremely processor intensive—even the fastest PC processors are brought to their knees by video compression unless you work with "postage-stamp" sizes of video windows. Fortunately, there has been a lot of development of special-purpose *coprocessors* for video compression and decompression. One of these coprocessors is an essential element in a practical PC digital motion video system that will display quarter-screen or larger motion video windows. Today, video coprocessors are available on add-in boards; in the near future they will be built onto motherboards in new PCs, and after that, they will become part of CPU chips. Thus, the cost of video compression will drop dramatically over the next few years. To be ready for that, you should begin working with digital motion video today.

An alternative way to create digital motion video is to use the computer to create the video from scratch. No video source is required—it is called *animation*. Animation has the advantage that it may save on the data required, but it has the disadvantage that it is difficult to create, and it may not be as realistic as capturing real video. Of course, with animation you can create objects and effects that would be impossible to obtain with a camera, so there are tradeoffs.

AUDIO

Audio is an important part of video. As you know from TV, motion video *needs* audio. In fact, if you turn off the audio on your TV, you will find that most of the message and a large part of the effect is lost. Just try watching a news program without audio! If we had to choose between video-only or audio-only to tell a story, we would usually choose audio-only. The video exists to enhance the message that is contained in the audio. Granted, it is a large enhancement, but we should not lose sight of the importance of audio.

Audio, like video, exists in nature as an analog phenomenon, and until very recently, all audio equipment was analog. However, like video and for the same reasons, on a computer we would like audio to be digital. Fortunately, the technology of digital audio is highly developed in the sound recording and musical instrument fields. Today, digital technology has almost completely replaced analog technology, and we have only to duplicate those technologies in the computer.

Digital audio for computers is widely available in the form of add-in sound boards. These cards not only support audio playback, but most also support audio capture from analog sources such as microphones or audiotape. Digital audio also takes a lot of computer data, but usually about one-tenth as much as video.

Another part of the digital audio field, which comes directly from the music equipment industry, is MIDI, an acronym for *musical instrument digital interface*. It was originally developed for communication between different types of musical instruments, such as keyboard and synthesizers. Most computer sound boards contain a MIDI synthesizer chip that allows the computer to directly create electronic music. The advantage of this is that high-quality music can be produced using very little data—as much as 100 times less than digitized real audio. If your application calls for music, you will want to consider using the MIDI capability of your computer.

You can see from the preceding discussion that hardware technologies for digital video and audio on personal computers are becoming highly developed, and a wide range of equipment is available. However, that proliferation creates a significant problem for a new user in choosing what hardware and software to use. The material in this book will help you understand the issues involved in making those choices for yourself.

SKILLS FOR DIGITAL MOTION VIDEO AND AUDIO

The skills needed for creation (called *production*) of digital motion video and audio are similar to those required for video and audio production in other media such as videotape, audiotape, or film. They include:

- Scripting
- Staging
- Camera operation
- Sound operation
- Lighting
- Directing
- Animating
- Editing

In addition, digital video production requires the skill to run the computer tools for digital video, including a special category of tool that I call an *assembly* tool. Assembly tools let you integrate your video into the rest of your work. (Many people in the industry call these tools *authoring* tools, but that is confusing because authoring is much broader than assembly.)

In professional video production, there is often a team of people with one or more person for each of these skill categories. However, I assume that you do not have such resources and that you will want to do it all yourself, or maybe with only one or two helpers. Therefore, you have to be the scriptwriter, the staging person, the camera operator, the sound operator, the lighting person, the animator, the director, the editor, and the computer operator. This book will help you to wear all those hats or manage the people who do.

APPLICATIONS OF PC DIGITAL VIDEO

Digital video on a PC is still new, but it is surprising how many applications have already appeared. Most applications require a means for distribution of digital video data to the end user. As I have already pointed out, digital video involves a lot of data—many megabytes. Therefore, most applications containing digital video are distributed on CD-ROM, which has capacity for 650 MB or more data. That's room for an hour or more of digital video, although most applications contain other kinds of data in addition to video, so their video content is usually less than an hour.

Application developers have to look for the widest markets, which usually means that applications are designed to work with certain minimum hardware capabilities that the developer thinks many users will have. Parameters such as CPU type and speed, RAM size, video capability, and audio capability are specified by most applications. If your system exceeds the minimum, most applications will run better. I'll discuss the minimum specification issue more in the paragraph on standards later in this chapter, but the point here is that current minimum specs do not include any special requirements for motion video hardware. As a result, most present "video" applications provide only small windows of software-only video—1/16th of the screen or less. This "postage-stamp" video can play on the typical system without any special hardware assist, but compared to television, this "video" is a joke.

Some applications provide larger video windows that will play properly on more powerful systems without hardware assist, but they will slow to a crawl on a minimum system. The small video window situation is not satisfactory and the industry is working hard on standardizing hardware and software that can be made broadly available so as to upgrade the "minimum" system. Although the software-only approach to motion video is good for the long term, when all PCs have processors even faster than today's best, the only way we will get good full-screen video on today's PCs is to add hardware for it. The companies who build video adaptor boards are working hard on this and motion video *accelerators* are beginning to appear as features of the newest video adaptors.

Let's look at some applications, grouped into categories.

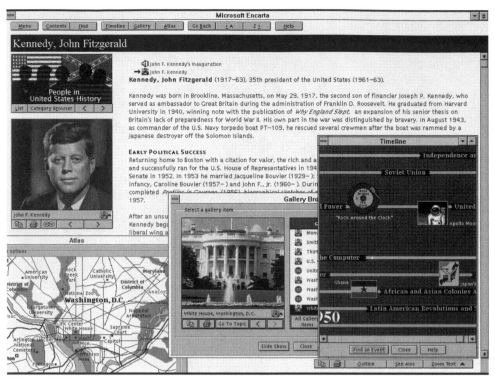

Figure 1.3 Sample screen from the Microsoft Encarta encyclopedia.

Information Delivery

The large data capacity of CD-ROM is a natural for many applications that distribute masses of data—this is called *information delivery*. For example, a residential phone book for the entire United States is available on CD-ROM. That application does not need any video, but it certainly exploits the large data capacity.

An information delivery application that does benefit from video is the electronic encyclopedia. The text content of a typical printed encyclopedia is less than 50 megabytes, so there is plenty of room on a single CD-ROM to include still images, audio, and video. For example, the encyclopedia entry for an important person, say John F. Kennedy (see Figure 1.3), can not only include photographs but also video clips containing segments from his most important speeches. Similarly, entries for historical events, locations, or actions can include stills, audio, motion video, or animations. Several CD-ROM encyclopedias are already on the market.

Other types of information delivery applications are these:

- Health and medicine—several CD-ROM applications allow the user to access different classes of health-related information. For example, one can look up various diseases and learn about their symptoms and treatment or explore a database about pharmaceutical items. Other health applications provide information about child care or exercise routines.
- Maps—street maps of every city in the entire United States are available on one disc. The user can interactively zoom in to detail on every street in a city. This is not motion video, but graphics are digital video. Some map discs reduce their scope to only a few cities or locations so that they can also include audio and video descriptions of highlights from each location. This is very helpful in planning a trip intinerary.
- History—many discs are available with information about historical events and people. The use of still photographs, audio, and motion video is widespread. The data capacity of one CD-ROM can provide many hours of exploration and research on historical subjects.
- Animals—discs that contain information about different species of animals are available showing text information, photographs, and motion video. Several discs even give information about extinct animals, such as dinosaurs.
- Travelogues—with a CD-ROM, you can explore travel locations and see maps, photographs, and videos about them. It is great for the armchair traveler.

This list just scratches the surface of digital information delivery. Almost everyone who owns collections of information is either already into CD-ROM or considering it. It is the publishing medium of the future.

Another class of information delivery is the public-access kiosk. These PC systems are built into a robust package (*kiosk*) and placed in public locations to deliver specialized information. For example, a shopping mall may have kiosks that present a map of the mall, allowing the consumer to search for the store(s) of his interest, learn about special sales offers, get directions, or otherwise get answers to questions about something in the mall. The search capability of a computer database allows shoppers to get answers to many questions and it makes the shopping mall seem friendlier.

Training or Education

Teaching by computer is not new, it has been used for 20 or more years in education and military or industrial training. Early computer teaching, called CBT, programs used text-only. As graphics capabilities were developed, they were added to CBT offerings, and analog audio and video overlay techniques were also included. The computer allows the student to interact with the information and navigate through the course at his own pace. At the same time, the computer can perform tests to confirm that the student is progressing effectively.

Today, digital video and audio technologies are being widely embraced in CBT, and many programs are available with these capabilities fully integrated. There are many instances where motion video capability enhances the teaching process or makes possible teaching a subject that would be impossible without it. The ability of the computer to display a window of video along with other information such as charts, text, or still photos creates a very rich teaching environment. In general, video is an asset whenever you are trying to teach a manual procedure or process.

Many teaching programs are being distributed on CD-ROM. For example, there is a disc that will teach you how to cook. It contains recipes for various dishes and will take you through the process, even showing motion video of the steps that are difficult to describe any other way.

Entertainment

Video games are often the applications that lead in exploiting new capabilities in digital display technology. This has been especially true in the use of high-speed graphics and sound and it is happening with realistic digital video, too. CD-ROM distribution is an important aspect because it offers low-cost distribution of the program and all of its data. However, no system ever fulfills all the performance desires of game designers, and they are anxiously awaiting the standardization of higher performance video hardware and software that will create a market for even more exciting games.

Productivity

Business applications such as word processing, spreadsheets, and databases are classified as *productivity* applications. PC video is used in these applications primarily for training purposes—in that sense it is a special application of CBT. Most productivity applications are adding capability to include audio and video objects in their documents, and this is spawning new uses for these programs. I have already mentioned how a database containing audio and video as well as text can become an encyclopedia. Similarly, a word processor document with multimedia objects in it can be a CBT application.

Figure 1.4 The MPC logo

Another class of productivity application is the business presentation. In this case, audio and video represent other ways to present or enhance the message of the presentation. A group of special programs has appeared for creating (sometimes called authoring) business presentations. With many of these programs you can begin with an outline and quickly build an entire presentation to which you can add other multimedia objects such as images, audio, or video.

STANDARDS

Because there can be infinite variability in the design of computer hardware and software, no two designers or companies would create the same system unless there were standards. Without getting into all of the political and technical reasons why standards don't always happen like we think they should, I have to say that standards are essential to the growth of any new technology such as the personal computer or its subset, digital video.

The standard for IBM-compatible PCs was started in 1981 by IBM's introduction of the IBM PC. Over the years since then, the "standard" has been enhanced and extended by the action of IBM and many other companies, with the final arbiter always being the market of millions of PC users. Enhancements are being proposed all the time (digital video is responsible for many proposals right now), and their acceptance is being tested in the marketplace.

Table 1.1 Digital video standards

Name	Playback Hardware	Software	Data Formats
DVI Technology	yes	yes	yes
Video for Windows	no	yes	yes
MPEG-1	yes	yes	yes
Motion-JPEG	yes	yes	yes
Quicktime for Windows	no	yes	yes
Ultimotion	no	yes	yes

There is no single standardizing body for PC standards, but one important initiative is contributing to standardization of the environment for digital audio and video—that is the MPC Marketing Council. MPC stands for *multimedia PC*, and the Marketing Council, composed of a large group of PC and add-in board manufacturers, has created a specification for a minimum PC capable of running audio, video, and animation programs (called multimedia). The current version of that is MPC 2. Manufacturers can place an MPC logo (shown in Figure 1.4) on any PC models that meet or exceed the MPC 2 specification, and software vendors can place it on their products that they guarantee will run on any MPC 2 system. MPC 2 stops short of defining any special hardware for digital video, so it still leaves us in the "postage-stamp" video era.

Several standards are in existence for digital video, and they all will be a factor in the growth of that part of the industry. Some of them are listed in Table 1.1 to support the discussion here—they will be covered more fully later in the book.

Two points can be made from Table 1.1. First, standardization for digital video must exist at several levels: software, data formats, and hardware. Software standards define a uniform way that application programs can talk to systems (called the *application programming interface*—API). Data format standards ensure that audio and video data can be transferred widely among programs and systems, and hardware standards define built-in or add-in capabilities that will support display of larger video windows, up to full-screen size without demanding more performance from the basic system.

The second point is that there are already multiple choices at each level. Competing products have been developed and some are already on the market. The industry groups working on standards have a real challenge to choose the best approaches.

So what does a potential user of digital video do? The simple answer is: You proceed carefully. That means you will have to make choices based on your application needs, your application user's hardware, what the forecast for the chosen approach seems to be, and your own experience and preferences. These issues will be covered thoroughly in later chapters, at the end of this book you should be fully equipped with the basic understanding to make your own decision about the digital video standards you will employ. I cannot give you the final answer to this because PC digital video is still very much a moving target.

It would be nice if this situation were simpler, but we are still at an early stage in the technology. A couple of years ago, digital video was already around, but most of these standards did not exist then—that slowed the acceptance. Now we have enough standards in place that large-scale acceptance and application can begin. Dealing with this is one of the prices of being an early adopter—if you want to wait a few years it may be easier (or maybe it won't)—but if you wait for that you will surely miss a lot of the opportunity for digital video that exists now.

SUMMARY

Digital video is a new and exciting capability available on your PC. It can enhance present applications and create whole new classes of application. However, it is demanding on all the resources of your PC and it requires consideration of special hardware and software to be successful. The opportunities exist now, the technology is ready, and you should make it part of your computing portfolio now.

2

Audio and Video Fundamentals

Audio and video exist in nature as the analog quantities known as sound and vision. To become usable by a computer, sound and vision must undergo two transformations: they must become electronic and they must become digital. Although you could use audio and video on your computer without knowing anything about how they got there, the processes of electronic capture and digitization cannot be avoided if you want to create your own materials. You will be much more comfortable using these capabilities if you understand some of the technical background and terminology. This chapter will introduce the fundamental concepts of electronic digital audio and video. You do not have to be a technical person to understand this chapter.

AUDIO

A sound source in nature generates minute rapid variations in air pressure that propagate in all directions from the source much like the ripples created when you drop a stone into a still pool of water. When those pressure variations reach our ears, we hear sounds. The human ear is a kind of *sensor* or *transducer* that converts sound into an electrical format usable by the brain. Similarly, a transducer that converts sound pressure variations into an electronic format usable by audio equipment is a microphone. The output of a microphone is an analog electrical voltage that varies with time in exactly the same way the impinging pressure waves vary. This electronic sound is called an audio signal, and it is a two-dimensional quantity—a voltage that varies with time.

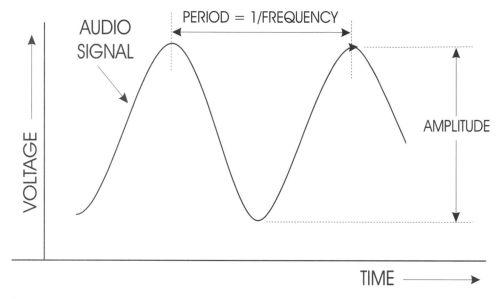

Figure 2.1 An audio signal

An audio signal from a microphone is very weak; however, it can be passed through an amplifier that will make it powerful enough to drive a loudspeaker for reproduction. It can also be recorded, for example, on a cassette tape. The tape can be played back through an amplifier for reproduction by a loudspeaker. These are the typical components of a home audio system, and they all deal with the analog audio signal. Another common home audio component is the Compact Disc (CD) player, which is actually a digital device, but it produces an analog output signal. That will be covered later in this chapter.

An audio signal can also be characterized in terms of two other parameters: frequency and amplitude, shown in Figure 2.1. Most audio signals vary periodically from positive to negative voltage and back again. The rate that this periodicity occurs is called *frequency*, and it is expressed in cycles per second. The unit of frequency—1 cycle per second—is given the name *hertz*, abbreviated *Hz*. The higher is the frequency, the higher the pitch of the corresponding sound. Thus a string bass instrument may create a frequency of 100 Hz and a violin may produce a frequency of 2,000 Hz. An audio system must reproduce a wide range of frequencies—this range is called the system's *bandwidth*.

For precise reproduction of natural sounds, an audio system must have a bandwidth that exceeds the full range of audible sound, which is from 20 Hz to about 16,000 Hz. High-quality systems often have a bandwidth from 20 Hz to 20,000 Hz—just to be safe. However, satisfactory reproduction of most sounds will be achieved with a bandwidth that goes from 60 Hz to 12,000 Hz. If a system

Table 2.1 Decibels

dB	Voltage ratio	Remarks
+10 dB	3:1	Overload point
0 dB	1:1	Reference (normal) level
-6 dB	1:2	
-10 dB	1:3	
-20 dB	1:10	
-30 dB	1:30	
-40 dB	1:100	
-60 dB	1:1000	Very quiet sound

is to be used for speech only, a bandwidth of 200 Hz to 5,000 Hz is usually enough. Telephone bandwith is even less than that, although recent developments are improving it.

The second parameter of an audio signal is *amplitude*, which is a measure of the loudness of the corresponding sound. Amplitude is measured by observing the maximum positive and negative swings of the audio signal's voltage. It can be expressed as a voltage value, but a voltage is meaningful only when compared to the capabilities of the circuit where it is measured, so it is far more common to express amplitude in relative terms. Furthermore, the usable amplitude of an audio signal can range over 1000:1 or more, so it is best to use a logarithmic scale for audio amplitude measurement. A logarithmic unit of relative measure is the *decibel*, abbreviated *dB* (pronounced "dee-bee").

The reference point for the decibel scale is called *0 dB*, and it usually is defined to represent a "normal" operating *level* for the signal (level is another word for amplitude). A signal at 0 dB would produce a comfortable sound—not too loud or too quiet. If the level goes too much above 0 dB, the sound may become too loud or the audio circuits may overload, producing distorted sound. However, the level may typically go much farther below 0 dB—that just represents quieter sounds. Table 2.1 shows a typical range of decibel values.

A real audio signal rarely has only one frequency or one amplitude value. That would correspond to a steady tone at a single pitch—really boring sound. Most signals contain a multiplicity of frequencies and amplitudes and both may vary rapidly with time. Some equipment displays this as a graph that shows the amplitudes existing at any instant in each of several ranges of frequency. That is called a *spectrum* display.

Reproducing natural sound by means of a single audio channel does not produce fully realistic sound because all the reproduced sound comes from the single point where the loudspeaker is located. The human ears are capable of recognizing where a sound is coming from and a single channel cannot convey the location information. Of course, the directional sensitivity of the ears comes because there are two ears that receive sounds slightly differently depending on the direction of the source. This can be approximated in an audio system by using two channels that carry sounds for each ear—this is called stereo audio. If the listener wears headphones, this theoretically will work perfectly, but stereo also works with two loudspeakers if they are placed sufficiently far apart. In a stereo system, each of the two channels is essentially the same as a single monaural channel. The stereo effect is produced when the channels are used together.

DIGITAL AUDIO

So far, we have discussed analog audio systems. Since sound in nature is analog and all audio transducers (microphones) produce analog outputs, analog is the starting point for all digital audio systems. To use audio in a computer system, we must convert the analog signal to a digital signal—a process called *digitization*.

Once an audio signal has been digitized, a computer can store it, replay it, or process it under software control just like any other kind of data. Also as with other digital data, digital audio signals can be copied or reproduced perfectly, without errors. The only possibility for losses is in the digitizing process itself. No special hardware is needed to store, replay, or process audio in the computer; however, an audio input/output card is needed to digitize audio or to provide outputs to speakers (unless the computer has this capability built-in, as many of the newer ones do).

Digitizing Audio

Each of the two dimensions of an analog signal (voltage and time) must be digitized. The time scale is converted to digital by a process known as *sampling*. To perform sampling, we take instantaneous readings of the voltage at uniformly spaced times, as shown in Figure 2.2. The *sampling rate* or frequency is the number of samples taken per second. The sampling rate theoretically must be at least two times the highest audio frequency to be reproduced. Thus to reproduce audio frequencies up to 10,000 Hz, we should have a sampling frequency at least 20 kHz (20,000 per second). In practice, the sampling rate is made a little more than

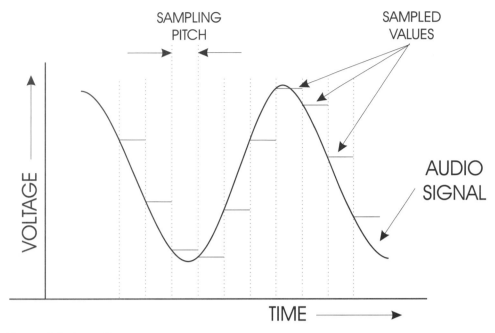

Figure 2.2 Sampling

twice the audio bandwidth, so the preceding example might actually use a sampling frequency of 22 kHz.

The output of a sampling process is a stream of *samples*, but the samples are still analog quantities because each of them exactly reproduces the analog voltage of the audio signal that existed at the instant of sampling. Now we must convert the sample values to digital—a process called quantization. Figure 2.3 shows how this works. The voltage scale is divided up into a number of equal-width bands or levels—the exact number of levels depends on the number of bits assigned to each sample. For example, if we use 8 bits to represent each sample, then the scale will have 256 levels ($256 = 2^8$) because each bit has only two values, 0 or 1. For simplicity, Figure 2.3 shows 16 levels corresponding to 4 bits per sample. The digital output for each sample is the digital code corresponding to the level lines that each sample value falls between. These are shown at the right in Figure 2.3. Notice that the digitzation process produces a stream of data whose *data rate* is (sampling frequency) × (bits per sample) ÷ 8. The result is in bytes per second.

Quantization produces an approximation of the sample value because it rounds off all analog values that fall within one level to the same digital value. Any difference between the original analog signal and its digital representation is called *distortion* and it will be noticeable if you do not use enough bits per sample.

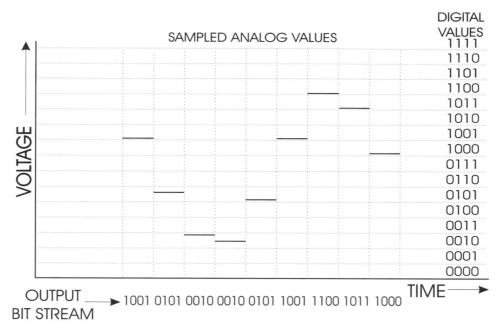

Figure 2.3 Quantizing

This particular kind of distortion is called *quantization noise*. It causes the audio to sound somewhat gravelly. Quantization noise is easily heard at 8 bits per sample, but it is essentially inaudible at 16 bits per sample.

A digital audio system that performs simple sampling and quantization and stores and replays the resulting bit stream without further changes is called a *PCM* audio system. The acronym stands for *pulse code modulation*, a term derived from digital communications theory. PCM is one *algorithm* for digital audio. Other algorithms, or methods, are possible; they require some amount of additional processing, which is done either to improve the quality at the same data rate or to reduce the data rate or compress the data. That will be covered in the chapter on data compression.

A circuit that performs sampling and quantization is called an *analog to digital converter* (ADC). For audio use, ADCs usually operate at sampling frequencies between 11 kHz and 44.1 kHz and between 8 and 16 bits per sample. The highest numbers conform to the Compact Disc (CD-Audio) standard, which delivers extremely high quality audio. The lowest numbers are compromise values that trade lower quality reproduction for much lower data rates; they are suitable for speech use only. Other values between the lowest and highest are satisfactory for more general use.

For replay of audio to speakers or headphones, the digital audio must be converted back to analog. This requires a digital to analog converter (DAC). A DAC circuit must be built for the same number of bits per sample as the incoming digital audio. If the DAC cannot process all the bits in the audio data stream, the audio ouput quality will be degraded.

MIDI

So far, I have been discussing only sound that has been picked up from nature with a microphone. However, the computer adds the possibility of synthesized sound—sound created artificially in the computer. That can be done very successfully for instrumental music and, with somewhat less success, for speech. The musical instrument industry has heartily embraced synthesized sound and the techniques are highly developed and widely used. Since this technology is digital and in existence long before there was any interest in good audio from computers, it is reasonable that the same technology should simply migrate to the computer world. That is just what has happened. The technology is called *MIDI*, an acronym for musical instrument digital interface. It was made part of the MPC standards and is implemented in almost all sound boards for computers.

MIDI is a serial digital interface for the control of musical instruments—it is not actual sound, only control. On the stage and in recording studios, it is used to interconnect all kinds of electronic musical instruments: synthesizers, drum machines, samplers. A MIDI signal is simply another data stream that can be stored, edited, replayed, and processed in a computer. In a computer sound board, it is used to control a synthesizer module. The MPC specification calls for an FM synthesizer; in music industry terms, that is a low-end synthesizer, with limited capabilities. There are better synthesizer of other types on the market for computers, such as those that use *wavetable* synthesis. Or, by using an external MIDI cable connection, the computer can connect to any MIDI-capable musical instrument. I will discuss the use of MIDI further in the chapter on audio production.

VIDEO

An image in nature is a parallel phenomenon—all the objects in the image are reflecting the surrounding light at the same time. The human eye is also a parallel sensor because the rod and cone receptors in the retina are all simultaneously active. The optic nerve contains millions of connections to deliver the information in parallel to the brain. However, in the electronic world, a parallel connection requiring millions of circuits is totally impractical. A single connection or, at most, a few connections is all that is reasonable to handle. A monochrome video sensor (camera) contains the means to convert an image that is basically parallel into a single electrical voltage to generate a video signal. That means is called *scanning*.

Scanning

An image may be captured electronically by sequentially reading the brightness values of a series of points in a pattern that covers the entire image. This is scanning, and it delivers a single analog voltage that represents the brightness of image points as they are being scanned. The electronic image may be displayed by performing a similar process: A point of light (spot) is made to scan in the same pattern that was used during capture. The video signal controls the brightness of the scanning spot of light. If the process is done rapidly enough (30 to 60 times per second), the eye will see it as a continuous image. Typically, the display device is a *cathode-ray tube* (CRT), although other devices are also used.

The scanning process just described is a fundamental concept of television, and it is also the basis for all computer displays. The rapid scanning not only tricks the eye into thinking it sees a continuous image, but it also allows the image to convey motion because each successive complete scanning of the scene provides an update of all the objects in the scene, thereby reproducing any motion that has occurred.

Figure 2.4 shows a typical scanning pattern. Scanning of a display begins with the spot positioned at the upper left corner of the image and proceeds horizontally across the top of the image. When the scan reaches the right edge of the image, completing one *line* of the scan, it snaps back to the left edge (this is called *horizontal retrace*). However, because there is a simultaneous vertical scanning motion at a much slower rate, when horizontal retrace occurs, the scanning spot is now positioned below the start of the previous line, ready to begin another line. The process of line scanning continues until the vertical motion has brought the spot to the bottom of the image. At that point, a vertical retrace and a horizontal retrace occurs and the spot jumps back to the top left corner of the image. This completes one frame of scanning.

What has just been described is called *progressive* scanning, and it is the method used by most computer displays. However, television is slightly different—it uses a technique called *interlaced* scanning. In interlaced scanning, the vertical scan rate is doubled so that one vertical scan scans only half of the lines needed for the image. At the point of vertical retrace, the spot moves to the top center of the image, to start another vertical scan that places a second series of lines exactly between the previous ones. After two vertical scans (called *fields*), a frame has been

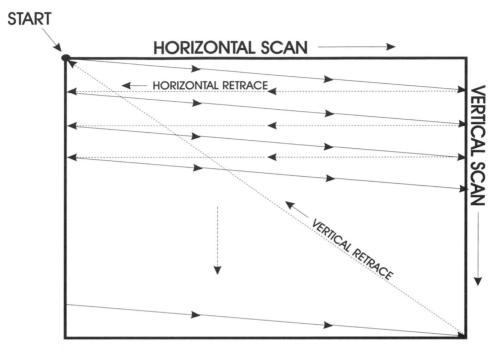

Figure 2.4 Progressive scanning

completed. This sounds complicated, but it is not—the precise positioning of the interlaced lines occurs automatically by choosing an odd number of total lines and making the vertical scanning exactly twice the frame rate. In United States television, there are 525 lines with 29.97 frames per second. The horizontal scanning rate (frequency) is $525 \times 29.97 = 15{,}734.26$ lines per second, and the field scanning rate is $29.97 \times 2 = 59.94$ per second. The funny numbers for field and frame rates are required by certain considerations of the color TV system that are beyond the scope of this discussion. It is usually OK to round the numbers off to 30 and 60 for most purposes. Appendix A gives the scanning numbers for other TV systems around the world and also for computer display systems.

The reason television uses an interlaced scan is that it allows the frame rate to be cut in half, which (as we will see later) allows the bandwidth required for the video signal to also be cut in half. The reduced bandwidth allows us to have twice as many TV channels, which has proved to be very valuable. However, interlacing is not appropriate for computer displays because it causes sharp horizontal edges or lines to flicker. Some computer displays offer interlacing, but it is not a good choice and should be avoided. Appendix A explains this further.

Resolution

The scanning process does not give a perfect reproduction of the original image because of the finite size of the scanning spot, the bandwidth of the video channel, and the number of scanning lines in the height of the picture. All these factors combine to determine the *resolution* of the video system, which relates to how well the system reproduces fine detail in the picture. In television, resolution is specified in TV *lines per picture height* (TVL), which is the number of black and white lines that can be reproduced in a distance corresponding to the picture height. That elaborate definition is necessary because resolution has to be specified in both horizontal and vertical directions. The reasons for that are covered in Appendix A. Typical resolution numbers for television equipment are these: broadcast video camera, 600 lines; home camcorder, 250 lines; and television receiver, 320 lines.

These resolution numbers correspond to the maximum bandwidth of the video system. For example, the bandwidth of a broadcast camera is 7.5 MHz, the camcorder is 3.2 MHz, and the TV receiver is 4.0 MHz. With standard TV scanning, these numbers are easy to remember because the TV system has a theoretical resolution of 80 TVL for each 1MHz of bandwidth. However, the circuit bandwidth is not the only resolution-governing factor—the video sensor and the optical system must also have enough resolution performance or they will be the ones limiting the system.

Video Cameras

Electronic video capture is done with a video camera. As shown in Figure 2.5, a monochrome video camera consists of a lens that focuses the scene onto the photosensitive surface of a camera tube or solid-state sensor (also called *charge-coupled device* or *CCD*). The sensitive surface converts the light image into an electronic charge pattern, which is an electronic image that is just like the optical image except that each point of the image is an amount of electrical charge proportional to the light at that point. In computer terms, the charge image is a parallel operation, because the charge at all points exists at the same time. The charge pattern is read out serially by scanning with an electron beam in a vacuum-tube sensor or electronically in a CCD. As the scanning passes over each point on the surface, the charge at that point is converted to a voltage on the output line. Figure 2.5 shows the signal that results from scanning across a white rectangular object against a gray background. Notice that the signal is inter-rupted each time that retrace occurs—these interruptions are called *blanking*

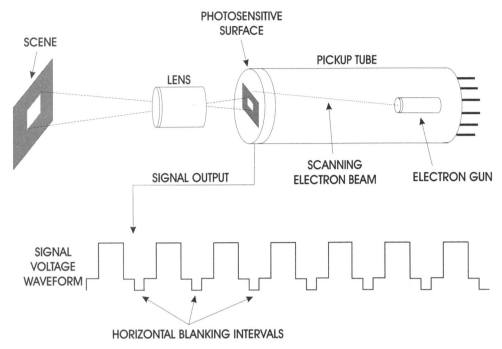

Figure 2.5 A monochrome video camera and its output signal

intervals. They introduce a pattern or structure into a video signal that makes it easier to perform certain processes on a video signal.

There are two blanking intervals in a video signal—horizontal and vertical. Horizontal blanking occurs for every line retrace, and vertical blanking occurs for every vertical (frame or field) retrace. In standard TV scanning, the blanking intervals represent a significant amount of time: Horizontal blanking is 18% of the time and vertical blanking is an additional 6% of the time. The periods between horizontal blanking intervals is called the *active line* time, when the actual picture information is transmitted. The large amount of time devoted to blanking is required for other functions needed by a TV system, such as synchronization and supporting data transmission. This is discussed further in Appendix A.

COLOR VIDEO SYSTEMS

So far, I have described monochrome video systems. (Do you remember black and white television?) Most video systems today reproduce colors, which is done using the *tristimulus* theory of color reproduction. That is based on the fact that there are three types of color receptors in the human eye, which, in combination, allow us to see all colors. As far as the eye is concerned, any color is a combination of specific amounts of three *primary colors*. The primary colors for color video are red, green, and blue. Lights of these colors can be combined to reproduce any color.

In grade school, you probably learned a different set of primary colors—"red", "blue", and yellow. These are the ones used in painting and they are different because they are based on placing pigments on white paper to produce colors by subtracting colors from the white light reflected from the paper. This is called the *subtractive* color system, whereas the system used in video is called *additive*, because colored lights are added to create any color. The subtractive primaries "red" and "blue" are not the same as the additive red and blue. In color video they are magenta and cyan, respectively.

Color video reproduction is accomplished with three cameras looking at the same image, using an appropriate color filter in front of each camera so that it sees only one primary color. To achieve three cameras viewing exactly the same scene, a light-splitting device such as a prism is used, shown in Figure 2.6. This is called a *three-sensor RGB camera*.

For display, the three output signals from the camera are connected to a color display that has RGB inputs. Color display monitors use a color CRT that has three scanning beams (one for each primary color) where the faceplate of the CRT is designed so that each beam falls on a phosphor pattern of the appropriate color. The phosphor pattern is an array of dots or lines small enough so the viewer does not see the individual areas of color, but instead the colors appear to be combined. Both computer displays and television receivers use this display technology.

Something similar to the three-dot color display can be used to make a single-sensor color camera. A pattern of color filter dots or lines is placed over the imaging surface of the sensor as shown in Figure 2.7. When the sensor is scanned, the video signal is a sequence of the three colors. This signal is processed electronically to separate it into the three RGB signals on three separate wires. The electronic processing removes the color pattern from the output—there is only a slight loss of resolution. All low-cost color cameras and camcorders use this approach. Professional cameras, which are more expensive, usually use three separate sensors to avoid the loss of resolution of the single-sensor system.

The three-wire RGB video setup just described is not appropriate for television broadcasting where each station has only a single broadcast channel. Therefore, color TV uses a system of *encoding* that combines the three color channels into a single *composite* signal for broadcasting. In the United States, this is called NTSC encoding. NTSC stands for *National Television Systems Committee*, a group that

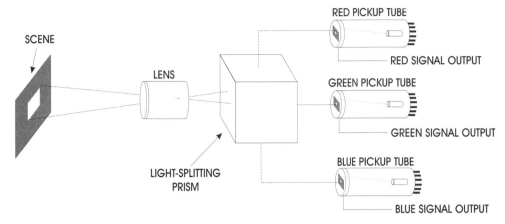

Figure 2.6 A three-sensor color camera

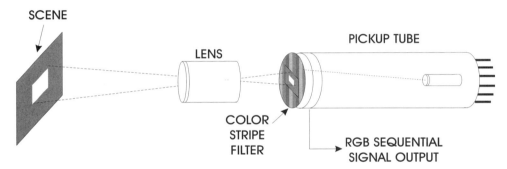

Figure 2.7 A single-sensor color camera

chose standards for color TV in the US in 1953. The NTSC signal has the unique characteristic that it can also be received by a monochrome receiver, which was important when color TV started because most receivers then were monochrome. In other parts of the world, there are different encoding standards, called *PAL* and *SECAM*. Appendix A has more detail about composite encoding systems.

Although composite encoding works well for color TV, the process of squeezing three signals onto one channel involves some compromises. This particularly affects the sharpness of colored edges in the picture, and it becomes very noticeable when you compare an NTSC image with a computer graphics image that does not have any loss of color edge sharpness. This comparison is easily made when you display composite video in a window of a computer screen that is otherwise all graphic. Since the video is considered acceptable when viewed by

Figure 2.8 An image, with pixels enlarged at the right

itself, you have to learn that it looks different from a computer screen and accept that difference when they are seen together.

DIGITAL VIDEO

An analog video signal (monochrome) is similar to an audio signal except that is has the inherent structure of lines and frames caused by the scanning. The process of digitizing is exactly the same as was described above for audio—sampling and quantizing. However, the sampling rate is chosen to produce a specific number of samples for each scanning line. These samples represent individual dots in the picture, which are called *pixels*—a contraction of "picture elements." Figure 2.8 shows a picture with an area enlarged to make the individual pixels visible.

For example, we may wish to have 640 pixels for each line. If the source signal uses standard TV scanning, that would mean the sampling frequency should be approximately 12.3 MHz. That is calculated by multiplying the line scanning frequency (15,734 Hz) by 640 and dividing by the fraction of a line period devoted to active line scanning (0.82).

In a digital video system, the resolution is determined by the number of pixels horizontally and vertically. This is specified by giving both numbers; for example, a VGA display has 640×480 pixels—that is its resolution—640 horizontally and 480 vertically. Notice that numbers of pixels and TV lines per picture height are not the same measures. It is beyond our scope to explain it here, but you should not try to equate the digital and analog measures of resolution (see Appendix A).

In digital audio, we spoke of bits per sample as another measure of quality. In digital video, the equivalent is *bits per pixel* (bpp) since each sample is also one pixel. A high quality monochrome image requires 8 bits per pixel—that corresponds to 256 levels of gray. Since a color system requires one monochrome channel for each of the red, green, and blue primaries, a high-quality color pixel requires 24 bits. That corresponds to 16,777,216 possible colors, including the 256 levels of gray! Some digital video systems actually use 24 bpp, but most use lower bpp values, with correspondingly fewer colors. It's surprising how much can be done with only 256 colors (8 bpp). Number of colors in a digital video system will be covered further in the next chapter.

The data rate of a video system is calculated (sampling frequency) × (bpp) ÷ 8. The numbers are gigantic, well beyond the capability of any personal computer. Data compression techniques must be used to play motion video on a PC. A great deal of technology has been developed for that purpose, which is one of the reasons for the existence of this book.

ARTIFACTS

There are many kinds of distortions to audio and video signals, both analog and digital. It is unnecessary to cover all the possibilities here, but it will help you to recognize some of them. The distortions are often referred to as *artifacts* because they are unnatural characteristics that creep into natural signals when they are electronically captured, processed, or reproduced. I have already mentioned some of them, but I will summarize the most important ones here. Let's begin with audio.

Analog Audio Artifacts

Some of the more common artifacts of analog audio signals are

- **Loss of bandwidth**—either (or both) the high-frequency and low-frequency ends of the audio band can be cut off by problems in analog circuits. You can experiment deliberately with this by turning down the bass and treble controls on any audio system. This is a familiar effect that most people easily recognize in an audio system. It most commonly results from misadjustment of controls, or if that is not the problem, it can be caused by bad circuits or cables.
- **Noise**—this is the familiar hiss that you sometimes hear in an audio channel, particularly when the signal is weak and the volume is turned up high to hear it. It is caused by unavoidable random fluctuations in electrical voltages

and in the atmosphere (with broadcasting), which become audible if too much amplification is needed. Since noise exists to some degree in all circuits, it is a common specification parameter. We refer to the *signal to noise ratio* (S/N ratio) of a circuit or system. This is normally specified in dB (since it is a ratio). S/N values for real systems range from 40 dB (100:1) for a very poor system to over 90 dB (30,000:1) for an excellent system. Most audio systems fall between these values.

- **Harmonic distortion**—this occurs if audio circuits become overloaded (too much level). A certain raspiness will be heard on loud passages or peaks of sound. Distortion is normally undesirable, but, in rock music, it is sometimes introduced deliberately to produce the "screaming guitar" or other effects.

Digital Audio Artifacts

Each of these analog artifacts has a parallel in digital system, but the effects are different. Since all digital audio originally existed as analog, it is possible for both classes of artifacts to occur together in a digital system. When an analog signal containing artifacts is digitized, the analog artifacts also get digitized and remain in the digital signal. In the following list, I will explain how the digital audio artifacts sound differently.

- **Aliasing**—this is a digital problem with bandwidth that occurs when the sampling frequency is too low and improper filtering is used in the circuits. What happens is that audio frequencies too high for the sampling rate get transformed to different frequencies that appear within the audio band. The effect is severe distortion and interference.
- **Quantization noise**—this occurs when there are too few bits per sample. It causes a gravelly sound.
- **Digital overload**—analog distortion usually develops gradually as the level or volume is increased. However, a digital system has a very precise range of level that it can handle—when the signal exceeds that by even a little amount, the excess signal is simply clipped off. This causes an immediate large distortion effect, sometimes sounding like a crash—as if the signal simply crashed into a brick wall.

Analog Video Artifacts

Because of the greater complexity of a video signal, there are many more types of video artifacts. A few of the more common ones are covered in the following list. Analog video comes first:

- **Frequency response effects**—for video it is important that the entire frequency range be accurately and unformly reproduced. The behavior of a system vs. frequency is called its *frequency response*, which must be uniform (called *flat*) over the band from 30 Hz to the highest frequency (4 MHz or more). An anomaly at any frequency will show in the video as an edge effect or a smear in the image (Figure 2.9b). The frequency response of an audio system is also important although audio is less sensitive to small anomalies.

- **Noise**—this is also important in video systems. It is often called "snow" and it appears as random flecks of black, white, or color in the picture (Figure 2.9c). In a motion video system, there is some degree of averaging of the noise from frame to frame caused by the eye's slow response. You will observe that a still frame taken from a motion video stream will often look very noisy (you can do this with a still-frame VCR), even though you didn't notice noise in the original motion video.

- **Overload**—when the video level becomes too high, the effect is that the highlight colors become washed out and the brightest points lose detail and simply become white (Figure 2.9d). Some of this is tolerable in an image, but when it affects large areas or areas where the detail information is important, it is objectionable.

Digital Video Artifacts

As with audio, digital video artifacts are different and will coexist with analog artifacts.

- **Aliasing**—this is the same problem as audio—the sampling frequency is too low for the frequencies being digitized; it appears in an image or motion video as jagged effects on vertical edges in the picture (Figure 2.10a). Proper filtering ahead of digitzing that assures too-high frequencies are removed will eliminate *aliasing*, but it will soften the edges in the picture (Figure 2.10b). Usually softness of edges is preferable to the annoying jaggies of aliasing, although this is a trade that any system designer can make her own decision about.

- **Quantization noise**—the effect of too-few bits per pixel (coarse quantizing) causes an effect called *contouring* in areas of smooth shading in an image. Since the low-bpp system has a limited number of colors it can display, you can see artificial edges or contour lines in a smoothly shaded area as the system has to jump from one of its colors to the next closest color to approximate the shading. This is very noticeable in 8-bpp (256 colors) images, especially on faces and the sky. At 16-bpp (65,536 colors) it is noticeable only in extreme situations, and with 24-bpp (16,777,216 colors),

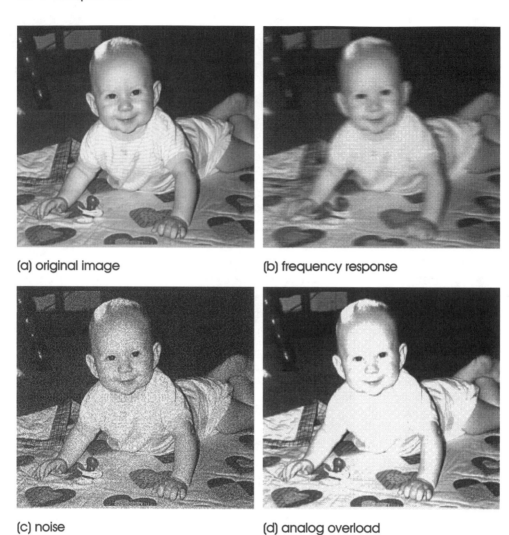

(a) original image

(b) frequency response

(c) noise

(d) analog overload

Figure 2.9 Analog video artifacts

most people will never see contouring. Figure 2.11 shows contouring vs. bpp for a monochrome image.

(a) aliased

(b) aliased and softened

Figure 2.10 Aliasing

- **Digital overload**—overload of a digital video system is caused when the signal being digitized exceeds the voltage range of the quantizer. It appears much the same in the picture as analog overload, except that it occurs more abruptly (Figure 2.12a). However, in some systems, overload of the quantizing range may cause an effect called *wraparound*, where a too-white spot will wrap around to become black (Figure 2.12b). This is highly objectionable, and most digital video systems are designed to prevent it.

There are many other artifacts of audio and video systems, but these lists should be enough to give you a feel for how some of them look and hear and what causes them.

AUDIO EQUIPMENT

Much of the audio equipment that you have in your home stereo system is usable with your computer system. That includes tuners, tape decks, record players, CD players, etc. Note that when you digitize audio into your computer, you are inherently making a copy of it. Most of the prerecorded material you have in your home library is not licensed for copying nor is the material you receive over the air. You must respect the copyright restrictions on all material that was produced by others. This cannot be overstressed.

(a) original - 8 bpp (256 levels of gray)   (b) 4 bpp (16 levels of gray)

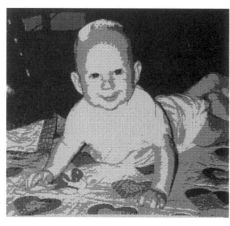
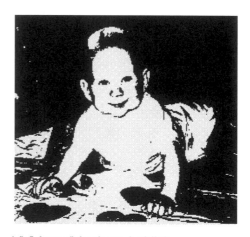

(c) 2 bpp (4 levels of gray)   (d) 1 bpp (black and white)

Figure 2.11 Contouring

I should point out that numerous libraries of *clip media* (audio, video, and images) are available and are licensed for free copying and often for distribution as well. Even with these, you should carefully read the license agreement to make sure your proposed usage complies with the license.

Although home audio equipment can meet many of your needs to work with audio on a computer, other classes of audio equipment, made for professional

 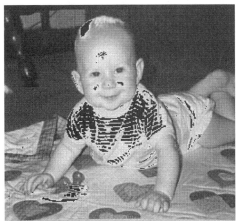

(a) Overload   (b) Wraparound

Figure 2.12 Digital overload artifacts

use, will deliver higher performance and other features that are useful. A later chapter will discuss this in detail.

VIDEO EQUIPMENT

Home video equipment, such as camcorders, cameras, and VCRs, is widely available, but it is not as satisfactory for use with as a computer as home audio equipment. This is because home video devices have to struggle to deliver even minimal performance at a consumer-market price point. Another reason is that video signals entering a computer will undergo much more complex processing than audio signals and that extra processing is sensitive to many video artifacts that might be acceptable when just viewing the video on your TV screen. This will be discussed much more when we get to the subject of video compression in Chapter 4.

As with audio equipment, some lines of professional video equipment offer greater performance in resolution, noise, and color rendition at higher price points. There is practically a continuum of products available from the consumer level up to the broadcast level. However, this represents a price range of more than 10:1. Your needs for video quality will determine how far up this price/performance curve you have to go.

SUMMARY

This chapter has discussed the theory behind electronic audio and video, both analog and digital. The presentation has deliberately been kept simple—just enough to introduce you to the concepts and the terms involved. This is important because I will now use the terms indiscriminately and expect you to know what I am talking about. Therefore, you should make sure you have understood this chapter before going ahead. You may find additional help in the glossary section at the back of the book, and Appendix A also gives more technical detail on many of the points if that is what you need.

3

Audio and Video
On a Computer

It takes more than simply acquiring digital audio and video for them to be effectively integrated into a personal computer. The data rates and storage requirements are prodigious, and replay of audio and video can use all the power of the fastest PCs, leaving nothing left for other tasks that may have to run simultaneously. This chapter will first review the architecture of personal computers and discuss the considerations of running audio and video on them. Then the various classes of special hardware and software for audio and video will be covered. Although the subject here is technical, as in Chapter 2, you do not need a technical background to understand it. What you will need, however, is a tolerance for acronyms and buzzwords. The computer hardware and software business uses them indiscriminately, as I will too, once I have defined them. Whenever you see an italicized term, it is something being defined, which will probably be used regularly in the discussion that follows.

PC PLATFORMS

The assemblage of hardware and software that provides an environment for running computer applications (programs) is called a *platform*. Hardware computers such as IBM PC/AT, Apple Macintosh, Commodore Amiga, and Silicon Graphics Indy are the basis for platforms. Within one of these hardware categories there is additional distinction of platform by the choice of different *operating system* (OS) software. The OS is the software that prepares the hardware for running applications. It provides input/output (I/O) functionality such as keyboard, mouse, and serial ports, and a file system for access to floppy and hard

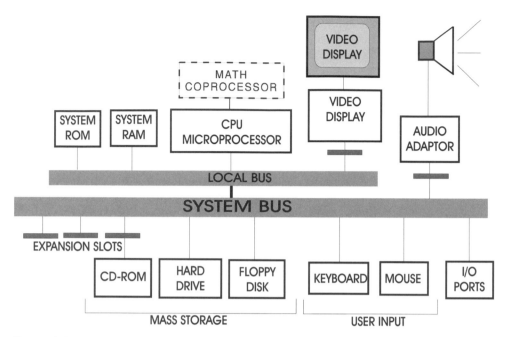

Figure 3.1 Hardware block diagram of a typical PC

disks. Finally, an OS includes an application programming interface, which is the means whereby an application program talks to the OS to access its functionality. Different OSs have different APIs, which is the reason why you must have an application program that matches your operating system. Examples of operating systems for the IBM PC/AT family of hardware are: DOS, DOS/Windows, Windows NT, and OS/2. Depending on your choice of OS, you have a different platform.

Most of the discussion that follows is specific to the IBM PC/AT and compatible hardware, which is the main focus of this book. Other hardware categories have slightly different architectures, although the underlying principles are generally the same. Figure 3.1 is a hardware block diagram of a typical IBM-compatible personal computer. As you can see, all the units of the system are connected by the *system bus*, except that some units that require the highest possible speed have their own *local bus*. Later, I discuss some of the units in more detail.

CPU

The heart of any PC is its *central processing unit* (CPU), which is a microprocessor chip that performs processing and control via software. That means it is programmable. Most PC platforms so far use CPUs from Intel Corporation's x86 family—386, 486, Pentium. These processors are all 32-bit units and will run all current PC software and most of the software dating back all the way to the original IBM PC in 1980. This *backward compatibility* of software has been one of the keys to the growth of the IBM-compatible PC market.

New processor types are being introduced to compete with the x86 family. These use the *reduced instruction set computing* (RISC) concept, which is an architecture where the internal instructions of the CPU are simplified so that they all can run in a single clock cycle (many x86 instructions take several or more clock cycles for execution). The simpler architecture allows a RISC chip to run at higher clock frequencies. The objective is to make the overall system faster.

Since a RISC instruction set is different, such CPUs cannot directly run x86 programs, and the inherent backward compatibility is lost. However, this is overcome by a software technique called *emulation*. A software module is written to convert the RISC API to the standard x86 API, so standard PC programs can then run on the emulator. This works, but the added software overhead of the emulator slows down the system. It can still be satisfactory, however, because the RISC machine is so fast to begin with.

The x86 family is not standing still, either. Intel is aggressively introducing competitors to the RISC devices while retaining the x86 compatibility, and you can expect that the CPU wars will continue for some time. The real winners are the PC users, who are experiencing tremendous acceleration in CPU speed as a result.

An important parameter for any CPU is its *clock frequency*, which is the speed in MHz that the processor runs internally. Clock frequencies today range from 16 MHz to 100 MHz, and higher numbers are coming. If everything else is equal (which it often is not), higher CPU clock frequency leads to proportionately higher performance. However, you also gain performance from the architectural improvements that have been added to the later members of the x86 family. For example, a 25 MHz 486 processor is several times faster than a 25 MHz 386 processor.

Figure 3.1 shows a *math coprocessor* connected to the CPU. This is an optional feature that speeds up floating-point math calculations by a large factor. *Floating-point* is computerese for math where the decimal point can be anywhere. It is important to any applications that require many calculations, such as computer-aided design (CAD), spreadsheets, and some forms of image processing. The 486 DX family of processors have a floating-point processor built-in; the 486 SX processors do not.

System Bus

Although the CPU is the heart of a PC, its main artery is the system bus, which is a multiwire electrical path on the system's motherboard that connects most of the components of the system. In addition to items directly wired to the system bus on the motherboard, there are usually a number of sockets or *expansion slots*, shown by the little gray bar symbols in Figure 3.1, to add optional plug-in boards. This is for such expansion items as audio or video boards, extra I/O, modem, or networking modules. All items in the figure that do not have the slot symbol are wired directly on the motherboard.

The components connected to the system bus are all electrically in parallel, but at any one moment only two are able to communicate. That action is controlled by the CPU, which (as one of its many tasks) continuously specifies who passes data over the bus. The system bus in most PCs is a standardized design called the *industry standard architecture* (ISA), which is based on the IBM PC/AT system that was introduced in 1984.

The CPU and the system bus are examples of system *resources* that basically perform operations *serially* (one after another). This serial nature means that they control the system's speed—the faster each one is, the faster the system can perform. If either one becomes overloaded with too much to do, it can bottleneck the system. This is especially true for the system bus, which must service every component of the system. As systems become more complex, with more devices on the system bus, it cannot keep up with the speed of the processor.

Because of the requirement for compatibility with older systems and peripherals, the ISA bus cannot be speeded up to match today's faster CPUs. It also has a data path of only 16-bits, meaning that each bus cycle transfers only 16 bits of data, even though present-day CPUs are designed to process 32 bits at a time. This has spurred several new and advanced bus designs such as the *microchannel* (MCA) bus used in IBM PS/2 systems, and the *enhanced industry standard architecture* (EISA) bus used in some PC/AT compatible systems. These new buses have 32-bit data paths and support faster speeds. However, they are incompatible with the old ISA bus and must use specially designed boards. This limits the flexibility of these new systems because they cannot use most of the add-in boards on the market, of which thousands of types are available. To improve their compatibility, most EISA machines retain some ISA board sockets, too.

Figure 3.1 shows a modification of the system bus, called a local bus, which is a feature of most new PC systems. This approach is based on the ISA bus, but adds a separate bus that connects only the components requiring the fastest speed, which are the CPU, RAM, ROM, and video display. This separate bus usually has a 32-bit data path and it runs at a higher speed. It also benefits because only a limited number of devices are allowed on it. One of the most important uses of a local bus is the video display adaptor. There usually is a special local-bus slot for a video display card.

Several local bus standards are in existence: the *Video Electronics Standards Association* (VESA) VL local bus, also called the *VESA bus*, and the *peripheral connect interface* (PCI) bus. It's beyond our scope here to discuss the details of local buses, but any new system you buy should definitely have one to get the best video performance possible at this time.

Memory

Another key system resource is its *memory* capability. Memory stores programs and data in the system making them available to the CPU for use as required, and putting them away in permanent storage when not in use. As with the system bus, software on the CPU controls what happens in memory. Memory is divided into three categories: random-access memory (RAM), read-only memory (ROM), and mass storage.

RAM

Random-access memory is the main working memory for the CPU. All data that the CPU needs must be placed in RAM, regardless of where it may normally be stored. RAM is made with solid-state integrated circuits (ICs), which makes it the fastest kind of memory. Depending on the system design, RAM can be as fast as the CPU itself. On the other hand, RAM is the most expensive memory, although its price continues to drop as the semiconductor industry makes improvements. At this writing, RAM is less than $45 per megabyte (MB), and the forecasts are that it will continue to drop about 2:1 every two years for some time to come.

At the same time that RAM is getting less expensive, systems are demanding more of it. The trend to the use of *graphical user interfaces* (GUIs) especially has upped the ante. This is because the graphical screen requires a lot of pixel data to be stored off-screen so that the system can respond rapidly when the user moves or uncovers windows, etc. Digital audio and video also add their own needs for RAM; a system handling digital video should have at least 8 MB of RAM; even larger RAM will improve the performance still more.

The reason having a lot of RAM is important is that RAM is at least 10 times faster than any other memory and the more of the system's program code and data that can be kept in RAM at once, the faster the system performance will be. Performance is drastically slowed down when the system has to go to hard disk all the time to get its working programs and data. With digital motion video this

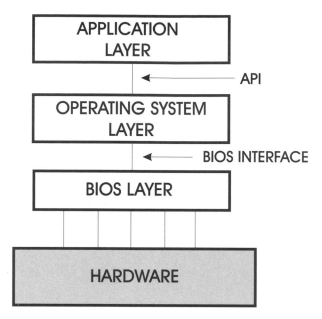

Figure 3.2 Software layers

can make the difference between the system working well or working almost not at all.

RAM is not permanent storage—when the power is turned off, everything stored in RAM is lost. This is called *volatile* storage. Therefore, a system cannot be built using only RAM storage (unless it is battery-operated and you make sure the battery will never run down).

ROM

Read-only memory is similar to RAM in some respects, it is also solid-state memory, but it is permanent (*nonvolatile*) storage and the system cannot change it by writing to it (it is *read-only*). ROM is used by the system to hold permanent program code that is required all the time. The most important code of this type is the *basic input/output system* (BIOS), which is the group of programs that mates the system's hardware to the operating system. The OS is usually loaded from hard disk, but the BIOS is a permanent part of the hardware (this is sometimes called *firmware*).

The BIOS is an example of a software *layer*. It is common for software to be built in layers, with a specified *interface* between layers. This is shown in Figure 3.2. The interface provides a standardized means of communication between layers. In this way, the BIOS, which is the lowest software layer in a PC, handles many of the details of the hardware and brings it out to an interface that is

Table 3.1 Mass storage characteristics

Type	Storage/Unit (bytes)	Access Time (milliseconds)	Data Transfer Rate (per second)
Floppy Disk	1.2–1.44 MB	500–1000	30 KB
Hard Disk	up to 2 GB	8–20	500 KB–4 MB
CD-ROM	680 MB	200–400	150 KB–600 KB

standard for an operating system. All operating systems designed for IBM-compatible PCs are built on the standard BIOS interface. Thus, any hardware system that has its own unique BIOS written to the standard will be able to run any OS. The OS itself is another layer (in fact, there are often layers within an OS); it has the standard API interface for running applications, which are yet another layer. Layers are one of several software design techniques that contribute to broader usage of the same software on systems of many types.

Mass Storage

Mass storage consists of hard disks, floppy disks, CD-ROM, and other forms of permanent storage. Some mass storage units have removable media (floppy disk, CD-ROM), some are read-write (floppy disk, hard disk), and some are read-only (CD-ROM). The characteristic shared by all mass storage units is that they offer large amounts of storage at a low cost per megabyte. The tradeoff is that they are generally slower than RAM or ROM, by 10 to 1,000 times. It would be nice if mass storage were faster (and it is improving over time), but system strategies have been developed for management of data transfer between mass storage and RAM so that excellent system performance is possible anyway.

The capacity of a mass storage device is usually specified in megabytes (MB). A typical hard disk today would be several hundred MB (they are available up to several thousand MB), and a CD-ROM disc can store up to 680 MB. Two other specifications for mass storage are access time and data transfer rate. *Access time* refers to how long (usually in milliseconds) it takes to read the first byte of the selected data block from mass storage and *data transfer rate* is how fast (bytes per second) you can read the rest of the bytes of the data block from storage. Table 3.1 lists the principal characteristics of the most common mass storage units. There are many other types, less used, that have characteristics outside of the ranges in the table.

In many cases the system will access the same area of mass storage repeatedly, so it is natural to think of keeping such data temporarily in a block of RAM to speed up the access. Such a RAM block is called a *cache*. Elaborate strategies have been developed for caching, and it is essential for best performance in modern systems. Many systems have a hardware cache built-in separate from system RAM, whereas other systems use the main RAM for this purpose. There is even value in doing both. The cache idea can also be extended to the CPU, and the latest CPUs, such as the 486 and Pentium, have some cache memory on-chip.

Plug-in Adaptors

The other two components of the system that we should discuss here are the video display adaptor and the audio adaptor. These are shown as plug-ins in Figure 3.1. That is the most common situation today, but some systems are building this functionality into their motherboards. Built-in functions are generally less expensive than plug-in functions, but this strategy ties you to the particular features that are built-in, while having plug-in features lets you choose from all the options available on the market. I'll leave it to you to decide whether you need that kind of flexibility.

Audio Adaptors

Dedicated audio (sound) adaptors are a recent addition to the market portfolio of PC add-in boards. PCs have always had sound capability, but it has generally been a single 2" or 3" speaker connected to a 1-bit signal source in the computer. This hardware was fine for making the beep sounds that we usually associate with computers, but it falls far short when we want to reproduce realistic voice, sound effects, or music, possibly even in stereo. The market for audio adaptors really opened up when the MPC Marketing Council announced the first MPC specification. The MPC 1 specification called for an 8-bit digital audio capability plus a simple music synthesizer for playing MIDI audio. Manufacturers rushed to bring out add-in boards with these capabilities or more. Because of the limitations of 8-bit digital audio, the ante was quickly upped to 16-bit stereo audio, which is now called for in the MPC 2 specification. I consider that to be the minimum requirement for any digital audio system.

Audio adaptors are generally plugged into a system bus slot, and they are connected externally to a set of small, but good quality speakers. Most adaptors have enough audio power output to directly drive small speakers, but there is also a good market for larger speakers that have their own amplification (*amplified* speakers).

Video Display Adaptors

From the beginning an IBM-compatible PC has required a plug-in video display adaptor. Although at first that seemed to be an unnecessary complexity, it was soon recognized as an advantage because the early video adaptors were very limited or else very expensive. However, as quantities increased and costs came down, improved adaptors became available at attractive prices and it was nice that you could simply plug in a new one. Only very recently have we seen systems with built-in video adaptors. These are usually VGA adaptors, which are now being superceded by Super-VGA (see later). That has only proven that it is still too early in the life of the PC industry to nail down something like a video adaptor. You can't hold back the trend of innovation!

The "standard" for video adaptors today is the *video graphics array* (VGA) adaptor, introduced by IBM with its PS/2 line of computers. However, VGA is no longer the preferred approach because it has limited colors. It's not even necessary to discuss the earlier "standards", but I'll mention them so you will recognize what they are if you come across their acronyms: monochrome display adaptor (MDA), color graphics adaptor (CGA), and enhanced graphics adaptor (EGA).

A display adaptor's basic task is to continuously read pixels from memory to support the scanning of the display monitor. This is called display *refresh*. For high-resolution, high-bpp displays, refresh represents a tremendous data rate because the display must be scanned 60 or more times per second to prevent flicker. For example, to support refresh of a $1024 \times 768 \times 24$-bpp display at 72-Hz rate calls for a data rate of 170 MB/second! There is no way that the CPU and the system bus could support such activity, let alone have anything left to do other tasks. Therefore, display adaptors have their own memory (display memory) on-board, and the refresh of the monitor is compeletely separate from the system bus and CPU. Of course, the CPU must still write to the display memory to put objects on the display. That is done in today's systems through the local bus, where the display adaptor is plugged in.

A VGA adaptor has a large number of different modes (including all the modes of the old adaptors already mentioned—backward compatibility). The most widely used mode is 640×480 pixels with 16 colors. This mode is quite satisfactory for graphic screens such as the Windows or OS/2 desktop screens, but it is not very useful for displaying any kind of real image or even high-quality drawings. That is because 16 colors is just not enough. VGA does have a 256-color mode, but the resolution must be reduced to 320×240 pixels, which gets blocky. The reason there are no better modes is that VGA is designed with only 256 KBytes of display memory. Within that memory size, one must trade off resolution to get more bits per pixel (colors).

There are several strategies for reproducing realistic images on a system with a small number of colors. These apply mostly to 4-bpp (16-color) and 8-bpp (256-color) systems. Video adaptors for 4 or 8 bpp use what is called a *color lookup table* (CLUT) or a color *palette*. In this kind of system, the video adaptor itself is capable of outputting more colors than can be distinguished by the bpp value of the image data. For example, a VGA adaptor has an output color range determined by 18 bpp (262,144 colors). However, the input data limit of 4 or 8 bpp means that only 16 or 256 of the 262,144 colors can be on the screen at one time. The values represented by the 4 or 8 bits in each pixel are used to look up the output color from the palette table or CLUT. This happens dynamically as pixels are read out to refresh the display.

With 256 colors, you can get surprisingly good reproduction of many images, especially if you choose the palette colors to match each image. There are a number of programs that can examine an image and choose the optimum 256-color palette for reproducing that image. Image4 in the \BOOK directory of the CD-ROM is an example of a 256-color image reproduced that way. On the other hand, image5 is an image that does not work well with only 256-colors. The real problem of customizing the palette for each image is that you have to change the entire screen's palette for every image and therefore you cannot display two images at the same time unless they use the same palette. When the palette is wrong for the image, the colors in the image become scrambled.

If the display adaptor is using only 16 or 256 colors, a different strategy can be used for reproducing a realistic image. This is called *dithering*. With dithering, the screen colors are approximated by varying the colors of adjacent pixels so the eye sees a mixture of them as the screen color. Image6 shows an example of dithering. You can see that the dithering does create colors that are not in the palette, but it trades off spatial resolution to do it. Neither 16-color dithering or 256-color custom palettes (or even both) really can reproduce good high-resolution realistic images.

The real solution to the problem of too-few colors is *Super VGA* (SVGA). SVGA adaptors are widely available and are even being built-in to some new systems. These adaptors remove the 256 K memory limitation and they have a selection of advanced modes going to 16 or 24 bpp. These modes become possible when you have more memory. The amount of memory on SVGA adaptors varies, but is usually at least 1 MB. Some adaptors can go to as much as 4 MB. Table 3.2 shows some of the mode choices on SVGA adaptors. The numbers in the table show how much display memory is required for each combination of resolution and number of colors.

Another display adaptor feature that is important to today's graphical interface systems (Windows, OS/2, etc.) is display acceleration. A *display accelerator* is a

Table 3.2 SVGA display modes and memory requirements in MB

		Number of Colors			
	bpp	4	8	16	24
Resolution		16	256	65536	16,777,216
640 x 480		1	1	1	1
800 x 600		1	1	1	2
1024 x 768		1	1	2	3
1280 x 960		1	2	3	4

special processor located on the display adaptor board to assist the CPU in drawing objects on the screen or changing the screen as the user creates, hides, or moves windows. Because those operations take a lot of CPU cycles, a display accelerator can speed up the system by 10 or 20 times by taking most of that work off the CPU. Acceleration is an essential feature of a display adaptor for digital video.

Another display adaptor feature that will be discussed in subsequent chapters is special hardware for video compression and decompression. Some display adaptors have such features, and other boards are designed to be used along with a display adaptor. In either case, the compression/decompression hardware assists the CPU in performing those tasks and substantially improves the speed and quality of digital video. As digital video becomes more widely used, more display adaptors will include these features.

DATA REQUIREMENTS

With the information just developed for video and audio, we can now look at overall data rates.

Digital Audio

Table 3.3 shows a number of possibilities for PCM audio algorithms. The lowest sampling frequencies and bits per sample values are good only for speech, and to obtain reasonable quality reproduction of general sounds, you should use at least 22 KHz sampling and 16 bps. The highest numbers correspond to CD audio. Notice that stereo always doubles the data—we simply add an identical second channel.

Table 3.3 Digital audio data requirements

Sampling Frequency (Hz)	Bits per Sample	Audio Bandwidth	Bytes per Minute	Stereo
11,025	8	5 KHz	662 KB	no
22,050	8	10 KHz	1.32 MB	no
22,050	16	10 KHz	2.65 MB	no
22,050	16	10 KHz	5.30 MB	yes
44,100	16	18 KHz	10.6 MB	yes

The bytes per minute column of Table 3.3 is the most telling. Here you can see how the data rates add up when you record reasonable amounts of sound. This data is what has to be stored on your hard disk, distributed on your CD-ROM or over your network. An application that has many minutes of audio will generate a lot of data, especially if you use the high-quality algorithms. As you will see in the chapter on data compression, these numbers can be reduced somewhat by the use of compression, however that requires a more sophisticated audio board. Fortunately, such boards are appearing and are low enough in price that they will probably become widely used. In the meantime, digital audio works perfectly well on most PCs if there is not too much other activity going on at the same time. The only problem is that it fills up your mass storage too fast.

Digital Video

The numbers for digital video will quickly convince you that it cannot work at all without some degree of data compression or other compromise. For example, if we wish to have full-screen 640 × 480 16-bpp video at 30 frames per second, the data rate is 18.4 MB per second. That would be 1,100 MB per minute! A 650 MB CD-ROM disc could only hold 35 seconds worth of video data! And we still have to add the audio data.

On a computer screen, you usually will want to have other information available at the same time as video is playing, so a reasonable compromise is often to reduce the size of the video window. Sometimes the video does not move too fast, in which case another compromise that works is to reduce the frame rate. Many scenes look reasonably good at 15 frames per second or even 10 fps. Below that, however, almost any motion will appear jerky. Table 3.4 shows what happens to the data rate with several combinations of window size and frame rates. Even with

Table 3.4 Motion video data rates (16-bpp, uncompressed)

Video Window Size	Frame Rate (per second)	Data	
		(per second)	(per minute)
640 × 480	30	18.4 MB	1,100 MB
320 × 240	15	2.3 MB	138 MB
160 × 120	15	575 KB	34.5 MB
160 × 120	10	384 KB	23 MB

the 160 × 120 video window (sometimes referred to as a *postage-stamp* window), which is 1/16th of a 640 × 480 full screen, the data rates are pushing what hard disks or CD-ROMs can do.

Reducing the bpp is another compromise that can be made. However, I do not recommend that for color images because of the problems with limited colors discussed previously. It is acceptable to reduce to 8 bpp for monochrome motion video—that cuts the numbers in half. Anyway you look at it, video compression is a necessity!

There are plenty of opportunities for compression of still images or motion video because the digital representation of both contains a lot of redundancy. Many algorithms have been developed that can compress video by as much as 100:1 below the numbers given in Table 3.4. However, they are extremely compute-intensive, to the point that most CPUs can run only simple algorithms and, even then, you have to give up all other concurrent activity when video is playing. A motion video accelerator or coprocessor is needed to help the CPU with video compression or decompression. As I mentioned, several of these are available, but so far none has had very wide acceptance. Most of the "motion video" we see today is of the postage-stamp variety and it's pretty bad. However, this will improve as better hardware comes out that supports larger video windows. This will be discussed further in the next chapter on data compression.

SYSTEM SOFTWARE

The performance of a system is determined not only by its hardware, but by its software. The operating system provides the primary interface to the hardware and is especially important. For example, the DOS (disk operating system) operating system, which began with the first IBM PC and has been regularly updated ever since, is very limiting to a modern system. DOS is a 16-bit system and cannot use the 32-bit capabilities of almost all of today's PCs. DOS is designed with the concept that only one program runs at a time and there is only one user at a time; you must stop one program and start another one whenever you need to move between programs. The one-at-a-time concept also means that whenever an application calls DOS to do something, the entire system is taken over by DOS until that operation is finished. So, for example, there is no way that you can have the system do something else while a long disk access is taking place. Also, DOS can directly utilize only the first megabyte of a system's RAM.

There are ways to circumvent these limitations, but they require that an application be programmed internally to go around DOS and directly access system resources. That makes the application more sensitive to the particular characteristics of the hardware, since the standardizing aspect of DOS is not being used. However, one thing you can say about programmers is that they are clever and resourceful, so many outstanding applications are written for DOS and many of them use all the system resources in spite of the OS.

An important recent advance in PC operating systems is the graphical user interface (GUI), shown in Figure 3.3. The first personal computer to have a GUI was the Apple Macintosh, introduced in 1984. (Other, more specialized, computers had GUIs before that, but they were too expensive for PC use until the Macintosh.) The Mac made its mark as an easy-to-learn and easy-to-use system, mostly because of the GUI and the uniformity with which it was implemented in applications. That happened because the GUI was built into the Mac OS. It took a while, but now we have several OSs or OS extensions that provide a GUI for an IBM-compatible PC.

Microsoft Windows

The most widely used PC GUI at this time is Microsoft Windows. Windows is not an OS itself, but rather an extension built on top of DOS. Because of that architecture, it retains some of the limitations of DOS, and it gets around some others. Windows (Version 3.1) overcomes the memory access limitation of DOS, and it provides for running more than one application at a time—up to a point. It does not get around the limitation that DOS stops everything else in the system when you access the disk, for example.

The ability to run multiple applications concurrently is called *multitasking*, and it comes in various flavors. Windows multitasking shares the system among several applications by periodically switching between them. This happens fast enough that you usually don't notice it. However, when one application gets the system, it can hold onto it as long as it likes; the OS cannot take the system back until the

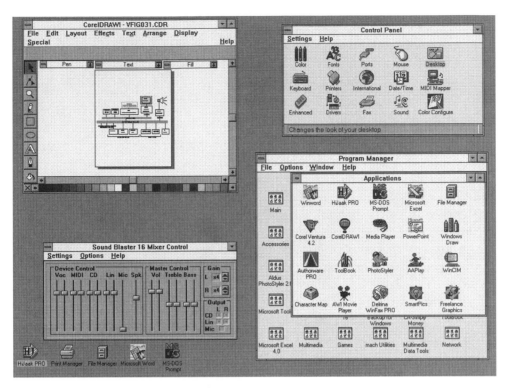

Figure 3.3 The Windows graphical user interface

application chooses to relinquish it. This only works well if all the applications are programmed to be well-behaved and avoid hogging the system. Some are and some aren't.

Many applications of digital video would like to have motion video or audio play while other activities take place in the application. This is effectively multitasking within the application, which also has a name—*multithreading*. Windows 3.1 doesn't do multithreading, but again ingenious programmers have found ways to get it inside their applications anyway. It works, but it can be upset if there are other applications running concurrently that don't play by the rules.

Although Windows lets each application have its own section of memory, no *protection* is applied, meaning that if an application tries to go outside its allocated memory space (usually because of a bug), nothing prevents the action. The result can be that the entire Windows system crashes and the system must be rebooted. Of course, any work that was in progress can get lost. This is not as bad as it sounds, because Windows applications are getting better and better and systems crashes are becoming rare.

In spite of these problems, Windows is an excellent environment that has a vast array of application program support, including some exciting digital motion video applications. Microsoft is well aware of the limitations in Windows, especially because some competitive systems have eliminated them. They have two initiatives to eliminate the problems. Windows NT is an advanced 32-bit OS that was introduced in 1993. It does not require DOS, it uses the x86 family CPU's built-in protection features to protect each application, and it has *preemptive multitasking*. Preemptive multitasking means that the system can interrupt an application at any time, no matter what it is doing. Therefore, the system can control the task switching to maintain priority of execution for each task. Windows NT also supports multithreading, so that applications can multitask within themselves using the system's scheduler for the purpose.

Windows NT's exciting features come with an entirely new API, meaning that programs have to be rewritten to benefit from some of the new things. However, a degree of backward compatibility is maintained, so programs written for Windows 3.1 will still run, and they do gain some benefit. Windows NT is definitely a high-end OS, and it has high-end needs for system resources. It takes a lot of hard disk space and RAM and runs well on only the fastest systems. Microsoft is not pushing it for general desktop PCs.

The second Microsoft initiative is Windows 95 (called Chicago during development), to be introduced in 1995. This also eliminates DOS, is 32-bits, and has preemptive multitasking. It will be an easier upgrade from Windows 3.1, without some of the high-end demands of Window NT.

IBM OS/2

The principal competitor to the Microsoft Windows scenario is IBM's OS/2 operating system. OS/2 in its present form (Version 2.x) has been around since 1992, and has gained something like 10% of the PC GUI market. It is a 32-bit OS with preemptive multitasking, multithreading, and memory protection. A typical OS/2 screen is shown in Figure 3.4. Note that it contains a mixture of Windows and OS/2 applications sharing the same screen. OS/2's system resource needs are competitive with Windows 3.1. OS/2 has its own unique API, so it requires specially designed applications to access all its features, but like Windows NT, it also will run Windows 3.1 and DOS applications and run them almost as well as Windows does. Because of these features, OS/2 is an excellent platform for digital video and audio. Its market share has grown large enough that some of the major applications are now being introduced in native OS/2 form. A new OS/2 release (called Warp) further improves performance while reducing system

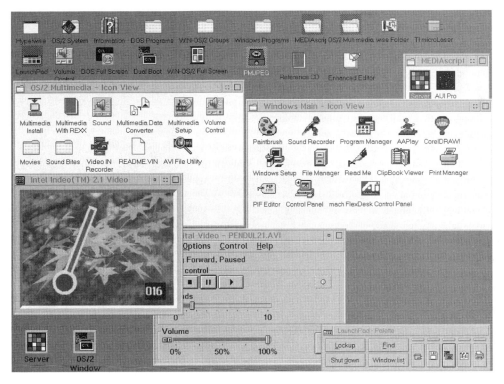

Figure 3.4 The OS/2 graphical user interface

resource requirements. That will further the acceptance of this high-performance operating system.

MCI

Digital video and audio capabilities are not usually built in to current operating systems. This is because they are too new and still changing too fast. However, GUI operating systems have included an easy way for users to add audio and video to their systems and make the capabilities available to all applications. For example, one can easily add audio annotation capability to any cell in a spreadsheet. Clicking on that cell causes a specified audio message to play. This is accomplished through an OS capability called *media control interface* (MCI).

MCI provides the means for any application to pass commands to a special class of driver called an MCI driver. An add-in hardware unit comes with its own MCI driver that is installed in the operating system the same as any other driver. For example, Figure 3.5 shows the Windows Control Panel screen with the

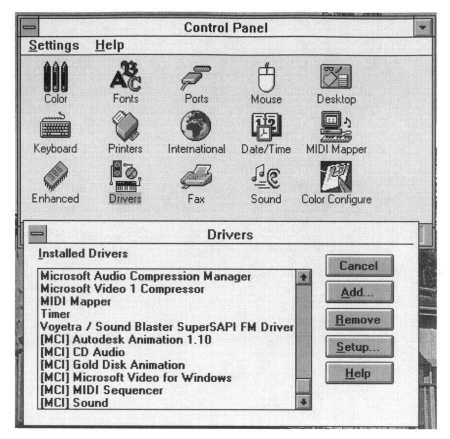

Figure 3.5 The Windows control panel, showing drivers

"Drivers" object open. The Drivers window shows a list of the MCI (and other) drivers that are installed on this system. Other applications in Windows can communicate with one of these drivers by sending an MCI message to the OS. The MCI message contains the name of the desired driver and a text string command to be given to that driver. The OS takes care of sending the message, so an application can, for example, tell the digital sound driver to play a specific file.

Neither the application nor the driver need to be specifically programmed for one another. The MCI command messages use a simple language, which the drivers are designed to understand. The language is extensible, so drivers having new capabilities can add new commands to the language. Also, all applications that will send MCI messages have to be designed to send messages to the OS MCI functions. Most applications designed or updated in the last several years have this capability. The users of these applications can cause them to send MCI messages by using their internal macro language, or other means that are provided to input MCI message strings.

There are other means for communication between applications in the GUI operating systems, including *dynamic data exchange* (DDE) and *object linking and embedding* (OLE). These protocols are more sophisticated (and more capable) than MCI, but they also require more programming to implement them. Nonetheless, the newer audio and video applications have support for them as well.

SUMMARY

This chapter has presented some of the PC architectural concepts that are important to digital video and audio. The hardware parameters that are important were highlighted, and numbers that relate them to the needs of video and audio were developed. Software architectures were also described, and the importance of operating system features to video and audio were pointed out.

4

Data Compression

The storage requirements for digital audio and, especially, video are mind-boggling as are the data transfer rates that must be achieved. Data compression is the solution to these problems. In the case of video, it is madatory—PC motion video is just not workable without it. In the case of audio, the system can run without using compression, but compression makes the job easier. This chapter will introduce some of the technologies available for audio and video data compression and discuss hardware and software for it.

WHY IS COMPRESSION POSSIBLE?

One reason for using digital technology in the first place is that data can be stored, copied, or replayed with absolutely no changes or errors occurring. Compressing data to make it smaller seems to be deliberately making changes or errors, so how can it work? The answer is that a data stream often may contain *redundancy*, meaning that there is repeated data or even unnecessary data. One way to compress is to find ways to change the data representation by eliminating redundancy so that there are, on the average, fewer bits. Probably the simplest example of this is *run-length encoding* (RLE).

RLE compression depends on there being a significant probability that adjacent data blocks (bytes or pixels) will repeat. For example, this often happens in video images, especially graphical ones, where a block of solid color will have many adjacent pixels of the same value. In that case, instead of having pixel after pixel with the same value, we can use a special code (called an *escape code*) that tells the system to recognize the next two pixels as a pixel value followed by a count of how many times to repeat that value. Figure 4.1 shows an example of RLE for 8-bit data. The escape code must be a pixel value that will never occur in an image, such as the maximum possible numerical value of a pixel (255 for

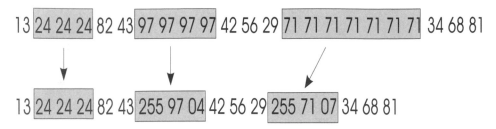

Figure 4.1 Run-length encoding for 8-bit data

8-bit pixels). The image is stored in RLE format, and when replayed and decompressed, the CPU will look for the escape code value in the data. Every time it is found, the CPU will perform the process of repeating the next pixel the number of times indicated by the following pixel. Then it will continue sending the data until it finds another escape code. This simple compression technique can often compress graphic images 2:1 or more, and the final image will be *exactly* the same as the original.

RLE is not very useful with audio, because an audio signal is constantly changing. At the most, it might compress the silent passages, or maybe some extremely low frequency audio. But most of the time, adjacent samples in audio will not be the same. Note that RLE as described produces no compression until a value is repeated more than two times. In fact, the escape code should not be used until there are at least four equal values in a row, for less than that, the escape code will only make the data larger!

LOSSLESS COMPRESSION

RLE and other compression techniques that reproduce data exactly when uncompressed are called *lossless* algorithms. RLE is a technique that works on any kind of data. It doesn't need to know what the data represents; so long as it can find repeated values, it will compress. There are better algorithms that look for repeated patterns, not just adjacent values. These techniques have been applied to compression of all data stored on a hard disk to effectively increase hard disk storage. One of these is the program called Stacker, published by Stac Electronics. Stacker can compress up to 2:1 on certain kinds of data. On most PCs, it can result in a 50% or more increase in hard disk storage. Note that a hard disk compressor adds processing to the task of storage and retrieval from disk, which takes time. However, the time to actually write or read the compressed data is less, so the total time to compress and store or decompress and retrieve may even decrease.

Compression algorithms always involve a tradeoff between degree of compression and the amount of processing required to compress and decompress. The amount of processing directly relates to how much time the algorithm will take—more processing, slower algorithm. It is possible to design compression so that the compression process takes longer than the decompression process. This is called *unbalancing* the compression and it is useful when it is important to have the fastest possible decompression, but the compression (that may be done only once for stored data) can be allowed to take more time. This is usually the case for audio and video, which have to be played back at a fixed rate for proper synchronization. Unbalancing can allow more compression without slowing the playback decompression.

LOSSY COMPRESSION

You can always "compress" simply by throwing data away. This isn't really useful unless you can find data that doesn't matter and delete it while keeping that which is essential. This is called *lossy* compression, and all the most powerful techniques for audio and video compression are lossy. Audio, and video especially, contains a lot of redundant data that can be modified or eliminated without affecting too much how the picture looks or the audio sounds. I don't intend to cover all of the techniques, but it is helpful to discuss some of the more important ones so you will be familiar with their names.

AUDIO COMPRESSION ALGORITHMS

Compression of speech audio has been extensively researched by the telephone industry, and it is an important part of modern telephony. One algorithm that grew out of that work is called *adaptive differential PCM* (ADPCM), and it is usable with general sound, not just speech. ADPCM works because most audio signals do not change by a large percentage between adjacent samples. I already pointed out that audio signals usually change between adjacent samples, but they usually do not change very much—only a small percentage of the total amplitude range. That means there can be an advantage in comparing adjacent samples and transmitting only their *differences*. This is where the differential in the name comes from. Since the differences are usually small, they can be coded with fewer bits than the total signal.

The differential approach works and can deliver up to 4:1 compression, but it has the fault that it will introduce distortion if the signal changes too fast between samples—that is called *slope overload*. That problem can be helped if the algorithm is modified by looking ahead during compression and adjusting the scale of the difference bits depending on the size of the changes that are coming. This is the *adaptive* part. It reduces slope overload distortion while retaining about 4:1 compression. However, it substantially complicates the algorithm so that a separate processor is usually required to do audio ADPCM. On the latest audio boards that implement ADPCM, a *digital signal processor* (DSP) chip is used for the processing, which is what is meant when you see the acronym DSP used in describing an audio board.

ADPCM is normally set up with 4 bits per sample to transmit 16-bit incoming samples, which means 4:1 compression. It does have some distortions on certain kinds of sounds, especially those that have sharp peaks of sound. You have to try it with the sounds you will be using to decide whether it is for you. This need to experiment is often the case with lossy compression algorithms—there's no substitute for actually hearing or seeing the result and evaluating it for yourself.

A second algorithm that came from speech-processing research is *subband coding* (SBC). SBC is based on a model of the human voice and really works only for speech. In that case, it can achieve compression of 10:1 or more compared to simple PCM. Because it expects the sound to fit the model of speech, where there is a fundamental tone that has been modified by the action of the human voice, SBC can produce some very strange results on other sounds such as music or effects.

STILL IMAGE COMPRESSION ALGORITHMS

Since a motion video stream is just a series of individual pictures at 30 per second, the techniques of still image compression represent a starting point for motion compression as well. A scanned image offers several opportunities for compression. In most images, there is a substantial degree of correlation between pixels that are near each other, both horizontally and vertically. Figure 4.2 shows an example using a drawing of a horse. The area around the horse's nose is expanded so you can see individual pixels. Notice how often adjacent pixels are the same both horizontally and vertically. Many techniques have been developed to exploit this.

One way to easily "compress" an image is to throw away alternate pixels, which simply reduces the resolution of the image. Depending on the viewing environment, the user may not see the lost resolution (because she is too far away from the screen). However, I don't accept that as valid compression—I prefer to talk of degree of compression that is achieved when the same number of pixels exist

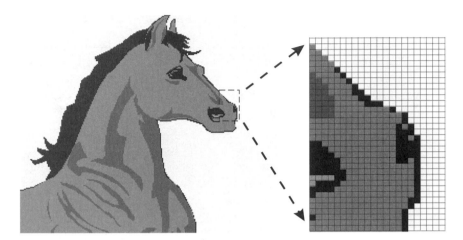

Figure 4.2 Adjacent pixels in graphics images are often the same

before and after compression. The degree of compression must always be stated along with the resulting picture quality. Compressing by throwing away pixels (throwing away quality) is not useful compression.

There are so many different ways to compress images that it becomes difficult and expensive to keep up with all the different algorithms that you might need to handle incoming image files. This has come to the point that there is a viable market for tools that do only still image format conversions. These tools often support more than 100 different formats. This indicates a serious need to develop standards for still image compression. The *Joint Photographic Expert Group* (JPEG) of the *International Electrotechnical Commission* (IEC) undertook this task. In 1992, the JPEG compression standard was adopted. Because there are so many different applications for image compression and each one has different requirements, the JPEG standard is not a single standard. Rather, it is *parameterized* to offer a range of options that allow it to fulfill the needs of many different industries. This makes the standard extremely complex. Depending on the choice of parameters, JPEG can be either lossless or lossy compression. The following lists some of the features of the JPEG standard:

- Lossless compression of images with wide range of size, aspect ratio, bpp, and content
- Lossy compression with same range of size, aspect ratio, bpp, and content
- Parameterization allows tradeoff of degree of compression vs. image quality

- Sequential encoding—the image is encoded in normal scan sequence
- Progressive encoding—the image is first encoded coarsely, with progressively more detail being added later
- Hierarchical encoding—the image is encoded at multiple resolutions

Of course, not all implementations of the standard have to provide all the options. When you are compressing an image, you have to choose the options from the list of which ones your system supports. When you decompress a JPEG image, however, the options are coded into the file header so the process is automatic unless, of course, the options in the file are not supported by your decompression software or hardware.

In the lossy compression mode on color images, JPEG compression can range from about 10:1 to over 50:1. In most cases, acceptable reproduction of high-quality images is achieved with compressions ranging between 10:1 and 20:1. Higher compressions produce too much distortion for most images.

The JPEG algorithms are highly compute-intensive. They are implemented in software in many current image-processing and image-using programs. With a fast processor, software JPEG takes anywhere from 2 seconds to 10 seconds to compress or decompress a full-screen image. Hardware processors are available in the form of chip sets that speed this up by 10 or more times. These processors are essential to use JPEG compression for motion video (motion-JPEG).

A set of sample images that show the performance of JPEG compression is included in the \BOOK directory of the CD-ROM accompanying this book. File image1.bmp is a 640 × 480 24-bpp original image. Files image2.bmp and image3.bmp show that same image JPEG-compressed and decompressed at 15:1 and 30:1 compression, respectively. Each image has an enlarged area that makes it easier to see the differences. The enlarged areas show clearly that compression has removed much of the detail of the woodgrain pattern. However, for normal viewing conditions, you can see that 15:1 compression gives excellent results, but more than that begins to show artifacts on most computer screens.

Note that the acceptability of compression depends on the size, or degree of enlargement, used in displaying the image. When an image is displayed small, or the viewer is a long distance from the screen, more compression can be tolerated. Of course, that is simply because the viewer cannot see as much detail in a small or distant image, so we might as well compress it out.

MOTION VIDEO COMPRESSION

In principle, motion video compression is simply repeating still image compression 30 times per second. However, in practice, that severely limits the ap-

(a) Motion video frames--the car is moving to the right

(b) reference frame (first) and difference frames (black areas represent no change)

Figure 4.3 Motion compensation

proaches available because most still image compression or decompression is too slow. Therefore, special fast algorithms have been developed for motion video. But you can do better than simply compressing 30 separate images per second by taking advantage of the redundancy between frames of a motion video stream.

Adjacent frames of motion video are often very similar to each other (see Figure 4.3(a). If part or all of the image is not moving, the frames or parts of them will be exactly the same. We don't have to keep sending the same still frame when nothing is moving. If the scene moves slowly, as when the camera is panning, each frame is just the previous frame moved slightly with a little strip of new information added. Figure 4.3(b) shows the frame differences determined from the stream of Figure 4.3(a). The first frame is a reference frame, so it is complete. The rest of the frames have to send only the movement of the car. You can see the possibilities of examining a stream of frames and removing the repeated information from one frame to the next. This type of compression is called *motion compensation*. The catch is that motion compensation is difficult and it takes a lot of processing. So most algorithms make compromises that take account of the available processing power.

Motion compensation compression causes each new frame to depend on the previous frame(s). This dependency makes it difficult to edit a video stream because the stream would always have to be played from the start up to the desired beginning frame of the edit. To alleviate this problem and also to prevent any errors or discrepancies in reproduction from accumulating, it is normal to periodically introduce *reference frames*. These are frames that are built from scratch—they do not depend on the previous frame at all. Too many reference frames will increase the data rate; normal practice is to have them once a second or once every 2 seconds. Then an editing system has to go back only 1 or 2 seconds to find a starting point to build up to the desired edit frame. Frames that are not reference frames are called *difference frames* or *delta frames*.

Software-only Motion Video

The ideal is to do motion video compression and decompression with the hardware already in a standard PC. This is *software-only* compression. Algorithms have been developed that work to some degree with partial-screen video windows. The degree depends directly on the power of the CPU and the speed of mass storage. For example, with the latest software-only algorithms, a 486 DX2 66 MHz system can play back a 320 × 240 video window at 15 frames per second. A Pentium machine can get the frame rate up to 30 per second. However, playback slows if you enlarge the video window; going to 640 × 480 pixels causes approximately 4:1 slowdown.

On the compression side, it is even more difficult to use software-only. Of course, you have to have hardware for receiving a video signal from a camera or VCR and digitizing it. This is called video capture, and there are many add-in boards for that. However, the problem with motion video capture is that the data rate between the capture board and mass storage is too high for the system unless you either use a very small window or you do some compression in real time while capturing. Table 3.4 in the previous chapter gives the numbers. Without any compression during capture, you are limited to 160 × 120 windows at 10 to 15 frames per second.

With the faster processors, you can do some compression during capture, which allows going to a 320 × 240 window at around 15 frames per second. Beyond that, you need hardware processing power to help with the compression.

The field of software-only compression and decompression is moving very rapidly with improvements and new algorithms appearing regularly. It is also subject to the advance of CPU, storage, and system power, which isn't standing still either. Products in this field must be very flexible, and we should expect that new algorithms and new hardware powers will have to be accomodated as soon as they appear. In 5 to 10 years, CPUs will be so fast that software-only motion video will fill most needs, but it isn't there today.

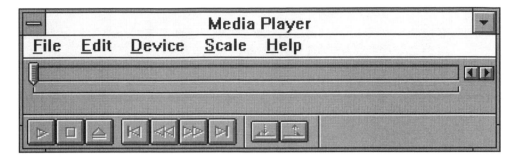

Figure 4.4 The main window of Microsoft Media Player

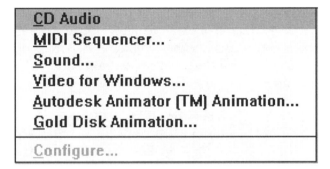

Figure 4.5 The device menu of Microsoft Media Player

Microsoft Video for Windows

Video for Windows (VfW) is the official motion video extension for Microsoft Windows. It is a software package that consists of drivers with installable algorithms and a set of tools for audio and video capture and editing. As new algorithms appear, they are installed in VfW, and new hardware offerings can include drivers that make them accessible to the system.

The key to VfW is an application called Media Player, which is supplied with Windows 3.1. The main window of Media Player is shown in Figure 4.4. It contains control buttons in the style of a VCR, a position indicator bar, and menus to choose what to play and how to play it. When you install VfW, it appears in the menus of Media Player, as shown in Figure 4.5. As you can see, Media Player is capable of playing audio, video, or animation. The items in the list of Figure 4.5 are all MCI object types—Media Player builds this list by searching for all MCI drivers installed on your system. If you install another item that fits the model of Media Player and it has an MCI driver, it will automatically appear in the Media Player menu.

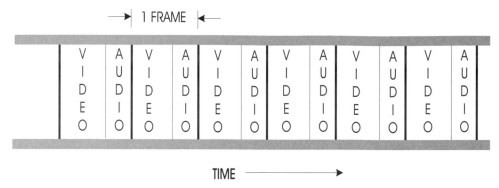

Figure 4.6 Interleaved audio-video data stream

Media Player also operates as a server to allow embedding of audio, video, or animation into the documents of other applications. This is accomplished via OLE communication between the other application and Media Player. By this means, the other application can call up Media Player to specify the item to play and how to play it. Upon closing Media Player, an icon is left in the other application's document. When the user clicks on that icon, the object will play.

The other programs included in VfW are VidCap, the video capture tool; VidEdit, the video editing tool; BitEdit, a bitmap editor; PalEdit, an editor for bitmap color palettes; and WaveEdit, a capture and editing tool for PCM audio. These tools will be discussed in detail in later chapters.

Video for Windows has its own special file format, called *audio-video interleaved* (AVI), that supports audio, video, or both together. Although the computer theoretically can play audio and video simultaneously from two separate files by having the mass storage unit seek back and forth between the two files as playback proceeds, that proves impractical with CD-ROM drives because the seek time is too long. There is a high probability that playback will be interrupted or synchronization will be upset during the seeks. This problem is solved by *interleaving* the audio and video into a single file (or data stream) as shown in Figure 4.6. The file is divided into sequential blocks, with each block containing both the audio and video data corresponding to the time duration of the block when it is played. Usually, the blocks correspond to single video frames, so each block holds one video frame and the associated amount of audio. Because you will not always capture the audio and video at the same time or you will need to edit them differently, the capture and editing tools support separate capture (as well as simultaneous), separate editing of audio and video, and the capability to separate or combine audio and video in AVI files.

When capturing video from a live video source, there is not much time per frame to run a sophisticated compression algorithm. For example, at 30 frames per second, you have only 1/30 second to process each frame. Therefore, real-time software-only compression algorithms tend to be limited in capability.

If you have a video source that can be stepped in single-frame increments, such as a laserdisc player or a professional VCR, you can run a more powerful algorithm by taking more time to process each frame. The VidCap tool supports doing that. Another way to get more compression is to capture frames to memory or to hard disk in real time without doing much or any compression. Then, the frames can be read back from memory one at a time and put through the compression algorithm. This takes a lot of memory, or an extremely fast hard disk. The large amount of data involved and the limited capacity of storage will still limit the length of a video clip captured this way.

Algorithms in Video for Windows

Four of the algorithms shipped with VfW are these:

- *Video 1* is the default compression method. It supports 8-bit and 16-bit video (24-bit is also supported, but it is converted to 16-bit), and a specified data transfer rate is produced. It also scales the playback quality to suit the capability of the current hardware.
- Microsoft *RLE Compressor* supports 8-bit video only. As the name implies, it uses run-length encoding and it is suitable for animations or for video that will be played on low-end (386SX) PCs.
- Intel *Indeo Compressor* always produces 24-bit video sequences. It is suitable for playback on high-end PC systems. It can be compressed in real time using the Intel Smart Video Recorder board.
- SuperMac *CinePak Compressor* is a high-quality compression method that cannot compress in real time, but it plays back in software on high-end systems. CinePak always uses the 24-bit format, and it produces excellent image and motion quality at 320×240 resolution and 15 frames/second at 150 KB/second data rate.

IBM Ultimotion

The standard motion video system for OS/2 is IBM Ultimotion. A media player application, called Digital Video, is built-in to OS/2. It supports PCM audio, video, or MIDI audio. The window of Digital Video is shown in Figure 4.7. Video can be played in IBM Ultimotion format or in Intel Indeo format. In both cases, the files are AVI format.

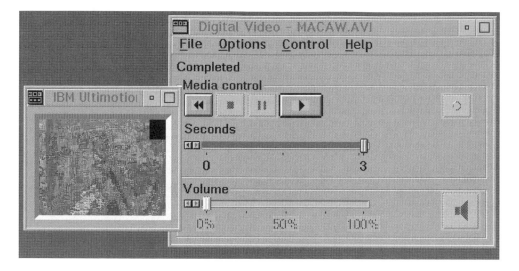

Figure 4.7 OS/2 digital video player

Capture of Ultimotion video is done with the IBM program called Ultimedia Video IN. This program is a combined capture and editing tool. The algorithms available with Video IN are:

- IBM *Ultimotion Asymmetric* is available only in frame-step recording from a laserdisc player or other frame-step device. It provides the highest quality compression at CD-ROM data rates, but the compression process is slow.
- Intel *Indeo* compression is the same as in Video for Windows.
- IBM *Ultimotion Real-Time* is used for recording from a live video source such as a camera or VCR. It operates without hardware support (except for a capture board) and can provide 320 × 240 resolution at 15 frames/second.

THE MPEG STANDARD

The motion video compression algorithms already described are not standards in the international sense, as is the JPEG standard. Rather, they are proprietary "standards" developed by individual manufacturers. There's nothing wrong with that, and to the degree that a manufacturer is successful, its algorithm may be widely used. However, a standard supported by a group that is independent of any one manufacturer or any one country is even better because no competitive or nationalistic stigma is attached to it. That is the objective of international organizations such as the International Electrotechnical Commission (IEC), which standardized the JPEG still image format. We need the same thing for motion video.

Another subgroup of the IEC, the *Motion Picture Expert Group* (MPEG), has undertaken that task. A first standard, MPEG 1 is complete—for PC motion video at data rates around 150 KB/second. This standard embraces many of the concepts of JPEG, including the parameterization feature. That will ensure the standard is applicable to many diverse fields. MPEG has used the same underlying compression techniques as JPEG, applying them to individual frames of a video stream. However, they have added a motion compensation technique, including the concept of reference and difference frames described earlier. The interframe difference concept has also been expanded by adding what are called *interpolated* frames, which are frames built by interpolating between a previous and a future frame. The use of the three frame types is too complex to discuss here, but it provides a high degree of compression while allowing for features such as slow or fast motion playback and bidirectional playback.

The MPEG algorithms are so compute-intensive that there is little possibility of real-time operation on present day PCs without special-purpose hardware support. Several add-in boards have been developed for MPEG 1 compression and playback, and programmable video compression systems such as DVI Technology are working on supporting it also. MPEG 1 compression provides the best performance yet, but it is still in an early stage while cost reduction and product design is taking place. The MPEG committee is also working on a MPEG-2 standard, which will deliver broadcast-quality motion video at somewhat higher data rates.

COMPRESSION HARDWARE

Add-in boards are available to enhance both audio and video compression. For audio, they allow compression to be used without burdening the CPU. In the case of video, the special hardware allows a powerful compression algorithm to be run in real-time while capture is being done. This eliminates the need to capture and compress separately. Except for DVI technology (described later), which has been on the market since 1989, video compression hardware is just appearing on the market. This hardware will make high-quality digital motion video really practical. CPU manufacturers are planning to include these capabilities in future CPU chips. When that happens, every new PC will be able to do full-screen motion video.

Audio Compression Boards

In Chapter 3, I described ADPCM audio compression. That can deliver up to 4:1 compression of PCM audio streams. However, doing ADPCM in software uses a lot of CPU cycles and is practical only on fast machines. Even so, it is now available in the latest update releases of Microsoft Windows and OS/2. Some audio cards have a digital signal processor on-board to perform ADPCM compression and decompression. There are no widely accepted standards for this yet, and audio compression is so far not widely used.

Intel DVI Technology

Several video compression boards are based on the Intel i750 Video Processor chips, which were developed as part of Intel's *DVI technology*. Those chips provide a powerful set of video processing functions that operate independent of the system CPU to perform real-time video compression or decompression. The chips are fully programmable in on-chip RAM so that they are capable of running numerous algorithms simply by changing the on-chip program. Special algorithms optimized for these chips have been developed—among other things, they can provide up to full-screen motion video at 30 frames per second.

The Intel *ActionMedia II* board is the top of the line. It includes both video and audio capture, compression, and playback capability on one board in either AT-bus or MCA format. It functions as a video display adaptor, but it is not a standard VGA. Since most PCs applications expect there to be a standard VGA, the ActionMedia II board has a special *keyed* mode where it works in parallel with a standard VGA or SVGA adaptor to provide combined VGA-DVI displays on one or two monitors.

Figure 4.8 shows how the DVI keyed mode combines the output from an ActionMedia II board (called the *DVI plane*) with a standard VGA (called the *VGA plane*). The color of each pixel in the VGA plane is used to control whether the monitor displays DVI or VGA for that pixel. If the VGA pixel is black, DVI is shown; for any other VGA color, VGA data is displayed.

DVI Technology is a package of chips, algorithms, and boards that implements full-motion video and audio using the unique hardware features of the i750 chips. It has its own software and file formats and has been widely used in interactive kiosks, military and industrial training, and information delivery systems. DVI Technology offers real-time compression on your PC. This is called *real-time video* (RTV), and it provides up to full-screen video. RTV performance is very satisfactory for most uses when the video is played at quarter-screen size or smaller, but it has limitations when viewed at full-screen size. The latest version of RTV is

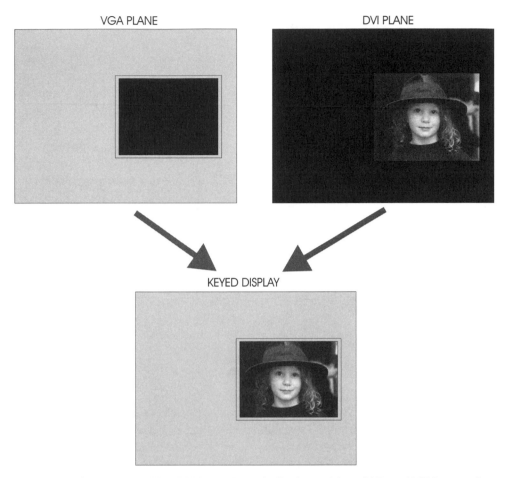

Figure 4.8 Operation of the DVI keyed mode that combines DVI and VGA on a single display

compatible with the Indeo compression available in Video for Windows and OS/2 Video IN.

To obtain the best possible full-screen video performance, there is another DVI compression algorithm called *production-level video* (PLV). PLV cannot be compressed on a PC; to use it you must send your video on videotape to a compression service that uses mainframe power systems to do the compression. The resulting PLV video file plays back on your DVI PC and delivers VCR quality full-screen video. The data rate of PLV can be as low as 150 kB/sec, suitable even for single-speed CD-ROM distribution.

DVI Technology is supported by IBM as well as Intel, but it has not been broadly marketed except in professional circles. However, DVI Technology is still the leading motion video system for PCs (more than 100,000 ActionMedia II boards are in use for information delivery kiosks, industrial training, and government and military applications), and it delivers the performance that the others are striving for. Several new products based on ActionMedia II are in development.

To create a bridge between the i750 chips and the software-only motion video field, Intel has developed the Indeo compression algorithm. Indeo can run on the i750 chips and the ActionMedia II board, but it creates a standard AVI video file that can play with the Video for Windows software applications. There is a version of Indeo for software-only use.

Intel is also marketing a low-cost product called the *Smart Video Recorder* (SVR), that uses the i750 processor to do real-time Indeo compression on any PC. It supports hardware-assisted video capture, but it does not assist playback, which is software-only. The SVR only does video, you need a standard PC audio board for your audio capability. The SVR is being widely marketed.

Other boards using the i750 chips are available from Creative Technologies and ATI.

MPEG Hardware

With the first MPEG standard nearly complete, some companies have designed custom chips to perform the algorithm and add-in boards are starting to appear. One of the first of these is the *RealMagic* board by Sigma Designs. It is a low-priced playback-only board that works alongside a VGA adaptor. It is optimized for playback at CD-ROM data rates. Most of the video software developers are working to support it.

MPEG capture hardware is still extremely expensive, and your best bet is to capture in another format (even analog) and have MPEG compression done off-line by a compression service house, as you do for Intel's PLV. I expect that will change soon and we'll see MPEG capture hardware suitable for desktop use.

Frame Grabber Boards

A large number of boards simply do video analog to digital conversion. These are used to display analog video on the computer screen or to capture a still image from a live analog video input (*frame grabbing*). With Video for Windows or Ultimotion software, these same boards can capture motion video. There is no hardware-assisted compression, so the results are limited to what can be done in software. On today's high-performance PCs, such a setup can capture up to 320×240 pixels at 15 frames per second.

SUMMARY

This chapter has described the basis for video and audio compression, both lossless and lossy. Various algorithms were described, and hardware and software for compression was discussed. Although software-only compression and decompression is becoming widely used, hardware support is necessary for high-quality or full-screen motion video.

Later chapters will cover the use of these items in more detail. I have now completed all the technical background, and you should be equipped with the knowledge and terminology to proceed with the main body of this book, which will discuss the actual tasks of using digital video.

5

Planning for PC Video Production

You are probably familiar with the professional method of producing video for TV or the movies. The scene of a large production studio is familiar to us all. With the masses of equipment, sets, lights, and dozens of people, it seems like the ultimate large, expensive operation. PC video production could be done the same way—and sometimes it is—but in this book I will stick to a much smaller scale. My scale of production is done by one person—you—maybe with one or two helpers. It is still a complicated process, and depending on the costs of the things you put in front of the camera, it can get expensive. There is no substitute for careful planning before you proceed to minimize cost and aggravation and guarantee a good result. This chapter is about the planning you should do before capturing the first second of video.

WHAT IS THE PURPOSE OF THE VIDEO?

You need to know precisely what you are trying to accomplish in producing a video. What does the video add to your application? Who will be looking at it? What message is it supposed to tell? You must start these considerations by stepping back and asking the same questions about the entire application in which the video will be included.

If you know the objective of the application, you can better decide where video fits into it, if at all, and from that you can develop the objective of the video itself. The most important thing about planning for video is deciding where in your application you will use video. For each piece of the application, you first decide what the application must present and then what medium to use to present it.

Maybe you already know these answers, but in case you don't, I will discuss some of the things you can do to get the answers.

In planning for the video content of the application you will need to know how much video the application can realistically contain. That will probably depend on how the application is going to be distributed, a subject covered fully in Chapter 14. You should create a budget for video—specify a total amount in seconds or megabytes. As you plan the application, you can allocate pieces of the video budget to parts of the application. This will help you when the inevitable tradeoffs have to be made. When your video budget gets tight, you may have to use alternate approaches in some places. The trick is in evaluating the different parts of the application so that the video is used in the best possible places.

Your application probably falls into one of the broad classes that were introduced in Chapter 1. Each of these has different reasons for using video.

Information Delivery

Many information delivery applications are dealing with the presentation of a body of information that already exists. If that information includes video, then the application must show video, and the purpose of the video is simply to be shown. This would be the case for an application that was presenting the news archives on a certain subject. When the archives contain video, the application must show it or else it is not doing a complete job of delivering the archives.

Sometimes, however, the application calls for video, but there is too much of it. An example is a database of information about movies, to be produced on CD-ROM for use by consumers in choosing movies to rent or buy. The database contains text information on 30,000 movies that have been produced since the industry began, and it would be nice to include video trailers for all these movies where available. Since trailers typically run several minutes, you can see that they could represent 1,000 hours or more of video, so it will be impossible to include more than a tiny subset on a single CD-ROM. You will have to narrow down the list of video trailers to a few hundred at most.

A different case of information delivery is, for example, a shopping mall kiosk that presents information to consumers about the features of the mall. Much of the material here could probably be delivered with text, audio, and still pictures. However, you might use video to "jazz it up" to make the kiosk more interesting and to better hold the consumer's interest. In that case, the purpose of the video is cosmetic, but that's exactly what the application needs.

Training and Education

The objective of these applications is to teach. To facilitate that, the content must be presented in the most clear and easy to understand way possible. Often that calls for video. For example, when the subject of the application involves actions or physical procedures, video would be the best medium to use. The reason for using video here is that it offers the clearest presentation.

When the training or education situation involves a simulation, there may be a requirement for realism that can be met only with video. In that case, the reason for using video is to achieve realism.

Teaching is most effective when the student becomes interested and involved in the process. Video can often help attract the student, which is another of those important "cosmetic" reasons for using video.

Entertainment

Entertainment use of video is a lot like training or education in that you have to convey realism, deliver action, and hold the user's attention. The difference is that the primary objective is fun, rather than learning. The user may be learning, too, but his first reaction must be that he is having fun. Most interactive entertainment applications solve this problem by making a game, which is simply a structured environment where the user is required to solve some kind of problem related to the subject of the entertainment.

When you are building a game environment, the playability of the environment over time will require that the environment be large. It must contain many optional paths to be found and explored, so that the user can play for hours without becoming bored. This is difficult to accomplish with video only because an application delivered on a single CD-ROM cannot have more than one or two hours of video content. Thus, you may want to base the bulk of the environment on less data-intensive media such as still images, animation, text, and audio. The video budget can then be allocated such that it comes into play at highlight points in the application. This is one place where you often would like to include more video than you can afford.

Productivity

Spreadsheets, word processors, databases, and other productivity applications have the purpose of collecting, cataloging, storing, manipulating, or presenting data. Usually the data being handled is not video, and the inclusion of video in these applications is somewhat incidental. It can be useful, however, for person-

Table 5.1 Reasons for using motion video

Video is content	The purpose of the application is to show video.
Clearest presentation	Video is the best way to show action or physical procedures.
Realism	Motion video is very realistic.
Personalizing	Include people in action that the user will recognize.
Cosmetic	Make the application interesting and attractive— usually to grab the user's attention.

alizing the presentation of the data as, for example, when a video clip is used to annotate a spreadsheet. This is important when it helps people other than the designer understand the content of the spreadsheet. Note that audio by itself is also useful for personalizing.

Productivity applications usually have a significant learning curve for their users. Most good applications include on-line help systems and tutorials, which are examples of information delivery and training that is included in the productivity application. In these situations, video serves the same purpose as it does in training or information delivery.

Summary of Reasons

The preceding discussion of classes of application has generated a list of reasons for using video, which is summarized in Table 5.1. Each of your uses of video should fit one or more of these reasons. If it does not, you should either use a different medium or come up with your own unique reason for why video should be used.

As you are going through your application and deciding on the places you will use video and why, start a list of all of them. The list should identify where the video is in the application, and a sentence or two about its subject. This will help you in the detailed planning later.

WHERE WILL YOU GET THE VIDEO?

There are other sources of video besides creating it yourself. These include in-house archives, clip video libraries, and outside production. With the exception of outside production, the other sources may be cheaper and faster than doing the video yourself. However, video requirements tend to be pretty specialized and unless you or your company have for some time been collecting video clips that apply to your work, it is unlikely that you will find what you need already available.

Thus, in most cases you will have to choose between hiring someone to produce the video or doing it yourself. If you are considering hiring someone, you can find about such people in your area by looking in the Yellow Pages under "Video Production Services." Although professional video production will deliver, well, professional results, it can be expensive. Thus, it is reasonable to consider whether you have the equipment, facilities, talent, and skill to do the video yourself, without going outside.

The equipment requirements depend on what kind of production you need. For example, if you can do the production in the vicinity of your PC, you can go directly to digital capture and eliminate the need for any analog equipment except the video camera. However, if the production has to be at a location where you cannot reasonably have a PC present, you will have to produce on videotape and do the digitizing later. That will raise the equipment ante considerably because you should use professional-level recording equipment to get the best results. It also means that there are more steps in the process of production.

The facilities requirements refer to the need for a studio, lights, sets, or studio props called for in the scene content of the video. If these things are available, you're home free. Otherwise, you will have to acquire them through construction or leasing from theater supply or other sources.

The talent, of course, refers to the people who will be in front of the camera. That may be you, someone else from your organization or family, or hired talent. If you are located in a metropolitan area, you will find many local sources of talent under "Theatrical..." in the Yellow Pages. If you will be doing a lot of videos, you should devote specific effort to learning about the sources of talent in your company and your area.

The skills to do the video involve the planning that we are discussing here, the collection of all the materials, facilities, and talent involved; the setup of the equipment, sets, and lighting at the production site; and the operation of the equipment during the production. All of these are things that you or anyone else can learn, but if your needs are sophisticated, you may have to consider professionals. Some of these subjects are covered further in later chapters, so you can learn some more about them before you decide how they will get done. I will continue this discussion under the assumption that you are at least involved in everything that gets done, if not actually doing it yourself.

THE PLANNING

The elements of planning that I will discuss in this chapter are the treatment, the type of production, the script, the location, who will be involved, the equipment, and handling the audio.

The Treatment

Depending on the number of people who have to approve the video production, it is a good idea to start the planning process by writing a narrative description of the project. This can be a one or two page text document that describes the general idea of the video segment in enough detail that people can see (and approve) what you are setting out to do. In production circles, such a document is called a *treatment*. If you are working for yourself and the project is simple, you can carry this in your head, but in most cases you should write it down.

The Type of Production

For simple productions, you can set up everything and run your complete video live while recording it with a single camera. This is the style of a stage show. It works if the action can reasonably be run continuously from start to finish, and if you don't want to do anything fancy with the camera other than panning or zooming. This is the simplest type of production, but it is seldom used in professional video work.

More typical is the production–postproduction style. Here, the production process concerns itself with getting all the parts of the video onto tape (or hard disk), without trying to put them together during shooting. After all the shooting is done, the recorded material is taken into an editing studio and assembled into the final video. This process, called *postproduction*, provides the flexibility to have different camera angles in the same scene, to combine material shot at different times or different locations, and to add all kinds of dynamic effects for camera transitions. Almost everything you see on TV except live news is done this way. It is a more complex process, it takes longer, and the equipment costs may be more than doubled (although costs are coming down, especially if postproduction is done on a PC). But the payoff in the results you can achieve is usually worth all that.

There is an in-between approach, sometimes called *in-camera editing*. In this style, you use the editing capabilities of most camcorders or VCRs to assemble the parts of the video during the shooting. This doesn't take any additional equipment, but it does take additional time, and that may be time while you have everything set up in the studio or on location and expensive talent or support people may be standing around. So it can cost more, and it really only works to do camera cuts between shots. There is no flexibility to combine prerecorded materials or to do dynamic effects. Except for very simple productions, in-camera editing is not a good deal. Most of the discussion that follows will assume that some amount of postproduction will be used.

The Script

The content of the video is described by the script. With an overall picture of the video sequence in your mind or in your written treatment, you should first divide it into *scenes*. A scene is any part of your video where the action on-camera flows continuously without change of location or interruption of time scale. During one scene, the camera may move, pan, tilt, or zoom, but the action it sees is continuous. It is not necessary that a complete scene be shot in one pass, but it should look like that to the viewer. Of course, it will be easier for you to shoot it all at once, but that will limit you in terms of the kind of effects that you can use. In professional work, most scenes are divided up into a number of *shots* for production. The shots are produced separately and put together in postproduction editing.

The Storyboard

It is often useful to first develop the script in *storyboard* format. A simple example is shown in Figure 5.1. One or more sketches is made for each scene, showing roughly how that part of the scene will look. If you plan to have several different camera angles used during the scene, you probably should make a sketch for each one. The sketches are accompanied by narrative text or notes that describe the considerations of each part. The type of transition between scenes can also be indicated on the storyboard. This is a good way to get a quick overview of the content of the total project and how it flows together. It is also useful when you need to explain the scene to others, such as your boss, your client, or your subordinates.

The Audio Script

If there will be audio with your video, you should begin mapping that out at the storyboard stage. Often the audio script will determine the time line for the video.

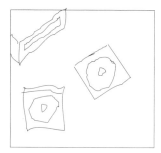 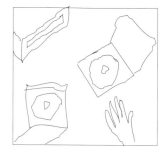 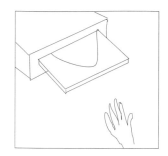

- Show still image
  (first frame of video)
- Start audio voice-over

- Open the jewel case
- open the caddy
- Transfer the disc
- Close the caddy
- Continue voice-over

- Insert caddy into drive
- Continue the audio

Figure 5.1 A storyboard

For example, if there is to be a *talking head* scene (a scene where a person is shown close-up on camera and talking), that scene will have to be at least as long as the time it takes for the person to say his message. For the smoothest, most professional-looking video, the audio and video timing should match exactly without the need to add "waits" in either of them.

A good technique for simple productions is to build the audio track first and then use that to establish the timing of the video. You usually have more flexibility during production to control the timing of video rather than audio, but if you cannot get the video timing to fit, you may have to rewrite the audio script. Of course, any scenes where synchronized audio is needed (such as the talking head), the video and audio will have to be produced at the same time.

The Video Script

Once a storyboard is agreed upon, the audio script can be written, and a video script can be developed. The video script should describe the setting for each scene, who will be on camera, and what they will do. With the video script, you can begin working out what the camera will do for each scene—will it be close-up or wide, does the camera angle move, such as in panning, tilting, or zooming. The handling of the camera is one of the places where professional experience will affect the quality of the production. I am not going to cover all these issues here—plenty of books, tapes, and courses are available on camera technique and video production design (see the Bibliography).

One way to learn about video production that is available to everyone is to study how some of the things you need to do are handled on television. You just have to learn to watch the production instead of the content. A good producer will handle things so smoothly that you may have to watch a video sequence several times before you can separate out what he did at each step. Of course, that's one of the objectives of good production—the viewer should be aware of the content only, the production itself should be invisible.

The final delivery medium significantly affects the design of a production. There are large differences between producing for the movies, producing for television, and producing for PCs. The differences are caused by the different viewing environments and the different technical capabilities of each medium. The special considerations of PC video will be covered as we go along.

The Location

The best place to shoot video or audio is a *studio*, where you can control the environment of the shooting—the background, the lighting, the sound. Although it is nice to have a fully equipped video studio, any nonpublic room that is large enough and has electrical power can serve as a studio. An unoccupied conference room is usually fine. The important thing is that is must allow you to control the environment, at least during shooting.

Sometimes, you cannot use a studio because the scene is where it is and is impossible to move or the natural environment is to be part of the scene. Then, you must shoot *on location*, which means you take all your equipment to the location of the scene and shoot there. Location shooting is more demanding because you are usually away from your sources of supply, and you cannot control all the aspects of the environment that will affect your production. Planning becomes even more important. But if the video content calls for location shooting, you have to do it.

The Equipment

The basic piece of equipment for video production is a video camera. However, outside of the broadcast field, most cameras today come in the form of a camcorder—a camera combined with a recorder. A camcorder is a good bargain and convenient to use, but you don't always have to use the recorder part because camcorders also have a separate live video output. In fact, except for high-end camcorders using the advanced tape formats like S-VHS, Hi-8, or BetaCam, you will get better results by not using the recorder and connecting the camera directly to your PC. However, this is not always practical, especially on location. I'll have more to say about cameras and recorders in the next chapter.

Other production hardware includes camera mounting equipment (tripod, dolly, crane, stabilizer, etc.), lighting equipment, audio equipment, monitoring equipment, and all the cables and other devices needed to connect items and mount them. If you will be doing a lot of production, you will want to own many of these items. However, most of this equipment can also be rented on a daily basis from local audio-visual equipment suppliers.

Handling the Audio

Except in the case of a talking head shot or other situations that must have synchronized (*lip-sync*) audio, the production of audio is a separate process. Audio and video are merged in postproduction. Even when the audio is shot with the video, there may be need for separate processing of the audio to enhance it or to mix in other elements, such as background music and sound effects. To facilitate separate handling of audio and for better quality, professionals often run separate audio recorders during video production. This works well, but you must provide means for synchronization of audio and video for each shot. This can be done with a device that marks both audio and video at the same time at the start of each recording. The *clapboard* slate that you often see in professional production is used for that purpose. The slate identifies the shot, the clapping of the lever is heard in the audio, and the exact frame where the clap occurs can be located visually in the video.

A more sophisticated means of synchronization during production and post-production is *time code*. That is a special track containing a digital code that is placed on all recordings to uniquely identify each frame of video and its associated block of audio. Time code is also the best means to identify edit or cut points in the video and audio during postproduction.

When the scene involves *voice-over* audio, it usually is best to record the voice-over track ahead of time, so that it can be played during the video shooting to make sure the video shots fit into the time line of the audio. If the video turns out to be too long to fit the audio, pauses can be added to the audio in postproduction, but it is much more difficult to fix the case where the video is too short for the audio. If you know that during video production, you may be able to do things to make the video longer, such as shooting different views that can be edited in to fill out the time. In the worst case, you might have to rescript and rerecord the audio.

AN EXAMPLE

Let us revisit the example shown by the storyboard of Figure 5.1. This is a scene from a training program for new computer users. The purpose of the scene is to show someone how to use the CD-ROM caddy included with some CD-ROM drives. This is a case where the use of motion video will effectively show the particular hand motions required to operate the caddy and the drive. You will be surprised by how many planning considerations apply even to a simple scene such as this.

You could do a scene like this by showing a person who describes the operation while he is doing it. Maybe the camera could zoom in on the person's hands as he opens the caddy and inserts the disc. That would be something that you could produce all in one shot, eliminating any editing.

However, because this will be a part of a large application with many other more important uses of video, the amount of video here should be minimized. We can save maybe half of the video if we have the scene begin with a still that is actually the first frame of the video. Voice-over on the still describes the task. After that, motion video begins with hands coming into the picture and loading the caddy. The last part of the scene, which might have to be a different shot, shows the caddy being inserted into the drive. Voice-over continues to complete the description. This approach requires one edit, which you might attempt as an in-camera edit. However, if you have postproduction capability available, it would give a nicer effect to use a dissolve to change the camera angles rather than the abrupt cut transition that the camera could do.

This scene is shown by setting up the presentation software to display the first frame of the video but not starting the action. Then start the audio and, on the appropriate cue, begin the video playing. Most of the presentation programs that are used for this type of application can do that.

The script for this example is shown in Listing 5.1. It is in a typical two-column format that places the audio and video scripts side-by-side with their time lines matched vertically. The audio script on the right is all to be read by the voice-over announcer; it is divided into sections so that the video action for each section can be described in the video script on the left. Of course, the announcer should read the script smoothly without reacting to the separate sections in the script.

You can see that a lot of thought can go into even a simple example such as this one. It will pay off in the quality of the resulting video, the ease with which you can accomplish its production, and the minimization of surprises during production.

Listing 5.1 Script for example of Figure 5.1

VIDEO	AUDIO
Closeup still shot of CD jewel case, CD caddy, and front of CD-ROM drive. This is actually the first frame of video.	Announcer: Some CD-ROM drives use a special carrier called a caddy to hold the disc in the drive. To use these drives you must first transfer the disc from its jewel case to the caddy and then insert the caddy into the drive.
Begin video, hands come into view and open the jewel case and the caddy.	Ann: Open the jewel case, then pick up the caddy with one hand, squeezing the two tabs on the end opposite the arrow. With the other hand, open the cover by lifting between the two squeeze tabs.
Hands transfer the disc to the caddy.	Ann: Transfer the disc to the caddy, keeping the label side up.
Hands close the cover	Ann: Close the caddy cover.
Hands open the drive door and insert the caddy	Ann: Now open the drive door and insert the caddy with the arrow end first and the disc label up.
Hands push the caddy in	Ann: Push the caddy in until it clicks into place.

SUMMARY

In this chapter you have learned about how to choose the places where video will be most effective in your applications and how to plan for the acquisition or production of that video. The planning includes writing treatments, scripting, choosing scenes and shots, picking shooting locations, equipment requirements, and the handling of audio. An example of a script for a simple scene was given. The next chapter will discuss the production process.

6

Video Production for PC Use

Once your script is completed and approved by all the parties involved, you are ready to approach the production task itself. This chapter covers the issues you face when doing or managing the production yourself.

ANALOG vs. DIGITAL PRODUCTION

The first question you have to answer is what kind of production you will do. Since your output is going to be digital video on a computer, it is reasonable to think that you should capture directly to hard disk during production. That is called *digital production,* and it means that a PC is present at the production site and all video and audio is captured directly to hard disk. The alternative is to record the production on analog videotape and audiotape and do the digitizing at a later time, before postproduction. This is *analog production*. There are pros and cons for each.

The advantages of digital production are that it eliminates a separate digitizing step and avoids any possible quality degradation from analog tape. It also needs no tape equipment, so it saves cost in that area. The disadvantages are that you must take a PC to the production site and, if you have a lot of repeat takes that you want to keep, it fills up your hard disk. Because of this latter problem, you will probably feel constrained during the production and will want to make decisions that reduce the amount of total time you record. Such an issue has nothing to do with the production itself. It is a diversion.

The advantages of analog production are that you need not have a PC around during production, and tape equipment, especially a camcorder, is very convenient and unobtrusive. Also, tape is inexpensive and reusable, so you don't have to worry about how much recording you do. The disadvantages are that for the best results you need professional-quality recording equipment, which is expensive, and postproduction activity is necessary to assemble your final sequence. Even if you produce the entire scene in one shot, you'll need postproduction to digitize and cut the scene to length.

More than anything, I think this decision depends on how much video production you will be doing. If you expect to be doing only a few short sequences at a time and you can design them to be shot in a simple manner, you would choose to do digital production simply because it avoids the expense of recording equipment and postproduction and the total job will be quicker.

On the other hand, if you will be doing a lot of video and expect much of it to require postproduction activity anyway, then you can justify the expense of recording equipment, and the production process will be simpler and more flexible as a result. Today, practically all professional videomaking uses analog production followed by postproduction.

HOW MANY CAMERAS?

The image of the live television production with multiple cameras and lots of people is not the way most video is produced. Generally, video production uses one camera at a time, recording onto tape or hard disk. The effect of multiple cameras is created in postproduction where all the individual shots and camera angles are put together. There are many reasons for "single-camera" shooting, but they all relate to the fact that you can optimize everything about the shot for the viewpoint of the single camera. Therefore your lighting, staging, and acting plays only to the one camera and everyone does not have to worry about making things look good for several cameras at the same time. If your postproduction plan calls for several views to be used in the same scene, they become separate shots during production.

However, there are circumstances where using more than one camera is necessary and desirable. This occurs when you want to have multiple camera angles on a scene that is not repeatable. Then you should have a separate camera for each camera angle you will use in the final video, all recording while the scene is run. You will then pick the shots to use from the multicamera output during postproduction. Even though you may not use most of the output from some of the cameras, it is still desirable to record them all continuously throughout the scene. That will make it easier to synchronize when you are playing back for postproduction—you simply run all the tapes at the same time and do your postproduction as if you had a multicamera live shot going.

EQUIPMENT FOR ANALOG PRODUCTION

Analog production equipment includes video cameras, camcorders, and stand-alone recorders.

Video Cameras

The types of cameras were discussed in Chapter 2. They come with tube or solid-state (CCD) sensors, single, two- or three-sensor configurations, and combined with a recorder (camcorder) or not. Let's deal with the sensors first.

Few tube-sensor cameras are being sold any more, except at the very high end of the market, which is for cameras used in television broadcasting. Tube cameras are large and generally take more skill to operate than solid-state ones. However, until very recently, they gave the ultimate in performance, so plenty of them are around. Solid-state cameras are now capable of equal or better performance than tube ones, and they have the advantages of small size and reliability. All cameras that you might consider for PC video production have solid-state sensors. So that choice is easy.

Single-sensor cameras arc the least expensive and dominate the home market. However, the single-sensor design has inherent tradeoffs in picture quality because of the need to divide the sensing elements between the three colors. In a single-sensor camera, everything else being equal, you should look for the highest number of pixels in the sensor. The current state of the art for single-sensors is 380,000 to 410,000 pixels, which delivers horizontal resolution performance slightly more than 400 lines. That is consistent with S-VHS or Hi-8 recorders, and most single-sensor camcorders for those standards have such sensors. S-VHS and Hi-8 camcorders are intended for low-end professional and high-end consumer markets, an area often called the *pro-sumer* market.

Home-market single-sensor cameras have sensors in the 200,000 to 300,000 pixel range and deliver TV resolution specifications in the range of 250–300 lines. This matches VHS or 8-mm home VCR performance, and it is good enough for many purposes. If you will be producing video for display in small windows, such as 160×120, this camera performance will not be limiting at all. However, if you plan on larger video windows (320×240 and up), then home-market camera performance will cause a noticeable loss of resolution. Resolution losses will accumulate, so even if the PC resolution is about the same as the camera, the combination will be less.

To achieve still higher resolution, you have to go to more sensors. The three-sensor configuration is the best—these cameras are now available starting at about twice the price of single-sensor cameras of equivalent features and offer horizontal resolution performance up to 700 lines. This is a good deal, and I would recommend a three-sensor camera for anything except the small-window video production.

Many other features on cameras deserve your consideration. Some of these are discussed in the following.

Video Output Format

Nearly all cameras provide NTSC format video output, simply because that is the format used by video recorders and TV monitors. (In most of Europe, the equivalent format is PAL.) An NTSC output can be connected to most any other video device, but it is not the best you can do for digital video because NTSC encoding causes an unavoidable loss in picture quality.

RGB video output, which requires three cables, is the best format for picture quality. However, few low-price cameras have RGB outputs because it is never used in analog video applications. Many PC video digitizing boards do support RGB, and ideally we will soon see more cameras delivering it.

In between RGB and NTSC is the *S-video* format, which uses a special connector and cable. It is a two-wire component signal format where the luminance signal and the chrominance signals are on separate wires in the cable. Because the worst quality loss of NTSC is caused by the limitations of combining *luminance* and *chrominance* on a single cable (see Appendix A), the S-video approach avoids a lot of the degradation of NTSC encoding. Many cameras and PC digitizing boards have this format. It is a good choice. In any case, you should make sure that your camera and your digitizing boards support the highest quality output format you can get.

Lenses

Nearly all video cameras have a zoom lens. They deliver zoom ranges up to 10:1. A zoom lens is very convenient for framing shots, but the zoom feature can get overused if you zoom dynamically during a shot. The reason is that the zoom effect is unnatural to the human eye and can be distracting or even upsetting when used too much. If you watch zoom use in television productions, you will see that it seldom occurs except in sporting events. Change between closeup and wide shots is done mostly by cutting or dissolving between shots that are taken at fixed focal length.

The principal limitation of the zoom lenses provided with most cameras is that they do not support extremely wide angle shots. This can be important, particularly in interior shooting. If you have need for extreme wide angle shots, you should check this out on any camera you consider. Low-priced cameras have single-speed zoom lenses. If you need a lot of zoom work, single-speed will get boring. Better cameras will have multiple zoom speeds; some even are continuously variable. With multiple or variable zoom speeds, the type of controller provided becomes important. If you are considering such cameras, try out the zoom controller to make sure you like the way it works.

Automatic Focus and Exposure

The automatic exposure and focus features are very convenient, but you will find many situations where you want manual control. Make sure that the cameras you consider have manual override for both of these features. Some do not have manual control at all, and others achieve manual operation in unusual ways. Try out the manual controls on any camera you consider and be sure it works the way you think it should.

High Speed Shutter

A television camera normally integrates the light over an entire field period, which gives an exposure time of 1/60th second. This causes blurring of the individual frames when there is rapid motion in the scene. You're not aware of such blurring in normal viewing because the motion itself hides the blurring, but if you are going to use still frames from the motion sequence, the blurring will be quite noticeable. Many cameras have a *high-speed shutter* feature that allows the effective exposure time of the camera to be reduced to much less than a field time. Some cameras go to 1/1,000th second or even shorter. This will produce sharper still frames, but of course the shorter exposure means that you must have more light to get a good picture. Because of that, the feature is most usable in outdoor shots.

Another use of the high speed shutter feature is to force the camera to open its lens aperture fully in order to reduce the optical *depth of field* (the distance range over which the lens is in focus). For example, when you are doing a closeup shot of a person who is standing in front of a very busy background, the interest of the scene can be better placed on the person by causing the background to be blurred (see Figure 6.1). In full sunlight, the camera lens aperture will probably be nearly fully stopped down, which may cause the background to be completely in focus. You can improve on this by moving the camera away from the subject and using the full telephoto capability of the lens to achieve your closeup. In that situation, the depth of field of the lens will be the least. However, if the background is still in focus, you can use the high-speed shutter feature to cause

Figure 6.1 Making the background out of focus enhances the foreground subject.

the lens aperture (in automatic mode) to open fully. When that happens, you will get the least depth of field from the lens.

Image Stabilization

Some cameras have an image stabilization feature built-in. This is particularly intended for handheld shooting, where the image may jump around because you cannot hold the camera steady enough. Image stabilization, which may be optical, mechanical, or electronic, can substantially improve the steadiness of the image. If you will be doing handheld shooting, you should consider this feature. Electronic stabilization approaches often have a tradeoff in picture quality because they derive the output picture from less than the full area of the sensor. Check that the stabilizer has an "off" mode that eliminates the loss of quality. Mechanical or optical stabilizers may not have any loss of picture quality, but they tend to be heavier and more expensive.

Stabilization can also be achieved by using a mechanical stabilizer that is separate from the camera, which is a special floating camera mounting that allows you to walk with the camera and still achieve smooth motion. The most popular one of these is the Steadicam Jr., which is a low cost version of the Steadicam product used professionally. This product is very effective, but it adds additional weight for you to carry, and it takes some practice to use it well. The Steadicam Jr. includes its own larger viewfinder that you can see without holding the camera up to your eye.

Electronic Zoom

Some cameras have an electronic zoom feature that effectively extends the zoom range by typically 2:1. Thus a camera with a 10:1 lens can do 20:1 with the electronic zoom added. This feature has a noticeable resolution tradeoff, since the zoom is obtained by not utilizing the full area of the camera's image sensor. Except for sporting events, it is not a valuable feature for professional shooting.

Low Light Sensitivity Features

As the light level of the scene goes down, the camera will open its lens aperture to achieve a full-level output. When the lens becomes fully open and the light level continues to fall, the signal output will drop. Some cameras have a "high gain" feature that will boost the video output back to normal. Some cameras can add up to 18 dB (8:1) gain for this purpose. The effect of this is that the output picture remains bright, but it becomes noisy—you are trading picture quality for sensitivity.

Since a noisy picture will not compress as well as a clean picture (the compressor uses up a lot of its data trying to compress the noise), this is not a good feature when shooting for digital video. You would only use it when there was no other way to get a picture that you needed. In that case, before compressing in postproduction you should probably do some filtering of the video to trade noise for less sharpness.

Viewfinders

All video cameras have an electronic viewfinder, which is a small monitor (1" to 1½") that usually is viewed through an eyepiece. Most viewfinders are monochrome. A few are in color, but the small screen size means that they have to trade off resolution, which can make it difficult to know when the camera is in sharp focus. Many viewfinders have an optical magnifier, which is good, but it means that you cannot see anything on the viewfinder unless your eye is right on the eyepiece. Note that with automatic focus, you don't have to use the viewfinder for focusing, only for framing the shot. A low-resolution viewfinder may be good enough for that.

A few of the latest home cameras have a larger (3" to 4") LCD color viewfinder. That allows a lot of freedom in holding the camera, since you no longer have to keep it against your eye. The tradeoff is that the viewfinder is more subject to being washed out by ambient light. To obtain the greatest freedom of camera movement, you can add a separate monitor, even a large one, so you don't have to look into the camera and you don't have to be close to the viewfinder monitor at all.

Camera Mounting Equipment

Although not a part of the camera itself, mounting equipment such as tripods, dollies, or booms can significantly affect the quality of your camera work. A tripod is an essential item—it should be used whenever possible to hold the camera solidly. This is especially important for digital video use because even the slightest camera movement will reduce compression performance. The camera should not move unless it is supposed to as part of the script. Be sure you have a tripod sturdy enough to hold your camera without vibration or flexing.

When the camera does have to change its angle, such as in a pan, it should rotate smoothly to create the best visual effect. That is accomplished by using a *fluid head*, which is a tripod head that contains fluid dampening. A good fluid head will deliver silky smooth camera movements, controllable at any speed.

A dolly is a set of wheels that support a tripod; it facilitates smooth movement of the entire unit in any direction. A boom or crane is a large device that allows the camera height to be changed smoothly, often with camera angle changes at the same time. These are mostly used in professional production.

Camcorders

As cameras and recorders became smaller, it became practical to combine them into a single unit—a *camcorder*. Today, camcorders weighing less than 2 pounds are available, and the format has become so practical that few camera-only units are available outside of the full-professional field. That is not to say that low weight is always good—a certain amount of weight in a handheld object helps the user hold it steady and move it smoothly. But too much weight quickly becomes tiring. Because of these considerations, camcorders range from 2 pounds up to 15 pounds or more. The heavier units are professional ones that have large optics and large-format recording. They are typically designed for shoulder holding rather than hand holding (see Figure 6.2). Shoulder mounting is a more stable way to hold a portable camera, but it inherently requires a larger camera package because of the distance between your shoulder and your eye where the viewfinder has to be. If you will be doing a lot of handheld shooting, I recommend that you go for a camera that can be shoulder held.

(a)   (b)

Figure 6.2 (a) hand-held camera, (b) shoulder-held camera (Courtesy of Pana-sonic Broadcast & Television Systems Company)

Recording Formats

There are several tape formats used today. All are outgrowths of the original VHS and Beta recorders that were developed for the home. Although Beta recorders are no longer made for the home, the Betacam format is one of the most popular formats for broadcast-quality portable recorders. Betacam is a component recording format—the luminance and chrominance are recorded separately. Other broadcast-quality formats are M1 and M2—they are descendants of the original VHS format. There are also some older formats such as the U-Matic 3/4" tape format and the 1" Type C broadcast format. Although these formats are in use in specialized areas, for PC video the smaller formats are more suitable.

In the home market, the formats are VHS, VHS-C, and 8-mm. VHS is the same as it always was, having a cassette that is approximately $7\frac{1}{2}" \times 4" \times 1"$ that can record for up to 6 hours depending on your quality choice. VHS-C is a smaller cassette using the same tape as VHS; it was designed specifically for portable recorders and it can be played in a standard VHS unit by using an adaptor. The VHS-C cassette is approximately $3\frac{1}{2}" \times 2\frac{1}{4}" \times 1"$ and it will record up to 1 hour depending on your choice of quality. Usually you do not want to use the long-playing versions of the formats. In that case, VHS is 2 hours and VHS-C is 30 minutes.

The 8-mm format was also developed specifically for portable recording, but, unlike VHS-C, it is not compatible with any other format. However, that incompatibility allowed the designers to achieve longer recording time (2 hours) in a smaller cassette than VHS-C. As a result, 8-mm recorders are slightly smaller than VHS-C units. The size difference is insignificant, but the recording time difference may be important.

When you record in the field with the small cassettes, you will bring them back to a studio to perform postproduction. Thus, an important consideration is the variety of equipment available for use in postproduction. In that case, VHS-compatible formats have a slight edge over 8-mm.

For the semi-professional and industrial markets, there are upgraded VHS and 8-mm formats that provide higher picture quality; these are S-VHS, S-VHS-C, and Hi-8. All three provide better audio and video performance using the same cassette sizes (the tape inside is different, so you have to buy new cassettes to use the new formats). There is no backward compatibility; for example, an S-VHS recording will not play back on a standard VHS machine. (Some recent VHS machines have a feature called *quasi S-VHS* that can play back an S-VHS tape but does not deliver the tape's full bandwidth.) I recommend that you get S-VHS or Hi-8 for PC video work.

In-camera Editing Features

All camcorders have the capability to perform in-camera cut edits. Some perform better than others at this. Many cameras have more advanced editing transitions including fades, dissolves, wipes, and other digital effects. The value of all this depends on whether you are going to do in-camera editing. If you are, the fancier effects can liven up your productions, although they are not as elaborate as you can do in postproduction. However, none of these features will get around the inherent awkwardness of in-camera editing. If you do a bad edit, you must rerecord the entire sequence to fix it. In-camera editing is suitable only for simple projects that have only one or two edits.

Audio Recording Features

All camcorders record audio. Most have built-in microphones, and the newer cameras using the upgraded formats also record stereo. These features are all usable in PC video production, but there are inherent limitations in recording audio at the same time as video. The limitations will be discussed in the next chapter on audio production. If you do intend to record audio with your video, you should make sure the camera you consider has a jack for external microphones—this can help you get around some of the limitations.

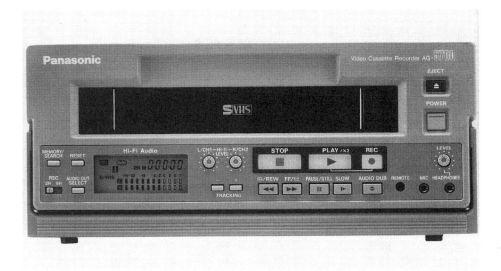

Figure 6.3 A desktop or portable S-VHS VCR (Courtesy of Panasonic Broadcast & Television Systems Company)

Remote Control Features

Many recent camcorders have infrared remote control of their functions. This is a valuable convenience feature that will help you do your production with fewer people. Get it if it's available on the camera you choose, but don't compromise anything else to get remote control.

Stand-alone Video Recorders

All the recorder issues just discussed also apply to stand-alone recorders. However, if you will be using separate camera and recorder units, there are some other considerations. First, since you will be connecting camera and recorder with cables, the signal format considerations discussed for cameras apply to the recorder as well. Be sure you have the desired signal format compatibility.

Not very many separate recorders designed for portability are available in the small tape formats (VHS and 8-mm). This is because those formats are focused on camcorders. Separate recorders in those formats are designed for playback or editing and the units are packaged in either tabletop or rack-mounted formats (see Figure 6.3). These machines may require special handling for field use. However, if you can ensure that they will not be mechanically or environmentally abused, they will work fine.

Rugged field recorders are available in the Betacam and M-format types. These are designed for professional use in news gathering, documentary, and other field situations. They are expensive, but if you can afford them, the performance is excellent.

THE LOCATION

Production can take place either in a controlled private location (a studio) or in a public location, indoors or outdoors (referred to as *on location*). Generally, you would prefer to use a studio because it gives you the best control over your production, but often the location itself is the subject and you cannot bring that into the studio. So you have to work in both situations.

The Studio

There are numerous advantages to studio production. You have complete control of the environment, all your equipment can be at hand, and you can create permanent setups to use again and again. If you will do a lot of serious production, you should have a studio. Of course, that takes some investment— you have to find the space and furnish it with equipment, lights, sets, and so on. Some of these items will be discussed here.

Lighting

Lighting equipment can range all the way from reflectors you purchase in the hardware store through photo lights to professional lighting designed for video production. The choice will depend on how large an area you need to light, how often will you use lights, and how much money you can spend. In addition to the lights themselves, you will need various mounting devices such as tripods and stands. A good professional photo store is the place to begin with this.

Probably the most important thing about lighting is controlling the harshness of the light. This calls for a variety of diffusing and reflecting devices, which again can be jury-rigged with common hardware and art supply items or you can go in for professional devices. For lighting small areas, you can do wonders simply by bouncing your lights off white bristol board sheets from the art store or even bounce it off a white ceiling. Lighting is an art in itself, which I won't go into here, but you can learn from the many books that are available.

Sets

There will probably be certain kinds of scenes that you will use often, such as a desk setup for talking head shots or a tabletop setup for shooting equipment or hardware. These are easy to build and don't take much space. In fact, you could probably design one set that served both purposes.

In either case, the most important element is the background that you use. For best results with compressed digital video, backgrounds should be kept simple so they do not contribute a lot of detail to be compressed and use up your data stream. (Everything in a compressed picture requires some data—for this reason, you should not allow anything to appear in your picture that is not essential to the scene. The result will be better picture quality for the items that do appear in the scene.) The simplest background would just be a flat sheet of material—wood, hardboard, or just paper. It should be of a fairly neutral or pastel color and should not have seams or folds that will create shadows when you light it. Preferably the background should be some distance behind your foreground person or object so that you can avoid shadows of the foreground falling on the background, and distance will make it easier to keep the background slightly out of focus. This requirement takes the most space, and it will cause the background panel to be a lot larger than the actual scene. Figure 6.4 is a diagram of a desk set that shows the space allowances for the desk, person, background, and camera. It grows to a considerable size.

I recommend that you construct a basic set as shown in Figure 6.4 with a perfectly flat background. If you need to change the color of the background, it can be covered with paper hung from rods. To add a few items to liven up the background, place them separately so they can be taken away when not required. Similarly, simple foreground objects can be added by placing them on the desktop. The desktop itself should be a nonreflecting material; you can change it by using overlays.

The principles just discussed for shooting a desk scene do not scale up very well to larger scenes. If you want to shoot a group conference, for example, you will have trouble finding a large enough space to have the background far enough away to avoid shadows. The solution is always to diffuse the lighting; that takes care of shadows, but it can make the scene rather boring. Experiment to find something you like.

Using a desk set for tabletop shooting poses the problem that it will be difficult to keep the rear edge of the desk from showing unless the camera is almost directly above the desk. For this kind of work, it is best to have a large flat space behind the table, at the same level, and then cover it with paper that you gently raise up at the rear to create a background. You will still have to use very diffuse lighting to prevent an awkward shadow from being on the background. Depend-

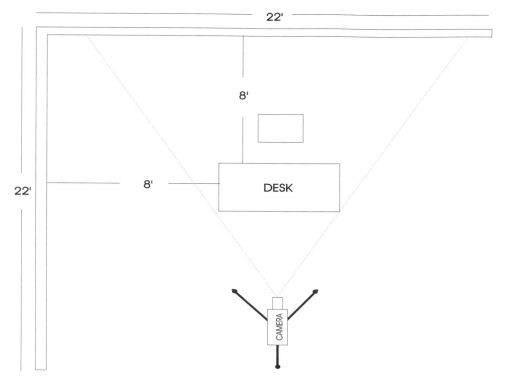

Figure 6.4 Set layout for a desk scene

ing on the type of objects you will be shooting, you can experiment to learn what works.

On Location

Location shooting is so varied that it's difficult to make many generalities. However, the guiding principle is to obtain as much control over the location and the environment as you can. If you are in a public location, you may have to be concerned with crowd control, because as soon as cameras come out, everyone wants to see what is happening. If this is going to be a problem, make arrangements ahead of time to get help from the local community.

If you are doing wide shots or scenery shots, you can do little about lighting except to plan to shoot at the best time of day. This may require a trip to the location ahead of time to decide when things will be best. When doing closeups on location, you can bring in lights (if there is electricity) or you can add reflectors to help the natural lighting. There are many possibilities—people with a lot of experience in location production have answers for them all. You do the best you can; presumably the location itself is important enough to you that you will accept a tradeoff in quality if that's the only way.

THE SHOOT ITSELF

On the day of the shoot, you have to get all the equipment and people together in the studio or on location, set up, shoot, and tear down. This is where all the planning considerations just discussed get put to the test. Good planning is not a guarantee that nothing will go wrong, but it will certainly minimize that possibility. Video production is full of surprises, so you always need to be ready for the unexpected.

I have really only scratched the surface of the planning subject, but I hope I have made you think about some of the issues so that you can carry the subject further by yourself. I will not discuss the artistic elements of shooting any more here, but there are some important considerations about managing the resulting tapes or files.

MANAGING THE OUTPUT

Apart from the setup of the scene and the direction of the actual shooting, which I'm not going to say any more about, the main issue about the shoot is keeping track of the tapes or files that are produced. This can become messy if you don't follow an organized system to identify scenes, shots, and takes. During postproduction, you need to quickly find the pieces of your production, without having to search tapes or files for them. A good system is important.

You can begin by numbering the scenes and shots—numbers are better than names because they will be easier to handle in file names as you digitize. If you are not working with an OS that supports long file names, you will need to keep the numbers small so that 8-character file names will work. Similarly, during shooting, you should number the takes for each shot. A simple naming scheme might use a code letter (that can have any meaning you like) followed by six numerical digits—two for the scene, two for the shot, and two for the take. Thus, the name S010411 would mean scene 1, shot 4, take 11.

Ordinarily, you should keep all the takes, even ones that appear bad at the time. That is because you may see something that you would like to fix in your best take when you review it in postproduction, or maybe after several takes you

Figure 6.5 Setup for producing the Chapter 5 example

Figure 6.6 The opening shot of the Chapter 5 example

decide that an earlier one was really best and you want to go with that one. Also, one of the bad takes just may have what you need to cut in a fix during editing.

A numbering system lets you identify the takes, but it doesn't tell you anything about them. To accomplish that, you need to keep a log sheet during production. The log would have one line (at least) per take, which contains the take number (as previously explained), a description of the take, the reel of tape it is on, and the position of the take in that reel. The latter can be in terms of tape timer readings, or if you are using time code, it can be a time code number.

The description field of the log sheet is the part that could grow to more than one line. In it, you should write down anything about that take that you might want to remember during postproduction. Of course, here is where you would indicate which take you thought was the best one (that's not always the last one).

AN EXAMPLE

Figure 6.5 shows a setup for producing the CD-ROM caddy example described in the previous chapter. This is a tabletop setup, using a paper background. You can see the lighting that is provided and the camera positioning. Figure 6.6 is the opening shot showing the CD-ROM jewel case, the caddy, and the drive. The shot has been framed tightly so that the important objects fill the frame. Since the background has no purpose other than a background, it is kept plain to avoid generating additional compressed video data.

SUMMARY

This chapter has covered the issues of video production for PC digital video use. The distinctions between analog and digital production were explained, and analog production was described in detail, including the equipment required for it. Digital production has many of the same considerations, but the actual techniques are presented in the next chapter.

7

Audio Production
For PC Video

A video production is incomplete without audio. The audio is not just something that you capture with the video and it then "goes along for the ride." It is often as important as the video—it can carry the message of the scene and it can augment, highlight, or enhance the video. Audio production deserves and often requires the same attention as video. This chapter will discuss the considerations of audio production.

ANALOG vs. DIGITAL PRODUCTION

The question of whether to digitize audio during production surfaces many of the same considerations as video. To digitize during production, you must have a PC at the production site and you have to worry about its operation during the production. Of course, if you have already decided to digitize video, then you might as well do the audio that way, too. That will restrict you, however, to simultaneous audio and video recording and only one track of audio. If your production requires any special treatment of the audio, you will have to use separate audio recording equipment. I favor digitizing in postproduction anyway, and I recommend analog audio recording for most production. The quality can be excellent and postproduction deals with many more problems than you would want to handle during production.

ELEMENTS OF A SOUND TRACK

A typical sound track is made up of one or more of the following elements:

- Dialog is made up of the voices of the performers and announcer. This element usually carries the message of the scene.
- Music is often added for effect. If there is no voice element, this track may carry the message of the scene.
- Effects are sounds other than music or voice that are added to mark or highlight actions in the scene or to enhance the environment.
- Ambiance is the sound you hear when no other element is active. It is the background sound of the environment.

The elements can be produced all at once in a single live recording, but there is more flexibility and you can achieve higher quality if they are produced separately and combined (mixed) in postproduction. The discussion that follows applies to production of any or all of the elements. Later, I will discuss the special considerations of producing each type of element by itself.

PRODUCING AUDIO AT THE SAME TIME AS VIDEO

All video recorders and camcorders have the capability to record audio while recording video. Camcorders have built-in microphones, so the process of recording audio can be nearly invisible. There are times when this is a perfectly satisfactory way to get your audio, but often it is not. The greatest reason for not capturing audio with the video is that the environment of a video production is usually not suitable for high-quality audio recording. There will be ambient sounds that you cannot control, and the actions of the video production itself may create sounds that you do not want in the final recording. Once unwanted or extraneous sounds are mixed in with your audio, it is extremely difficult to remove them.

If the final audio is not being recorded during the video production, the director of the production can give voice commands during video recording, which makes it easier for him to control the production. You have probably seen scenes of motion picture production from the days of silent pictures where the director is shouting through a megaphone to control what the actors are doing. Because of separate audio production, it can still be done that way today.

Another reason you cannot capture audio during your video is that the desired audio may be completely different from the sounds occurring at the video location. For example, you may have an off-screen announcer explaining what is happening on the screen. This, called *voice-over*, is a widely used technique. Because the voice-over announcer is not visible on-screen, the requirement for precise synchronization of the audio with the video is eliminated. That simplifies the production and postproduction.

On the other hand, there are cases where you do want to capture audio with the video. The most important of these is where a person speaking is seen by the camera and you must have exact synchronization between audio and video (called *lip-sync*). In this situation, you have to shoot audio with the video. If you are shooting in a studio, you can control the environment well enough that the audio quality will be satisfactory, but if you are outdoors there may be audio interference you cannot control. Sometimes microphone technique can solve the problem, sometimes you can fix it in postproduction, but other times you cannot.

The last resort is a technique the professionals call *automatic dialog replacement* (ADR). To use ADR, you record the actor's speech along with the video, but then you take the actor into a studio where you can play back the video and audio from the shoot. The actor wears headphones to hear the original audio, he looks at the original video of himself speaking, and he tries to voice the speech the same way he did it originally. His efforts are recorded, and the process is repeated until he gets it right. Experienced actors learn to do this very well and it is a widely used technique in movie and TV postproduction. With ADR you get a clean recording of the actor's voice by itself that can be merged with separately produced background sounds in postproduction.

Another case where recording audio with the video is valuable is when the action creates sounds that you need in the final scene. Examples are when something is dropped, or a machine is being shown that makes sounds that must remain synchronous. Sometimes, the original sounds might be replaced in postproduction with something more spectacular, but having the original makes the exact synchronization easier. In these cases, what you are recording with the video is called the *effects track*. Effects are sounds that highlight events occurring in the scene, both on-screen and off-screen.

EQUIPMENT FOR AUDIO PRODUCTION

Audio-with-video production can be done using the built-in facilities of camcorders, but often this does not give the best results. You may need to use a separate microphone, and you may wish to use a separate audio recorder. Such equipment is discussed here.

Microphones

Sound pickup begins with the microphone—your audio can never get better than what your microphone picks up. Ideally a microphone will exactly reproduce the sound that arrives at its sensitive element. The first problem is that the sound arriving at the microphone may not be the sound that you want. For example, if the microphone is on the camera, it is usually some distance from the subject making sound in your scene, which means that it also receives sounds from other directions that are not in your scene. Worse yet, it receives sound from you and the camera, both of whom are much closer to the microphone than your subject. These are the main reasons for not using the microphone built-in to your camera. To capture the best sound, *you should get the microphone as close as possible to the sound source*.

But getting close to the source may mean that the microphone becomes visible in the picture. Sometimes that is OK, as when the audience expects it to be there anyway. Other times, you don't want the microphone to be seen, or at least it should be unobtrusive. There are many solutions to this problem, which fall into the category of microphone technique or *miking* as it's called in the industry.

There are at least three ways to categorize microphones: by the type of sensing element they use, by the type of pattern they have, and by the type of mounting. Additional distinction is in the type of cable connections used.

Sensing Elements

The two main sensing technologies used in microphones for video cameras are dynamic and condenser. A *dynamic* microphone has a sensor consisting of a magnet containing a moving coil responding to the sound waves. This approach performs well, and it is rugged and reliable.

A *condenser* microphone has two plates spaced closely together (forming an electronic condenser); one plate moves in response to sound waves. An electrical voltage must be impressed on the condenser plates for this to work, which means that this type of microphone usually requires a battery. However, the battery life is very long. There is also a special type of condenser mike called an *electret* that does not need a battery. Condenser mikes have the widest bandwidth and high sensitivity.

Patterns

The *pattern* of a microphone describes how it responds to sound coming from different directions. For example, an *omnidirectional* microphone responds equally for sound coming from any direction. Such a microphone would be used when it is necessary or desirable to receive sound from all directions during the same take. You might use this if you were recording sound from a group of people seated around a conference table.

Directional microphones respond better to sound coming from specific direction or directions and they come in many varieties. A common directional pattern is the *cardiod* (the diagram of this pattern is heart-shaped), which receives sound over almost 180 degrees in the horizontal plane. It is good for the talking head situation because it will reject sound coming from the camera or anything in that direction while responding to the person on-camera, even when he moves about a little.

The idea of the cardiod is extended in the *supercardiod* and *hypercardiod* patterns. These are more sharply focused in one direction and would be used in a talking head setup when the microphone could not be placed close to the speaker. A camera-mounted microphone is usually of this type. The highly focused pattern is carried to the extreme in the *shotgun* microphone (which looks like a gun). This microphone often can pick a single voice out of a noisy crowd.

There are also *bidirectional* microphones, which respond to sound from two directions but reject sound coming from perpendicular directions. This might be used in a one-on-one interview so that there was good sound pickup for the two speakers. The TV news interviewer often carries this type of mike.

Most microphones are single-channel (monaural). However, there are also stereo mikes that have two channels built into one unit, with patterns that capture left and right sounds. Stereo mikes are most common in camera mountings, although there are a few for handheld use. Holding a stereo microphone is a little tricky, because it is hard to keep the stereo fields from shifting as you move around. Generally, finished stereo tracks are created in postproduction by mixing a number of individual monaural sounds; postproduction mixing techniques are available for positioning each sound in the stereo field. However, a stereo mike would be good for capturing sounds that you cannot capture and process individually, such as crowd noise at a sporting event.

Mountings

The types of mountings are handheld, camera-mount, headset, and lavalier. Handheld mikes have a handle where the cable comes out that makes them convenient to hold when you are speaking or singing yourself or when you are holding the mike for someone else to speak.

Camera-mount mikes are usually adapted to fit the expansion shoe that is on most camcorders. They have a short cable that plugs into the camcorder's microphone jack.

Headset mikes are for the same purpose as handheld mikes—one person making sound himself. They apply in situations where mike must be held close to the mouth (noisy locations) but the user wants to have his hands free, so the mike is mounted to his head. Many pop singers use them on stage.

Lavalier mikes are also for individual speakers in quiet environments where the mike can get good pickup from a location such as the speaker's lapel. They clip on so the speaker's hands are free, and he can move around within the limits of the cable.

Cables

A wire is the usual way to get the signal from a microphone back to the recording device. However, there are also wireless microphones that use radio-frequency (RF) transmission to return the signal. These offer the greatest convenience for the performer, but they are more expensive. The RF transmission link must be well designed and used within its range limit or it will introduce noise or interference into the audio signal. Wireless mikes come in handheld form where everything is in the handheld unit or in lavalier mounting where a short cable goes to a small box that is usually mounted to the user's belt.

When cables are used, there are two types—*balanced* and *unbalanced*. Unbalanced cables are the most common; they have a single wire surrounded by a shield that is the second wire. They usually have phone plug connectors that go into a single hole jack in the equipment. Balanced cables have two signal wires inside a shield; this is an improvement that reduces interference picked up in cabling. The connectors for balanced cables are the XLR type, which is a larger plug that connects to a multiconductor jack. You can get adapters to connect XLR cables to phone-plug jacks. If your recorder does not have XLR jacks, you can use an adapter at the recorder end of a balanced mike cable and still gain most of the advantages of using balanced cables.

You can see that the combination of all the microphone characteristics could produce a mind-boggling array of different products. That's just what has happened in the market, and you can find almost any combination you want. The task of microphone selection and placement for use is almost an art form in the industry.

Audio Recorders

The S-VHS and Hi-8 camcorders have high-quality stereo audio tracks. If it suits your needs to record audio at the same time as you record video, then the camcorder audio tracks will do fine. You can still separate them out during postproduction for special audio-only processing if needed. However, if some of your audio is not going to be recorded with the video, it makes no sense to run videotape to record audio (although that is possible). You should have a separate audio recorder.

Any type of audio recorder can be used, but you should make sure it is compatibile with the audio player you will use in postproduction. The postproduction machine should be remote controlled and have other editing features that are not necessary for the original recording.

You can also get digital audio recorders to use in production. They are fine, but they have their own unique data formats that are different from those used in computers. To go into a computer, you will probably have to take the analog output from your digital audio recorder and digitize it again to get the proper format into the computer. You can also buy audio postproduction equipment that works at the same format as the digital recorders. Then you can complete your audio in that environment and convert at the end to the computer format needed to merge with the video.

Multitrack Recorders

Most audio recorders have at least two tracks for stereo use. As you move into the semi-professional and professional fields, you will find recorders with four, eight, or more tracks. Figure 7.1 shows a typical semi-professional four-track cassette recorder. These are widely used in analog postproduction, but they may also be used in production when there are multiple microphones in use. For example, you may have three actors in your scene and each is carrying a wireless mike. You could simply mix the outputs of the three wireless units and record on a single track. However, that is not wise because you lose control of the volume balance between the voices once the production is completed. By recording separate tracks for each voice and doing the mix in postproduction, you have a lot of flexibility to achieve the desired balance between the voices. Of course, you could use a separate audio recorder for each actor, but this is more equipment to worry about during production and it means there are three audio sources to synchronize in postproduction rather than one.

PRODUCING A DIALOG TRACK

Dialog can either be the voices of actors who are visible on-screen or it can be the voice of someone off-screen (voice-over). As I explained, the usual production approach for voice-over is to record the audio track first and then use it as the

Figure 7.1 A semi-professional four-track tape deck and mixer (courtesy of Yamaha Corporation)

time line for recording the video. The audio script in Listing 5.1 is an example—this script runs approximately 17 seconds. To get a professional sound for voice-over, you should hire a professional announcer or use someone you know who has been trained in announcing.

Recording actor's voices on-screen must be done at the same time as video to achieve lip-sync. If the quality is not good enough, you may have to use dialog replacement later. The principal consideration of recording on-screen is the placement of microphones. If the scene requires that mikes not be visible, they either have to be hidden on the performers, hidden on the set, or positioned just off-camera but still close enough to get good pickup of the voices.

Setting up a Sound Studio

When you are recording off-screen dialog or other sounds, you should have a sound studio to give you a quiet environment for recording. This can be any quiet room of 100 to 200 square feet. The room should have some sound deadening material in it, such as drapes, carpet, and acoustic ceiling tiles. Too many reflecting surfaces such as windows and smooth painted walls are to be avoided. Too large a room is also not desirable, unless it contains a lot of sound absorbing material. The preferred approach is to obtain a recording that is pretty *dead*, meaning that there are no echoes or *reverberations* (repeated echoes). If the dead recording does not sound right, these effects can be added in a controlled way in postproduction.

For recording an announcer's or an actor's voice, use a unidirectional microphone placed about one foot in front of the person speaking, who should be seated at a small table in the center of the room. If possible, the recording equipment and all other people should be outside of the room so they will not contribute to background sounds.

Recording

To do a take, you start the recorder running and cue the announcer visually (or with a light, if there is no way to do a visual cue from outside the room) to begin speaking. Run the recorder a few seconds beyond the point he finishes. Don't worry about making the recording exactly fit the speech; if you record too much it is easily cut out in postproduction.

For multiple takes, the easiest thing to do is to leave the recorder running continuously. However, you need a system to locate each take on the tape. This can be done with tape timer or time code readings written down at the start of each take or by having the announcer identify each take verbally before he begins the scripted speech. The last approach is not as good because you will have to play the entire tape at normal speed to find a take. A log sheet as described in Chapter 6 for video production is desirable to keep notes about each take. As with video, you should retain all the takes—you never know what you might need in postproduction.

If there are things in the script that you are not entirely sure about, you might make several different versions of the script and have the announcer do several takes for each of them. This will not cost very much while the announcer is there and everything is set up, compared to what it might cost if you have to do it all over again later.

This all may seem pretty obvious, and if you have given it any thought, it is. But remember, even the simplest and best thought-out production can give you a surprise when you go to carry it out. It's best to think through everything, even the things that seem obvious.

PRODUCING A MUSIC TRACK

An entire chapter or even a whole book could be written about this subject. You can choose between using existing music, hiring a musician to compose custom music, or doing that yourself. Except for the last case, make sure that your music comes with the proper rights for its use in your application and for the type of distribution you contemplate. The music industry is extremely sensitive to rights issues and they cannot be ignored.

There are many sources of music in PC digital formats. CD-ROMs containing libraries of music with rights for PC use are widely available. Even so, you should carefully read the license agreement to make sure that it applies to your particular class of use. PC audio can be in either PCM or MIDI format. However, MIDI format is not supported in AVI interleaved audio/video files. To use MIDI audio in an AVI file, you must convert MIDI data to PCM by playing it into an audio capture device. You can do that on your PC with most audio capture tools. Of course, that eliminates the data size advantage of MIDI compared to PCM. With a multitasking operating system such as OS/2 or Windows NT, you could try playing video and MIDI audio as two separate devices, it may or may not work for you.

If you are somewhat of a musician (or you know someone who is), its quite reasonable to create your own MIDI music using one of the MIDI *sequencer* programs on the market. (See Figure 7.2.) With such programs, you can enter music either from a music keyboard or with the computer's mouse or keyboard. In the latter case, you deal with notes one at a time, placing them on a music staff the same way you would write on paper. The difference is that the computer will help you edit your work and at any time you can have it instantly played by the computer. Many tasks such as repeating, transposing, or changing tempo can be handled automatically by the computer.

PRODUCING AN EFFECTS TRACK

Sound effects can contribute greatly to your audio by enhancing or highlighting actions on the screen. Sounds made directly by the action can be recorded while video production goes on. If you can accomplish appropriate miking, such sounds could be recorded separate from any dialog that you may have. By editing those sounds together in their own track during postproduction you can produce a separate effects track. (It is best to do this as a separate track so that you can adjust it without affecting the other audio elements.)

Often the sound effects you record live are not as powerful as you would like. Then you have to use artificial effects, either from a sound effects library or from special recordings you make. Many sound effects libraries are available in PCM format. You should have several of these for when you need special sounds and

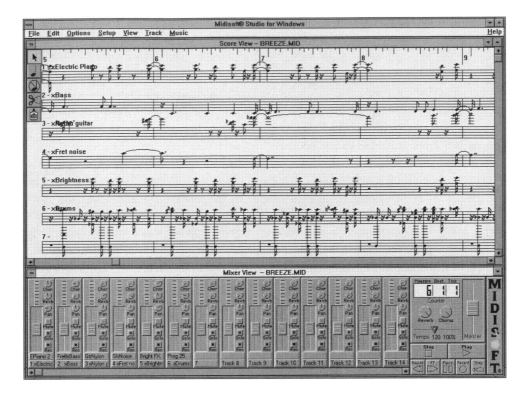

Figure 7.2 A screen from Midisoft Studio for Windows, a MIDI authoring program

do not want to make them yourself. As with all libraries, make sure the rights you get are consistent with your class of use.

Professional audio producers have special rooms for making sound effects, called *Foley* studios. Such a studio contains all kinds of devices for making sounds such as footsteps, breaking glass, thunder, or crashes. You have probably seen or read about these if you are at all interested in movie production. Often a sound is produced by unusual means, such as shaking a large sheet of metal to make thunder sounds. An operator in the Foley studio works with the devices there, and the sounds he makes are recorded on separate tracks. Sometimes, in cases such as footsteps, it is necessary to synchronize the effects with the action, so a Foley studio will also have means to display the video footage in synchronism with the audio recording. Just as in ADR, the Foley operator learns to synchronize his actions with the video.

PRODUCING AN AMBIENCE TRACK

Sound effects libraries usually have many sounds that you can use to build ambience tracks. For example, a forest ambience should have insect and bird sounds, maybe rustling leaves, possibly even some animal sounds. You can select such sounds from a library and build your own track by placing them randomly into a mix. You can often build 30 seconds or a minute of such a track and simply repeat it if a longer playback is required.

Another possibility is to go out to the right environment and record the ambience live. That would probably be a lot of fun, but the results might not be a good as you would like. Ambient sounds in nature are often rather faint and are easily masked or interfered with by human-made sounds. You have to give it the same consideration you would any recording—choosing proper mikes, eliminating your own sounds, and so forth. But if you need a certain sound and you can't find it in a library, getting it yourself is worth a try.

SUMMARY

This chapter has presented the considerations of audio production for PC video. You have seen that there are just as many issues and caveats of audio as there are for video. The sound production industry has been around longer than the video production industry and techniques are highly developed. I discussed microphones and microphone technique, audio recorders, and production of the audio elements of dialog, music, effects, and ambience.

8

Audio and Video Digitizing

At some point in the processes of production and postproduction you have to run the appropriate tools to digitize analog audio and video. When you do this depends on how far you have decided to go in the analog domain. Digitizing is often called *digital capture* or simply *capture*. This chapter discusses PC digitizing tools in detail. Tools for Windows, DOS DVI, OS/2, and OS/2 DVI are covered.

DIGITIZING AUDIO

Most video digitizing tools provide for simultaneous capture of audio, so if you are producing audio and video together, the audio does go along for the ride. Your only concerns for audio in that case are to set the level and choose the sampling parameters. However, there are many audio-only tools that you can use to capture audio by itself. These are discussed here.

General Audio Digitizing Considerations

In an analog audio system, the louder the sound is, the more signal voltage there will be in the system. However, if the signal voltage becomes too high, the system will begin to overload and distortion will occur. In analog systems, there is no abrupt threshold for overload, rather the distortion increases gradually as the signal level increases and slight overload is usually acceptable. On the other hand, a digital system has a brick wall threshold beyond which the signal cannot increase. If the signal level hits or exceeds the threshold, even for a moment, there is a crash of extreme distortion that is very objectionable. Therefore, level control in digital audio is very important.

Controlling Signal Levels

For the best performance of a digital system, the signal level being digitized should be as close as possible to the maximum system capability but should never hit the maximum. If you watch the level meters on an audio system you know that levels fluctuate wildly, so how can you meet this criterion? One way is to constantly adjust the level during digitization to keep it always near the maximum. This is called *riding the level*. It is extremely difficult to do, even if you practice the segment many times, but it is also undesirable because it removes much of the dynamics of the audio. Silent passages become loud and loud passages get subdued. Quite simply, you should not try to ride the audio level during digitization.

The correct approach is to set the audio level at a point where the loud passages are near the maximum and quieter passages fall where they may. You set the level once and then leave it there. If you are digitizing from analog tape, you can preview the segment and find the level setting that will accomplish the objective. Progressively raise the level until you hear distortion in loud passages; then back off until the distortion just stops.

If you are recording live, you can do a level check before starting by having the actors speak in their normal voices while you set the level. However, once you begin capturing, you are at their mercy—if they speak louder than you set levels for, you may get overload and have to do a retake. This is a good reason to avoid digitizing audio from a live source.

Providing for Synchronization

There are two ways of synchronizing: cue marks and time code. If your equipment supports the use of time code, that is by far the best approach. However, you must use a digitizing tool that handles time code, and most of them don't. Of the tools discussed here, only Touchvision CineWorks can use time code.

When recording audio and video together from live sources, you should use a device such as a clapboard that makes a simultaneous mark in both audio and video. If you did that, be sure and include the clap mark in the digitized audio. If the audio was recorded by itself, there is no clap mark and you will have to work from the start of the audio clip or file. Once you get both audio and video into the digital domain, you can use video frame numbers as a form of time code. You have to manually position your audio for proper synchronization, which mates the start of audio with a particular video frame number starting from the beginning. After you do that, most audio/video editing systems will maintain sync.

Table 8.1 Choices of audio sampling parameters

Purpose	Sample Freq.	Bits/sample	Stereo?	Bytes/minute
Intelligible speech	11,025	8	no	662 KB
High-qual. speech	11,025	16	no	1.32 MB
Music (mono)	22,050	16	no	2.65 MB
Music (stereo)	22,050	16	yes	5.30 MB
CD-quality (stereo)	44,100	16	yes	10.6 MB
Speech (ADPCM)	11,025	4	no	331 KB
Music (ADPCM)	22,050	4	yes	662 KB

Choosing Sampling Parameters

All audio digitizing tools give you a choice of sampling parameters. Your choice depends on the type of material you are digitizing, your needs for sound quality, and (in the case of ADPCM) the capability of your hardware. Table 8.1 shows some typical choices for different types of material. The table also shows the resulting digital data rates for each choice, so you can see the price you pay for higher quality.

Input Selection

Some sound cards have more than one audio input, and they may support both line and microphone levels. This usually means that you have to choose the input and its type. Line inputs are for signals coming from devices such as mixers or recorders. Microphones require additional amplification, so a board that supports microphone levels must switch in an additional amplifier. That's usually done by a software switch.

Audio Digitizing Tools

The following audio digitizing tools are discussed here:

- **Sound Recorder**—this is a program supplied with Windows 3.1.
- **Wave for Windows**—this is primarily an audio editing tool. It's capture module is described here, the rest of the program is described in the next chapter.

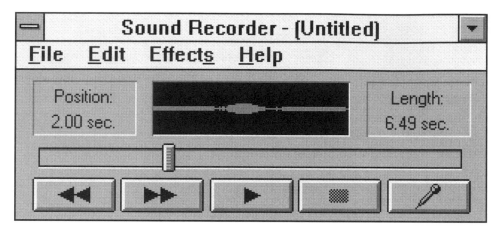

Figure 8.1 The main window of Microsoft Sound Recorder

- **Digital Audio**—this is the audio recording tool that is included with OS/2 2.1
- **MEDIAscript OS/2**—this is an OS/2 authoring program that supports DVI technology audio and video. It's audio capture module is described here.
- **wrec.exe**—this is a DOS audio capture tool that comes with the Sound Blaster 16 card.

Microsoft Sound Recorder

The main screen of Sound Recorder is shown in Figure 8.1. It provides a simple control panel with VCR-type controls for recording and playing the captured audio. There is also a window that shows a simplified view of the audio signal during recording or playing. A slider bar shows the position in the recorded data. The button with the microphone icon on it is used to begin recording.

Sound Recorder records audio into memory. It limits the length of any one recording to 60 seconds. When a recording is completed, you have to perform a separate Save operation from the File menu to save the audio to disk. Some of the other tools record directly to disk, which extends the length limitation out to whatever your disk will hold and a separate save operation is not necessary.

You access the parameters selection dialog by choosing New from the File menu. The dialog shown in Figure 8.2 appears. It allows selection of mono or stereo and three choices of quality level. More selections are available if you click the Custom button, which causes the dialog to expand to that shown in Figure 8.3.

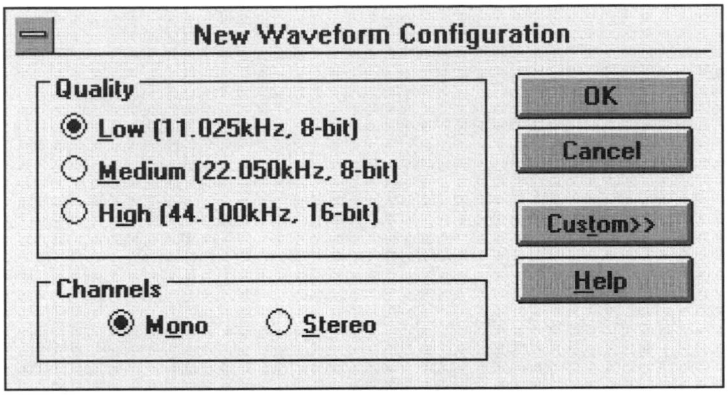

Figure 8.2 Sound Recorder's Sampling Options window

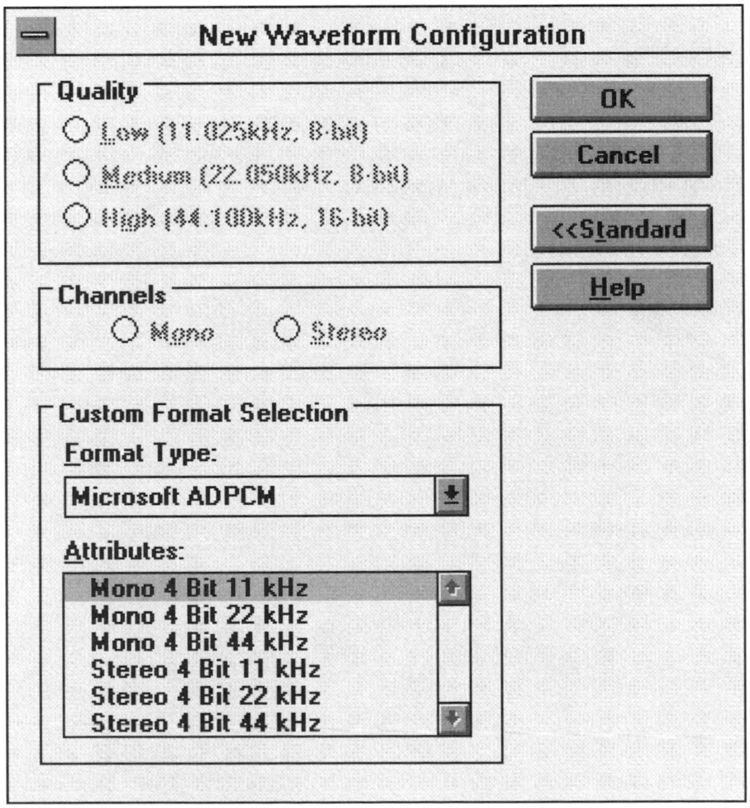

Figure 8.3 Sound Recorder custom options

Figure 8.4 The Sound Blaster Mixer Control

The expanded dialog offers a choice of algorithms—you can choose between Microsoft PCM or Microsoft ADPCM (shown). The list box of selections below changes based on your choice of algorithm.

Level control of the audio being recorded must be done outside of Sound Recorder. The machine being used here has a Sound Blaster 16 ASP card, which has a Mixer Control utility, shown in Figure 8.4. The sliders at the left are used to establish the levels of the different sources available on the card. The resulting mix goes into Sound Recorder according to the software switches in the dialog of Figure 8.5, which you get by selecting Recording from the Settings menu of the Mixer.

Figure 8.5 Sound Blaster Mixer routing switches

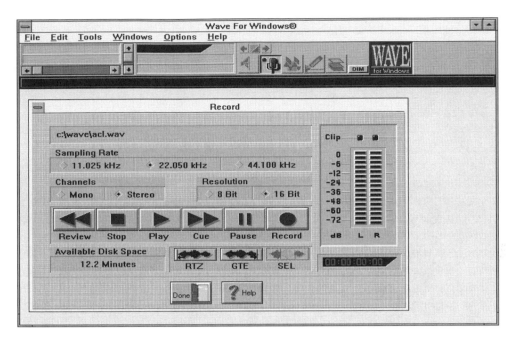

Figure 8.6 Wave for Windows Recorder dialog

Once the switches and levels are set, you begin recording by clicking in the Sound Recorder main window on the button that has the microphone icon. The slider begins moving and the Position window shows elapsed time while the waveform window gives a representation of the sound waveform (the latter does not happen if you are using the ADPCM algorithm).

Turtle Beach Wave for Windows

Wave for Windows is a full-featured audio editor. It has a Recorder module that captures audio to hard disk; the main window with the Record dialog open is shown in Figure 8.6. The usual VCR buttons are provided for recording and reviewing the material. Sampling parameter selection is in the same window, along with stereo and mono selection. A nice feature is a bar-graph level meter at the right of the dialog. There is also a little light (Clip) for each stereo channel that blinks if the maximum level is exceeded during recording. A window below the level meter shows the elapsed recording time in hours:minutes:seconds:frames format. At the left bottom a text window shows the maximum recording time available on the hard disk.

Consistent with the editor metaphor of this program, you create a new recording by first opening a new edit window using New from the File menu.

Then you select the Record icon (the one shaped like a microphone) from the tool bar of Wave for Windows to open the Record dialog. Before you actually get to the Record dialog, you are presented with a dialog to enter a file name for the new audio file. This is necessary because Wave records directly to the hard disk. After you enter a valid file name, you see the Record dialog.

In the Record dialog, you first make selections for sampling rate, mono or stereo, and resolution (bits per sample). Your choices are remembered from one session to the next, so if you always do it the same way, you have to do this only once. Of course, if you have opened an existing file to add on to it or to overwrite it, these choices are determined by the file and cannot be changed.

To monitor the incoming signals and set levels, you click the Pause button, which turns on the level meters and audio monitoring. Now run the incoming source for a test and adjust it to set levels so that the bar graphs go up as high as possible without activating the Clip lights. When your levels are OK, you can rewind the source and begin the recording by clicking the Record button. When the source signal ends, click the Stop button to end the recording.

A recording can be immediately previewed by using the Review (rewind) and Play buttons. You can append to the end of an existing recording by clicking the GTE (go to end) button before starting the new recording. Similarly, you can overwrite the existing recording by clicking the RTZ (return to zero) button before recording. There are many other features in Wave for Windows that are specific to editing; these will be covered in the next chapter on postproduction.

OS/2 Digital Audio

Digital Audio is the audio recording and editing tool for OS/2. Figure 8.7 shows the main window of Digital Audio when it is in the record mode. Record setup choices are in the Options and Type menus. Choices are provided in the Type menu for mono or stereo and three combinations of sampling rate and bits per sample labeled voice, music, and high fidelity. The Options menu lets you choose the input source and gain (level) setting. Level can also be changed at any time by operating the knob control in the main window. Digital Audio records directly to hard disk, so the recording time is limited only by disk space.

MEDIAscript OS/2 Desktop Edition

MEDIAscript is an authoring tool for OS/2 that supports DVI Technology. It can capture audio and video using the ActionMedia II DVI hardware. The audio capture dialog is shown in Figure 8.8. DVI Technology uses its own audio and video file formats that have the file name extension .avs. The dialog provides for

Figure 8.7 OS/2 Digital Audio main window

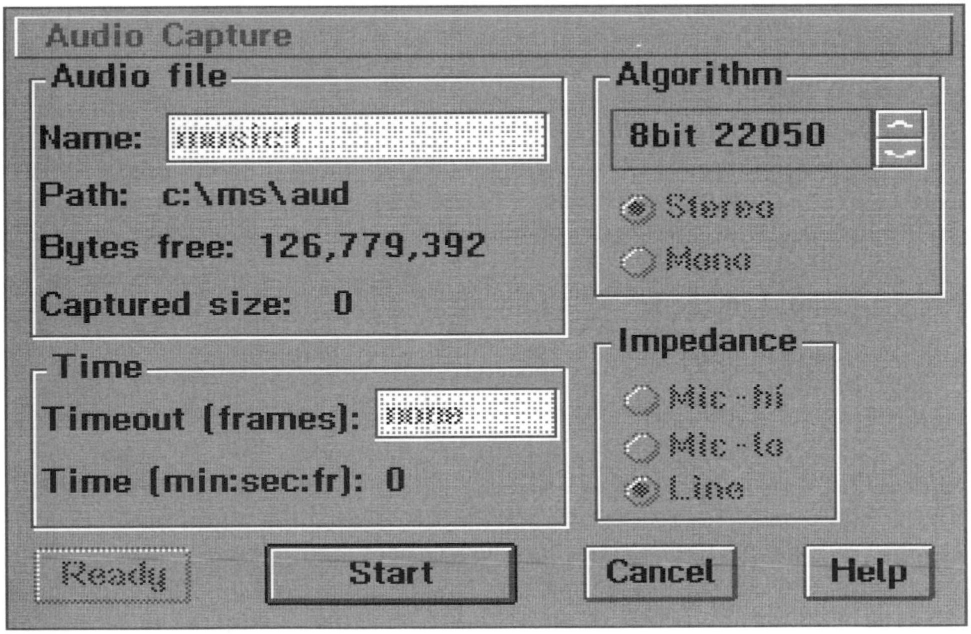

Figure 8.8 The MEDIAscript OS/2 audio capture dialog

selection of algorithm, mono or stereo (if supported by the algorithm selected), and input signal impedance (a selector on the ActionMedia II card). You can either specify a recording duration (Timeout) or run until you click a Stop button. To Record with this dialog, you set up an appropriate file and path to use, make the algorithm selections and click the Ready button. That turns on monitoring and readies everything for an instant start when you click the Start button. This is an important feature because any delay in starting makes it difficult to achieve accurate cueing. While you are in the Ready condition, the input audio is passing through the digital processing the same as will be done during recording. Therefore you can set levels because you can hear the overload effect if it occurs.

As soon as you start recording, the Start button changes to a Stop button. Thus you can use the same button for starting and stopping, without moving the mouse. Both of these operations can also be done using the Enter key on the keyboard.

Review of the recording in MEDIAscript is done by opening the Audio Player dialog. This can be opened during recording, but you cannot actually play anything during recording.

DIGITIZING VIDEO

Digitizing of video differs from audio in that three channels (usually R, G, B) have to be simultaneously digitized and their outputs combined. Also, sampling rates are 100 or more times higher than audio and data rates are proportionately higher. The rates are higher than most PCs can handle directly, which means that compression is not optional. However, the amount of processing needed for good compression is more than a PC can do while video is being captured at 30 frames per second unless there is dedicated hardware for the purpose. This leads to some compromises in the way capture occurs.

Non-real-time Video Sources

A live video source such as a camera runs at 30 frames per second, and there is nothing you can do to slow it down; your digitizing equipment has to take 30 frames per second. However, if the video is recorded, you could theoretically play it in slow motion to give more time to the compression process. Although most VCRs have slow motion features, the process is not very controllable and the performance is significantly degraded. Except with professional-level VCRs designed for single-frame use, this is not a practical approach to do digitizing and compression.

The only readily available device that will deliver high-quality single-frame performance is a laser video disc player. These units are inexpensive and easily controlled for frame-at-a-time compression. However, your material must first be put on a video disc, which requires sending the video out to a mastering center and paying about $300 to produce a half-hour disc. For most digital video applications, this is not practical either. Thus, you will probably choose to do the best you (and your PC) can do to capture video in real time.

General Video Digitizing Considerations

A video capture card must first separate the incoming video into its RGB components, if it is not already that way. The three component signals are then digitized separately and the digital outputs merged into the desired pixel format. At this point, the data rate for 30 frames/second will be too high to go to hard disk storage unless the picture is very small. The numbers for this were discussed in Chapter 3 and a few examples are listed in Table 3.4. From this, you can see that a 160×120 picture at 30 frames per second will generate more than 1 MB of data per second. A very fast hard disk could handle that, but a better approach is to have the CPU do as much compression as it can while the data is streaming in. Algorithms have been developed for that purpose and, with a fast PC and a suitable capture board, they allow video to be read to hard disk for 320×240 pictures at up to 30 frames per second.

Video captured that way is still at too high a data rate to allow full-speed playback on all but the fastest PC systems. Therefore, it is desirable to take the original data and run it through additional compression a frame at a time. Since the frames can be read from hard disk whenever necessary (there is no need to run at 30 frames per second), we can spend more time per frame to do the further compression. This results in a video data stream at a controlled low data rate that can be placed on a CD-ROM and played back on most systems.

If special hardware is available for compression, such as a DVI Technology board or an MPEG encoder board, the total compression process can occur in real time and the second step of compression is not needed. Such hardware usually also delivers better video quality because there is enough video processing processing power to avoid some of the compromises in doing it all with software.

With many tools it is possible to capture and compress with one algorithm and then recompress with a different algorithm. In general, this not a good practice because different algorithms create different artifacts that will simply compound the problems. If you must capture and compress separately, you should capture in an uncompressed format.

Algorithm Selection

It is difficult to make a general evaluation of capture and compression algorithms because there are so many different tradeoffs to consider. In the final analysis you will have to experiment with the algorithms that are available on your hardware and decide by looking at the kinds of material you will be digitizing. However, it is useful to discuss the general considerations:

- **Resolution and bpp**—all algorithms give a choice of resolutions and some offer choice of bpp also. Resolution choices are usually different divisions by 2 of the VGA full-screen size of 640×480 pixels. Thus the numbers 160 $\times$ 120 or 320×240 arise. The more advanced algorithms support 16-bpp or 24-bpp, although they will still display on less-bpp displays by a process of scaling down during playback (this may slow down the system somewhat.) The Microsoft RLE algorithm, however, only works at 8-bpp.

- **Speed**—there are speed considerations during compression and also during playback. During playback, the algorithm speed and the CPU speed will determine the frame rate that can be captured. With a small enough video window and a fast enough CPU, the capture speed will be 30 frames per second, but if you use a larger window or a slower CPU, the capture frame rate will slow down. If the capture frame rate is slowed, it cannot be speeded up by a faster playback system. This is why the system used for capture should be the fastest one you have. Most algorithms will automatically slow down the playback frame rate when running on a slow system. They will try to maintain the average rate of video by dropping frames that come too fast to be displayed in the time available.

- **Control of data rate**—algorithms that compress in a separate operation from capture can establish an exact data rate for the compressed video. The most common use of this is to match exactly to a CD-ROM data rate. This is done so that video can be played smoothly from the CD-ROM without the need for interruptions or seeks by the drive, which might interfere with the video because of the slow access time of a CD-ROM drive.

- **Quality tradeoffs**—in addition to the reduction of resolution that results than a less than full-screen video window, many algorithms make additional compromises to obtain additional compression. Often this tradeoff is adjustable in the compression software by setting a "quality" parameter. A lower quality reduces the data rate but it usually lends a blocky appearance to the video. There is no substitute to experimenting with this setting to decide what suits you best.

- **Platform considerations**—some algorithms are platform specific, while others produce data streams that can be played on different platforms using the appropriate drivers. For example, Indeo and DVI .AVS files can be played on both Windows and OS/2 platforms. If multi-platform use is important to you, that will limit your choice of algorithms. Fortunately, platform independence is a feature of many of the newest algorithms, but these are not yet as widely available as the older ones.

- **Difference frame compression**—algorithms that compare data from one frame to the next and compress out repeated data (motion compensation) deliver more compression. However, this technique is very compute-intensive and available only on algorithms that have dedicated hardware or do not run in real time.

Development of compression algorithms is continuing at a high pace. Nothing on the market is near to becoming the one universal standard, and there is probably still much room for improvement. Therefore, the task of choosing algorithms will be something you will have to do repeatedly for some time. Every time a new algorithm comes out, you will want to evaluate it for your needs.

Controlling Signal Levels

Video voltages are well standardized throughout the television and video industries, so much so that most equipment does not even have provision for adjustment. The standard video voltage is 0.7 volts peak-to-peak, white positive—measured from the blackest part of the picture (blanking level) up to the whitest highlight in the picture. Video cameras have automatic exposure systems that maintain the video level by adjusting the lens iris continuously during shooting. This will usually be satisfactory, unless you are striving for a special video effect of some sort.

To obtain control over video level, you have to turn off the automatic iris in your camera; most cameras have a switch for that. Then by manually adjusting the iris, you can increase or decrease the level to get the effect you are looking for. For example, if your camera is making your picture too dark because of some bright highlights that are affecting the automatic iris, you can go to the manual iris mode and try to open the lens a little to see if the picture can be improved before the highlights overload too much.

In professional video systems, video levels are monitored by using an oscilloscope or waveform monitor, which is a special display that shows the actual video voltage waveform. These monitors are calibrated so that you can set levels to exactly 0.7 volts; at the same time, the waveform view shows you how much of the signal is at the highest and lowest levels of the voltage range. This is an excellent approach if you have the equipment, but you can also do an adequate job by watching a normal picture display that has been carefully set up. The most

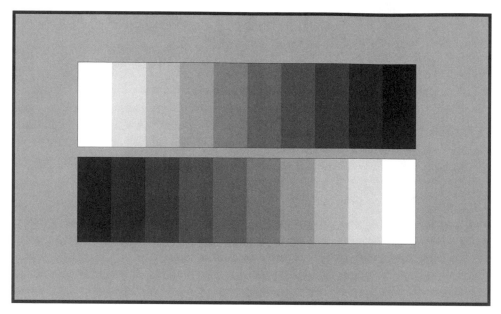

Figure 8.9 A gray-scale test pattern for setting monitor brightness

important part of monitor setup is the black level or "brightness" setting of the display.

For correct brightness setup, you need to make sure that the darkest part of the image just reaches black on the screen without going below black. The best way to set that is to use a 10-step gray-scale test signal. A typical gray-scale pattern is shown in Figure 8.9. Such a signal can be generated with most graphics drawing programs. When displaying the gray-scale, you adjust the monitor brightness all the way up until you can see that the black step of the gray-scale is not really black. Then back down the brightness until the black step just extinguishes, but not so much that the next step goes black, too. You should see each of the gray levels and the darkest level should be real black. With a little practice, this is easy to do.

The other adjustment on most monitors is the "contrast" control, which you adjust to set the level of the brightest highlight in your image. Again, you can do this with the gray-scale pattern; set it to give a pleasing level of brightness to the highlights. You should recheck the brightness setting after changing the contrast.

Once your monitor is set up, you simply adjust your camera to produce the most pleasing picture on the monitor. If you are using automatic iris, you can adjust the lighting to improve the picture, filling in dark areas or toning down highlights. When the picture looks good on your monitor, you should be seeing what you will get when you capture the video.

Video Digitizing Tools

There are many video capture tools, some are tied to one algorithm and some provide a choice of algorithm. The following video capture tools are discussed here:

Microsoft VidCap is a tool provided with Video for Windows.

IBM Video IN is a video capture tool for OS/2.

Touchvision Systems' CineWorks is a video capture tool that uses DVI Technology and runs under DOS.

Network Technology Corporation's MEDIAscript OS/2 is an authoring tool for OS/2 that supports DVI Technology.

Microsoft VidCap

Microsoft includes VidCap in its Video for Windows package. VidCap supports installable capture board drivers and algorithms. Therefore, it can stay up to date as new products emerge (as they are doing all the time). VidCap supports real-time capture from live video or capture and compression from a sequence of single frames. In the latter case, it also can automatically control a single-frame storage device, such as a laser video disc player.

Figure 8.10 shows the main window of VidCap on the left with dialogs open for setting up motion video capture. The Capture Video Sequence appears when you select the Video... item from the Capture menu in the main window. In this dialog, you select the desired frame rate for the capture and whether capture goes to memory or directly to disk.

Capturing to memory will be faster, but the segment duration will be limited by the amount of memory available. Capture to disk will usually let you capture a longer segment, unless your hard disk is already very full. To make disk capture as fast as possible, you should preallocate a capture file (there is an option for that on VidCap's File menu) and then defragment your hard disk to make sure that file is contiguous on disk. The best approach is to allocate a capture file that is as large as you ever expect to use. VidCap lets you use this file over and over by giving you the option to copy the contents of the capture file to another file with a different name. The file acl.avi indicated in the title bar of VidCap is my preallocated capture file.

The Capture Video Sequence also lets you set up an arbitrary limit on the capture time by clicking the Enable Capture Time Limit check box and setting the desired number of seconds in the spin box below. This is useful to make sure you don't run out of hard disk space or that you go beyond the end of your capture

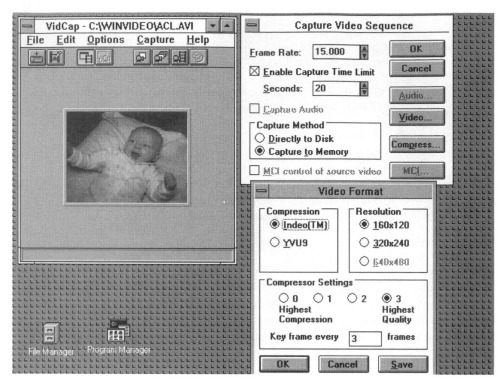

Figure 8.10 The main window of VidCap (left) with dialogs for setting up motion video capture

file (which it will otherwise try to do.) This dialog also lets you choose whether to include audio with your video. If you have audio, there are dialogs similar to Sound Recorder for selection of audio format.

Clicking the Video... button in the Capture Video Sequence dialog opens the Video Format dialog shown at the bottom in Figure 8.10. Here you can choose the resolution and the type of compression to be used during capture. With the Intel Smart Video Recorder board installed here, you can do Indeo capture in real time because that board provides hardware acceleration of compression. You can also make a tradeoff between degree of compression and picture quality by means of the buttons at the bottom of the dialog. Finally, you can choose how often you want Indeo to insert a key (reference) frame. If you plan to edit your video, you should insert key frames often; but if you will not be editing, you can increase the amount of compression by having key frames less often.

When you change the resolution setting in the Video Format dialog, the video window in the main window changes size. For higher resolutions, you might need to increase the size of the main window to see all of the video window.

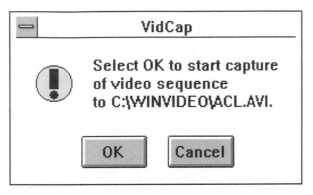

Figure 8.11 The dialog for starting motion video capture in VidCap

When you have made all the setups and closed the two dialogs, VidCap prepares to do the actual capture. When it is ready, the dialog shown in Figure 8.11 appears. When you click OK or hit Enter, capture begins. A prompt appears at the bottom of the main window to tell you that you can stop capture by hitting the Esc key. After capture is finished, the same prompt line tells you how many frames were captured and whether any frames were dropped during capture, which would happen if something in the system slowed the operation.

To see playback of the capture, you have to open VidEdit, which you can do from the File menu of VidCap. Doing that brings up VidEdit with your captured video already loaded. You can save the video to a different file name using either VidCap (if you do not need to edit it) or VidEdit. When you save with VidEdit, you have the option of doing further compression, and there is a wider choice of algorithms than during capture. This is discussed more in Chapter 9.

IBM Video IN for OS/2

IBM's video capture tool for OS/2 is Video IN. This program supports IBM Ultimotion and Intel Indeo real-time capture algorithms. Several frame-grabber boards are supported. The video source can be a video camera or VCR, a video disc player or an .avi file. The last case is used for copying or editing a file or changing its compression type or parameters. With either a video disc or a file source, the recording process is *frame step*, meaning that the compression algorithm can take as much time as it likes to compress each frame. That way, you can get higher quality and more compression than is possible in real time.

The main window of Video IN is shown in Figure 8.12. This particular example is set up for frame step recording, although the dialog is similar for live recording. The top part of the dialog defines the video source and has controls for it, the

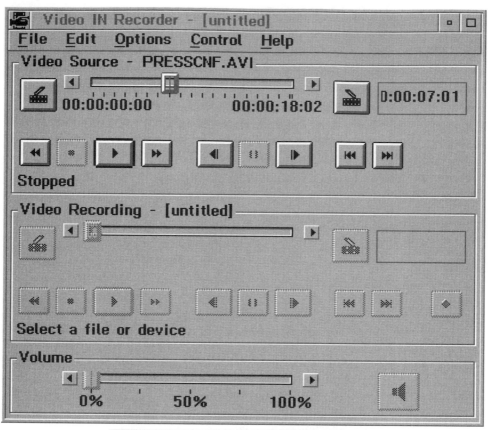

Figure 8.12 Main dialog and monitor window of Video IN (courtesy of IBM)

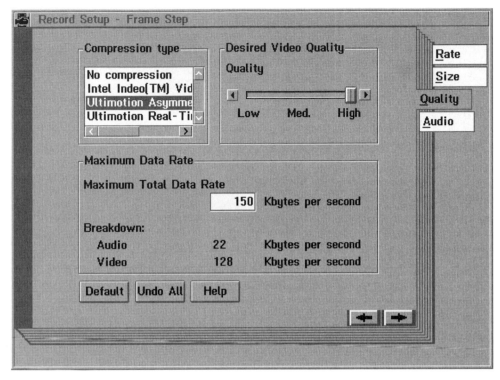

Figure 8.13 The Record Setup notebook dialog from Video IN

next part below controls the recording, and the bottom controls the audio. Slider bars show the file position in both source and recording.

Many options are controlled from the menu bar. For example, a Record Setup OS/2 notebook dialog is accessed from the Options menu. The quality page from that notebook is shown in Figure 8.13. This page allows choice of compression algorithm, setting compression parameters and compressed data rate objectives. Other pages in the Record Setup notebook set video image size, frame rates, and audio parameters.

Touchvision Systems' CineWorks

For the highest quality motion video capture, you should use DVI Technology or another hardware-based video compression system. CineWorks is a capture and editing tool that works with the ActionMedia II DVI board. It runs under DOS. Cineworks provides a complete environment for capture and editing and allows the production of video sequences that include DVI motion video, still images, graphics, and animations. It also provides full facilities for mixing and

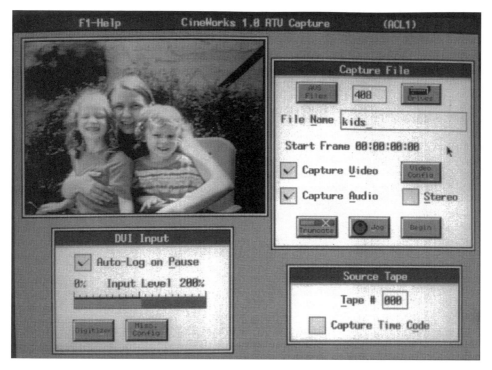

Figure 8.14 The RTV Capture dialog from CineWorks

editing up to four channels of audio. The output from CineWorks can be as a DVI .AVS video file (playable only on DVI-equipped systems) or a Video for Windows .AVI file (playable on any system running Windows) or as analog video for recording on a VCR.

CineWorks allows you to organize your work into a number of *jobs*, which are collections of all the resources needed by a particular editing project. Each job has its own directory on the hard disk, and all the files for that job must be placed there by CineWorks. Once the files are created, captured, or imported, they are available to all editing tasks on that job.

Video and audio capture in CineWorks runs from the RTV Capture screen shown in Figure 8.14. This is accessed from the Prepare to Edit menu and it supports either live capture from a camera, capture from a VCR, or automatic capture from a VCR with time code. The last mode allows you to return to your original source tapes after editing to produce an edited output in higher quality than you used during the editing process.

The RTV Capture window shows the live input in the upper-left window. To the right is a dialog box where you must specify the capture file. You can create a new file or you can add footage to an existing file. Below the live video window

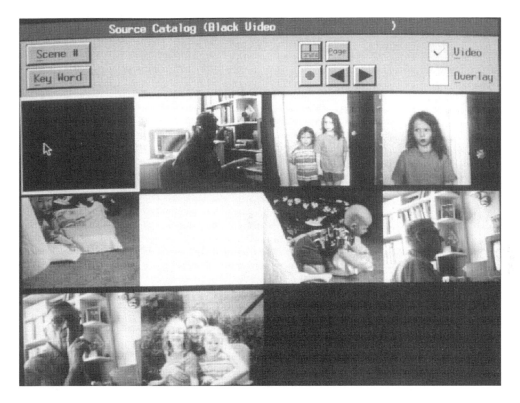

Figure 8.15 The CineWorks Source Catalog screen

is another dialog for setting DVI Input level and setting other parameters about the digitizing process.

One important feature here is Auto-Log on Pause, which causes a log entry to be made every time you pause recording. When you go to edit your job, all the files and log entries will appear in the Source Catalog screen, shown in Figure 8.15. This screen allows you to move instantly to any of your shots without having to search for them—they are all shown visually with still frames in the Source Catalog screen(s).

Once you have specified a capture file and selected other options, setup for capture is begun by clicking on the Begin button in the Capture File dialog. The screen changes to a full-screen display of the live video with only a narrow prompt bar at the top. Actual capture is started or paused using function keys on the keyboard. When you are finished capturing, you return to the RTV Capture screen by hitting ESC on the keyboard.

On the RTV Capture screen, you can review your most recent shot by clicking the Jog button in the Capture File dialog. This puts you in playback mode with CineWorks' unique jog controller on-screen. As you move the mouse from side to side, you control the speed of playback in forward (right) or reverse (left). As you do this, the current frame number is continuously displayed. You have smooth speed control from one frame at a time all the way up to 50 times normal speed!

CineWorks is a well-designed capture tool with the ability to output its work in a number of formats. Combined with its built-in editing capabilities (described in the next chapter), it is a very valuable tool.

Network Technology MEDIAscript OS/2

MEDIAscript OS/2 is a complete multimedia authoring suite that runs under OS/2 and supports DVI Technology. I will describe its capture capabilities here. Figure 8.16 shows the Video Capture dialog and its monitor window. Capture is directly to disk, so a file name must be entered to begin. Once a name is entered, the Ready button is enabled; clicking that brings up the Monitor window showing the live video input.

The algorithm selection offers choice of DVI RTV real-time compression algorithms and the video resolution can also be selected. If audio is enabled, there is algorithm selection and a stereo/mono choice for that. A Timeout entry field allows optionally specifying a maximum length for the video.

Capture is started by clicking the Start button (or hitting the Enter key)—capture begins immediately without delay. During capture, the approximate captured file size is displayed dynamically in the Captured size field. This can be compared to the Bytes-free field to judge how much disk space is left. Also, when capture begins the Start Button changes to a Stop button, so a mouse click on the same button (or an Enter keystroke) will stop recording.

SUMMARY

The considerations of audio and video digitizing (capture) were discussed, including setting levels, choosing algorithms, quality levels, and deciding when in the production–postproduction process capture should be done. Capture hardware was covered and several software tools for capture were presented.

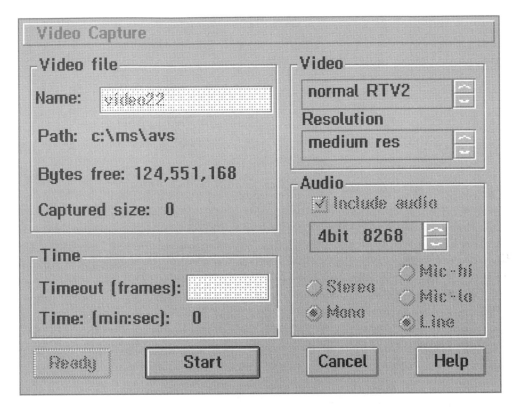

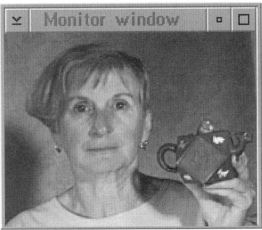

Figure 8.16 The Video Capture dialog and Monitor window of MEDIAscript OS/2

9

Postproduction

Creating video and audio programs for television almost always uses the production–postproduction technique, where the task of recording all the materials from live scenes is done separately from the task of assembling the materials into the program continuity. Even though this approach is slower and more difficult, the flexibility it affords pays off copiously in the quality and professionalism of the results that are obtained.

The production–postproduction approach is equally applicable to PC video and audio creation, and it has most of the same advantages. It is further attractive with PCs because you don't need any extra equipment—the same PC you use for everything else can do postproduction. In this chapter, I will discuss video and audio postproduction using both analog equipment and PCs.

TASKS OF POSTPRODUCTION

The process of postproduction can be as simple or as complex as suits your application and yourself. Figure 9.1 is a simplified diagram for postproduction that encompasses all the major task classes. Notice that any of these tasks can be done either in analog or digital, so digitizing can occur at any point from the beginning up until just before the final formatting. Ordinarily you would digitize andio and video only once—you would not go back to analog once you had become digital. I'll discuss the issues of analog vs. digital postproduction shortly.

The inputs to the process are audio cuts and video shots from your production takes or from your libraries or any other sources you have. These are in whatever format their original sources are—tape, disk, computer file, etc. The process of converting formats is part of postproduction and may occur at any point or even more than once. (Digitizing is one kind of format conversion.) Next, I will define each of the tasks in more detail.

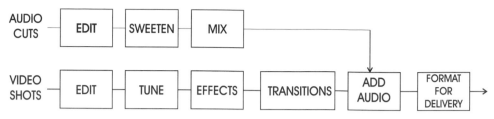

Figure 9.1 The tasks of postproduction (simplified)

Editing

The term editing is often used to refer to the entire postproduction process. However, I want to be a little more precise, so I will define editing as *the process of selecting and marking or cutting the exact segments that will appear, whole or in part, in the final program*. Thus, editing is where you choose your exact cuts and decide how they will go together. Sometimes you will have more than one segment of the same type (audio or video) appearing simultaneously in your program. In such a case, the segments overlap, and the edit marking of the segments must take account of the overlap regions.

In the early days of videotape, editing was done by physically cutting the tape and pasting the pieces back together. This required extreme manual dexterity on the part of the editor, and he only got one chance at doing it because the tape was ruined after one edit. Today, we have much better ways involving either rerecording in the case of videotape or fully electronic in the case of PCs. I will discuss both approaches later.

A particular case of editing is the building of the sound effects audio track from individual sounds specially recorded or from libraries. A separate track is usually made so that the timing of sound effects can be adjusted after the video editing has been completed. The effects track is not mixed into the rest of the audio until the end of postproduction. (Once it has been mixed in, it is very difficult to adjust timing any more.) An audio/video editor must be used for sound effects editing so that the video can be viewed in sync during the audio editing.

Sweetening and Tuning

Often there will be something about an audio or video segment that you would like to fix up a little. Maybe the high frequencies in your audio are weak or your video's color is not quite right. Correction of such things is easily done during postproduction; it is called *sweetening* for audio and *tuning* for video. Many tools are available for these tasks. These functions are also often built into digitizing or editing tools.

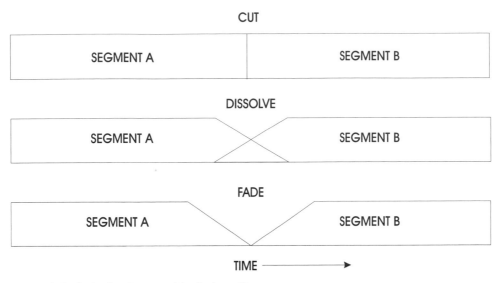

Figure 9.2 Cut, dissolve, and fade transitions

Audio Mixing

The process of merging separate dialog, music, effects, and ambience tracks into a single audio program is called *mixing*. In mixing you control the amount (amplitude) of each component that goes into the final output. Sometimes this is done with fixed settings and sometimes the amounts have to be continuously adjusted during the mix. Audio transitions are also accomplished during the mix. Of course the final output level has to be controlled to keep it from overloading the system or becoming too quiet. Audio mixing of many separate elements can take a lot of skill and experience.

Video Effects and Transitions

The simplest way to join individual video segments is to butt them to one another, with the transition taking place between one frame and the next. This is called a *cut*. The cut transition is abrupt and may interfere with the content of the program if not carefully placed. For this reason, a cut is often replaced with a *dissolve* or *fade* transition, which performs the transition over a period of 1 second or more. Figure 9.2 shows how cut, dissolve, or fade transitions operate on the two signals being joined. In a dissolve, one segment fades out while the other fades in at the same time. During the dissolve, both segments are partially present on the screen or in the sound. In a fade, one segment fades out *before* the other starts fading in.

The result is that the segments never appear simultaneously—the effect is to make a more deliberate change of scene.

In the case of audio, the fade and dissolve are about the only types of transition available. However, for video these are just the beginning—there are thousands of transition effects one can do by treating different areas of the picture differently. These are the various wipe-like effects produced by one or more transition lines that move across the image plane to switch the picture locally from one segment to the other.

Still more elaborate video transitions are based on *moving* one picture relative to another. These are often called *digital effects*, a name that comes from the television industry, where such effects were one of the first digital processes to be used in the analog video system.

A fade or dissolve effect is usually intended as an unobtrusive transition that gets the viewer from one scene to another with as little disruption of the continuity as possible. When more elaborate transitions are used, the transition can easily draw attention to itself. These are more often used in nondramatic programs such as news, sports, or commercials where the transitions add pizzaz to a presentation that might otherwise be dull. With the portfolio of video transitions available today, one has to be careful not to overdo that.

Adding the Audio

In general, audio and video should be kept separate until the very end of postproduction. Of course, this would not be true if they were recorded together and there was never any reason to process them separately. If you do process them separately and there is a need for synchronization, such as lip-sync, you should use time code or some other means to reestablish sync when you finally put them together. The assembly of audio and video is usually part of the process of building the final video format and is provided for in the video tools that you use to assemble the complete video.

ANALOG POSTPRODUCTION

Although this chapter is mostly about digital postproduction on your PC, it is useful to look at analog techniques first to understand some of the basic concepts and procedures of postproduction. In the analog world, the medium for both audio and video postproduction is magnetic tape. Tape is a *linear* medium, meaning that it is one-dimensional and different scenes or cuts are necessarily one after another along one or more tapes. Therefore you must run tape or maybe even change reels or cassettes to go from one place to another, which takes a lot of time. Most tape decks cannot go faster than about 20 or 30 times play speed and they are less controllable when they are going fast. In computer terms, the access time of magnetic tape is very long—sometimes measured in minutes.

Assemble Editing

In editing, you need to preview your various segments and select the exact portions that will be included in your final output. To do this, you play the segments and place marks of some sort to identify the start and end of each cut. These are called the *in-edit* and *out-edit* points. Once several in-edit and out-edit points are identified, you need to preview the segments together, so you can see how they look or sound in the final arrangement. That is a random-access task, but magnetic tape access time is too slow to do it the way we would on a computer. To get two segments from different places on the tape or on different tapes to play together, you must either use two tape decks set up to play the segments in sequence, or you must copy (rerecord) the segments onto another tape. The latter technique is the usual method because the multiple-deck approach might take one deck for every segment you have in your program.

Therefore, to cut and rearrange material on magnetic tape, you make a new recording with the segments arranged in the desired sequence. By setting up one deck to play back a selected segment and a second deck to record the output from the playback deck, you can assemble segments from various sources into the desired sequence on the tape in the second deck. This technique is called *assemble* editing and it requires two tape decks and an appropriate edit controller. Figure 9.3 is a block diagram of an assemble edit setup. The audio or video outputs of the source deck connect to the corresponding inputs of the recording deck. The edit controller manages the marking of in- and out-edit points and controls both tape decks to perform edits.

Edit controllers identify in-edit and out-edit points by counting pulses on the tape's control *track* (a special track that the VCR uses for its own internal control) or by using a time code signal recorded in its own track on the tape. The latter approach is more accurate and also more expensive.

Assemble editing is limited in that you do not have any choice of transition effects between segments—only cuts. The output from assemble editing is always a copy of the original material, so any distortion that occurs in the analog recording and replay process will accumulate. A copy of an original tape like this is called a *second generation* tape.

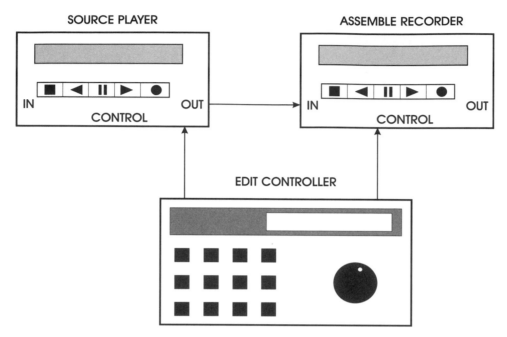

Figure 9.3 Block diagram of an assemble editing setup

The A/B Roll

A more capable technique is the *A/B roll* setup, whose hardware is diagrammed in Figure 9.4. There are three tape decks. Two are used primarily for playback and the third is used primarily for recording. An audio/video mixer connects the decks to add transition effects and an edit controller box controls all units.

With A/B roll, you build your final sequence in two steps. First you make the A and B tapes by assemble editing. These tapes have alternate segments from the final sequence as shown in Figure 9.5. Segments on the A and B tapes overlap appropriately wherever transition effects require both sources simultaneously. To preview the overall program, you play the A and B decks simultaneously under control of the edit controller, which also controls the audio/video mixer to combine the outputs from the A and B decks according to your script. You view the output of the mixer on a TV monitor. When you are satisfied with the results, the program is run once more and the output is recorded on the third tape deck to make your final tape.

A/B roll editing is very capable, but it is difficult to accomplish and a lot of equipment is involved. Because the output tape from this process is a *third generation* (a copy of a copy), you must use high-quality recording equipment such as S-VHS or Hi-8 or better to avoid too much accumulated distortion. Tape decks

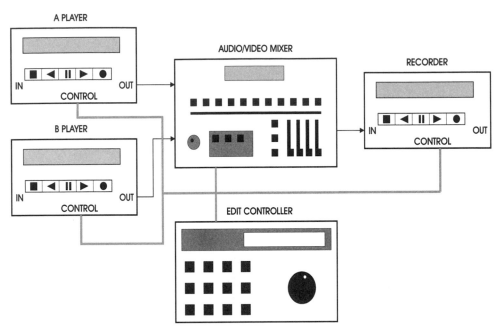

Figure 9.4 Block diagram of an A/B roll editing setup

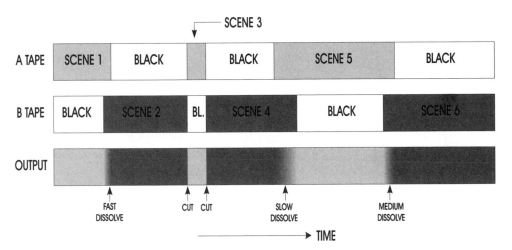

Figure 9.5 Sequence diagram showing how A/B roll editing works

for editing also must have remote control and fast tape handling. It will cost more than $10,000 for the minimum A/B roll editing setup, and you can easily spend two to three times that amount.

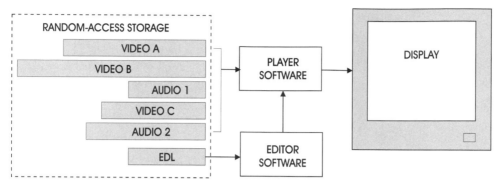

Figure 9.6 Diagram of nonlinear editing on a PC

NONLINEAR EDITING

In the linear editing approaches described so far, extra equipment and a lot of trouble in use has resulted from the fact that magnetic tape does not support fast random-access operation. This is the place where digital techniques make a real contribution to editing, because random-access is easy with digital storage and memory devices. However, to use digital storage, the audio and video must be digital! I have spent several chapters telling you about that, so you know it can be done and you should understand the limitations. But you should also understand that all the limitations of digital technology today are subject to that continuing curve of digital cost-performance improvement—two times every two years. The limitations are temporary. This is the reason why digital postproduction is so exciting.

Editing with random-access is called *nonlinear* because you can instantly access your materials at any point, without regard to tape locations, reels, or formats. You are not limited by linear locations on tape reels or cassettes. Figure 9.6 shows a diagram of nonlinear editing on a PC.

A proposed edit is previewed simply by building a command list that tells the digital memory where to start reading (playing) data and where to jump to at each edit cut point. Such a list is called an *edit decision list* (EDL). But it can go further than that, because the digital audio and video data can be processed to create effects and transitions. These things also can be placed in the EDL.

All audio and video information is digitized, compressed, and stored on hard disks. Playback software can play any segment from any starting point, at variable speeds, down to single frames. In- and out-edit points can be located to the exact frame number, and the playback software can jump from a frame location in one segment to another frame location in a different segment without missing a frame. Thus, you can view your material to locate edit points and you can quickly view an out-point adjacent to the next in-point to see if the transition will look the way you want it to. An EDL is automatically built while you are doing all that. When you want to preview a sequence, you can immediately play the EDL to view the overall effect. When you are all done, you can play the EDL to a VCR or to a new digital video file.

Nonlinear editing is so attractive that an entire industry has built up around computer workstations coupled with special hardware for digital video capture and processing. The special hardware provides the high-quality data compression and storage required to support operating at broadcast levels of picture and sound quality, but it is very much more expensive than PC video hardware. These systems are slowly replacing more traditional tape editing in broadcast and professional postproduction. Because nonlinear editing is so fast and flexible, this is happening even though the output from these facilities is still recorded on analog videotape. How much more desirable it will be when the desired output is digital, as I am talking about in this book.

DIGITAL POSTPRODUCTION ON A PC

When your objective is to produce video and audio for use on a PC, it makes all the sense in the world to do your postproduction on the PC also. Since you are going to have to digitize at some time anyway, do it right after production and then use your PC for all the postproduction. All the postproduction takes is software—the hardware you used for digitizing will do the job. This is a new field and its software market is still developing, but already a number of interesting products support nonlinear editing and all kinds of effects and transitions—all done on your PC. I will discuss three software packages for digital postproduction: *VidEdit*, the video editor included with Microsoft Video for Windows, *Wave for Windows*, a stand-alone audio editor produced by Turtle Beach Systems, and *Cineworks*, an audio/video editor by Touchvision Systems, Inc. that runs under DOS and DVI Technology.

Microsoft VidEdit

The main window of VidEdit is shown in Figure 9.7. The operation of VidEdit is somewhat like a magnetic tape assemble editing setup. You can use two instances of VidEdit running simultaneously to perform the functions of the source and record tape decks in an assemble setup. Having two copies of VidEdit at the same

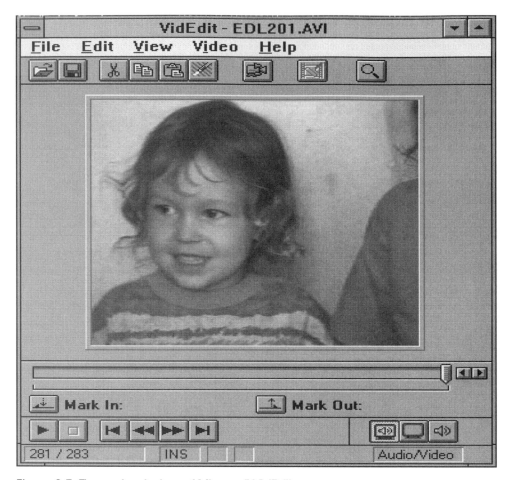

Figure 9.7 The main window of Microsoft VidEdit

time is possible because of the multitasking capability of Windows and the fact that VidEdit was designed to work this way.

To assemble a new sequence taken from several source files, you open each source file in one of the copies of VidEdit and use the playback controls to select the part of the file you will include in the output. Then you copy the selection to the Windows clipboard. In the second copy of VidEdit, you start a new file and paste the segment from the clipboard into it. You can continue that way to build your new sequence. As in assemble editing with tape, VidEdit only does cut transitions.

VidEdit never actually makes copies of the objects you are working with; it just identifies them on your hard disk and calls them up whenever you choose to play or view them. This is where the process differs from videotape editing. Because of the random-access capability of your hard disk, no copying is needed. However, the random-access allows something that tape editing will not do: you can insert new material at any point and everything beyond the insert will automatically move downstream. With tape, you would have to rerecord everything beyond the insert point.

Many features in VidEdit support merging of material captured in different formats, and a wide portfolio of compression algorithms are available for formatting the output. You can also edit audio and video separately or together.

Returning to Figure 9.7, the menu bar at the top of the window give access to file management, editing, options, and formatting features. The current video frame is displayed in the center of the window. Below the video display is a slider bar that indicates the current frame position in the total segment opened in the editor. At the right of the slider, two arrow buttons allow single-step moving in either direction. These help you locate an exact frame point in the video. Below the slider are two buttons (Mark In and Mark Out) for marking a selection region in the current video. The selection region is used by the Cut, Copy, and Paste controls in the Edit menu. When you mark a selection, its frame numbers (or optionally, its time location) are indicated to the right of the Mark buttons.

Below the Mark buttons, a series of VCR-type control buttons allow playback or rewinding of the entire segment or the selection. Three buttons at the right allow choice of whether audio, video, or both are currently being edited. Finally, the line at the bottom of the VidEdit window gives status information, including the size of the current selection, the entire segment, and various types of mode information.

Setting Compression Options

Normally you capture video in an uncompressed format and edit it that way also. When the complete scene has been assembled in VidEdit, you can then choose a compression format and save the final version as compressed. The compression and saving process may take some time, but it runs by itself, taking uncompressed frames from the hard disk, compressing them, and appending the compressed data on the end of the output file that is being built. There are many options in this process, as you can see from Figure 9.8, which shows the Compression Options dialog from VidEdit.

Starting at the top left in the dialog, the Target: selection chooses the way your final file will be distributed. The choices cover hard disk and CD-ROM at several different data rates (most compression algorithms will accept a target data rate for compression.) Then you can select the Video Compression Method (algorithm). The choices here include Microsoft Video I, Cinepak, and several versions

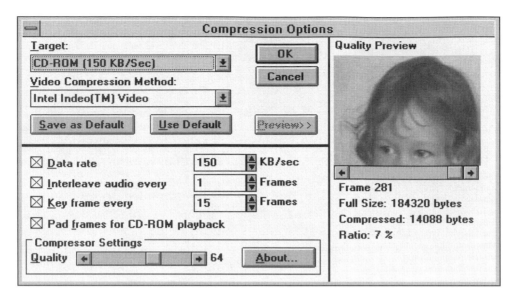

Figure 9.8 The Compression Options dialog of VidEdit

of Indeo compression. This list is actually a moving target because new algorithms can be added to your system at any time and they will appear in this list.

Below the algorithm selector are check boxes and spin windows for you to set exact data rate, audio interleaving, and key (reference) frame information. All of these parameters have default values that come up when you select an algorithm, but if you want to do fine tuning, they can be changed. At the bottom of the dialog, there is a slider bar to make adjustment of the quality vs. compression tradeoff. This appears only for algorithms that have such a tradeoff available.

At the right in the Compression Options dialog the current frame from the video in the editor is shown as it will look when compressed. A slider bar lets you change to other frames, and the compression statistics are also given. This is helpful if you want to experiment with the parameters and the quality tradeoff. When you are satisfied with this dialog, you click OK and your choices will then apply to any subsequent file saving that you do.

VidEdit is a good basic tool for cut-only editing of video and audio. It also has a good portfolio of output formats for Video for Windows use. It is inexpensive, but it leaves room for more sophisticated editors to provide transitions and other more advanced features.

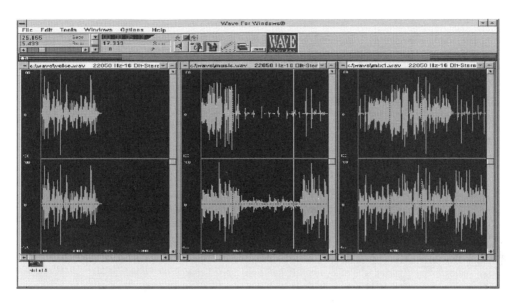

Figure 9.9 Wave for Windows main editing screen

Turtle Beach Wave for Windows

An audio postproduction studio has so many features that it is not reasonable to include them all in a digital audio/video editor. Wave for Windows by Turtle Beach Systems is an audio-only tool that goes head-to-head with almost any analog audio postproduction studio. It supports all types of audio editing, sweetening, and mixing. Figure 9.9 shows the main screen of Wave, with a setup that places voice-over with a music track behind.

The editing metaphor of Wave for Windows is a little different than what I have just described for VidEdit. Wave supports up to four soundfile windows, each of which displays the contents of one sound file on your hard disk. Wave edits the disk files directly; it does not bring sound files into memory. A *soundfile window* displays the audio waveform data directly; it displays two waveforms if the file is stereo. You can zoom in on the data as much as you like, even so much that you can see individual cycles of the sound waveform. Figure 9.10 is an example of that: it shows a waveform containing a loud noise spike (seen at the center of the top window), the second window has zoomed in on the spike and selected it, and in the third window the spike has been deleted. This kind of fix is easily done in Wave.

There are more audio processing and manipulation features in Wave than I can possibly cover here. As an example, Figure 9.11 shows the Tools menu. I will briefly explain what each of these does so you can understand some of the power

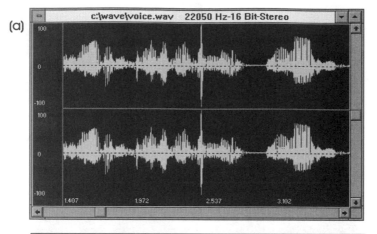

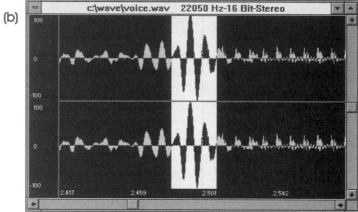

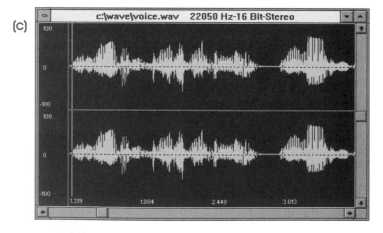

Figure 9.10 Editing in Wave for Windows to remove a noise spike: (a) a soundfile window showing a spike, (b) zooming in on the spike, and (c) the spike deleted

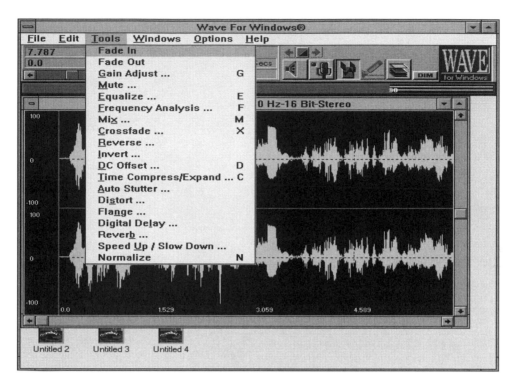

Figure 9.11 Wave for Windows screen showing the Tools menu

of this program. Most of the tools can be directed to operate on the entire sound file, a selected region, or a region identified by markers you can place in the soundfile window. The tools modify the sound file in the current soundfile window, but you can select the region of application using the dialog shown in Figure 9.12. Because a lot of processing is required for some of the tools, they can take considerable time to apply.

- **Fade in and fade out**—these tools fade the volume up or down in the selected range.
- **Gain adjust**—this tool adjusts the level in the selected range. The volume can be set at each end of the range and it will vary smoothly between those values. This tool was used in the example of Figure 9.9 to reduce the level of the music in the range where the voice-over was to be added.
- **Mute**—this tool erases the selected range of audio.
- **Equalize**—this tool is a four-band parametric equalizer in software.
- **Frequency analysis**—this tool does not actually modify a sound file; rather it creates a frequency spectrum display that shows the sound frequencies

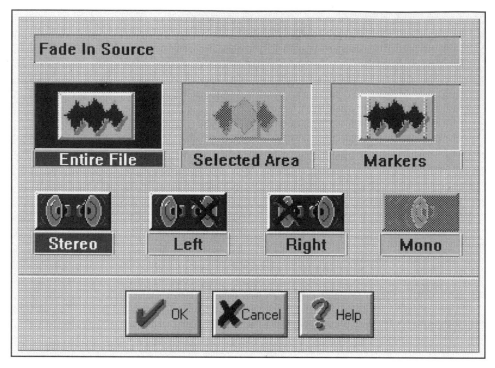

Figure 9.12 Wave for Windows' dialog for selecting the region of action

contained in the selected range of the sound file. It is used to study the characteristics of sounds.

- **Mix**—with this tool you can mix ranges of two or three sound files to create a new fourth sound file. It was used in the example of Figure 9.9 to mix the voice-over and the music tracks. You can adjust the levels and the timings of the mix.
- **Crossfade**—this tool fades one sound file into another.
- **Reverse**—this tool lets you reverse a range of sound so that it will play backwards.
- **Invert**—this tool reverses the polarity of a channel, which is sometimes needed to enhance the stereo effect.
- **dc offset**—this adds a fixed dc voltage to the specified range of sound. It is sometimes useful to fix distortion.
- **Time compress/expand**—this tool allows you to stretch or shrink the time scale of the selected range.
- **Auto stutter**—this tool chops the selected range into a specified number of blocks with blank space between them. It causes a stuttering effect in the sound.

- **Distort**—this tool introduces deliberate digital overload, which is sometimes used in certain types of music.
- **Flange**—this is a modulation effect that introduces a characteristic whooshing sound into music.
- **Digital delay**—this tool introduces an echo or slapback effect into the sound.
- **Reverb**—this tool introduces artificial reverberation into the sound to simulate various kinds of room acoustics.
- **Speed up/slow down**—this tool changes the speed at which a sound file plays. It also will change the pitch of the sound by the same amount.
- **Normalize**—this tool adjust the level of the selected region so that it is as loud as possible without any overload. It reads the entire region to find the highest peaks and then does its adjustment.

Wave for Windows will very likely fill all your needs for digital audio editing. Sound files produced with Wave can be inserted into your video by using the Insert File feature of VidEdit.

TouchVision Systems' CineWorks

The two editors described so far are not nonlinear editors in the sense that they create an edit decision list containing multiple edits of audio and video with effects and transitions so that a complete session can run from the EDL. They are more like assemble editors that do edits one at a time. CineWorks from TouchVision Systems, Inc., is a true nonlinear editor that will run on any desktop PC having an ActionMedia II DVI board. It was introduced in the previous chapter where its capture features were described.

DVI Technology has its own unique file formats that are not compatible with Video for Windows or Wave audio. The payoff of choosing DVI is that much higher video performance is available even when playing back on 386 PCs. Few programs offer conversion capability between DVI formats and others in the industry, such as Video for Windows AVI. CineWorks captures only in DVI format, but it is capable of exporting AVI files that will play on Video for Windows or OS/2 systems. Therefore, CineWorks is an excellent tool for capturing and creating Video for Windows sequences.

In addition to being an editor, CineWorks handles your file management for each editing project (called a *job*). All the source files for a job must be either created in CineWorks using the RTV Capture feature or imported into it from other applications. Every file is given a number, and it can have a description attached, which will appear on-screen during editing. You must choose an RTV quality level for a job, and all video files have to be at the same level. This choice will depend on how fast your system is and especially on how much hard disk

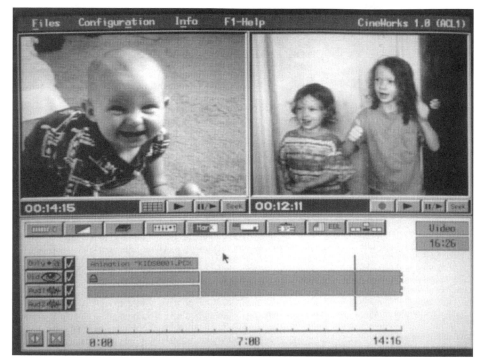

Figure 9.13 CineWorks main editing screen

space you have. To support a lot of editing, you should have several gigabytes of fast SCSI hard drive space.

The main editing screen of CineWorks is shown in Figure 9.13. This screen has two video windows, the left one is the Source window and the right one is the Record window. Editing occurs by selecting video in the Source window and then "recording" it into the Record window. Recording occurs whenever the Record button is activated in the toolbar below the video windows. Of course, no actual recording occurs, the editor is simply building an edit decision list that is played to show the edited output.

Both the Source and Record windows have controls for random-access playback. CineWorks has an unique controller for this purpose (also used in the RTV Capture mode) called the *Speed Control Indicator*. This is activated by clicking the second button from the right of the four-button group in either video window; it is shown in Figure 9.14. When the Speed Control Indicator is active, horizontal movement of the mouse controls speed forward or backward from one frame at a time up to 50 times normal playing speed. The white vertical line in the display shows the current speed setting. Playing is paused when the line is in the center

Figure 9.14 The CineWorks Speed Control Indicator

of the indicator as shown in the figure and it moves to the right or left as the playing speed is increased forward or backward, respectively. The color of the display changes to indicate stopped, normal speed, or jog/slew; and the current frame number is always shown next to the display. This control is very responsive, and once you get the hang of it, you can rapidly move to an exact frame location in any part of your video sequence.

The bottom of the Main Edit screen shows a time line display of the edit in progress. There are lines for an "overlay" track, one video track, and up to four audio tracks. Each is individually editable or, if the source is appropriate, they can be edited in groups. The overlay track is a special one for adding graphics or animations (produced by other tools and imported into CineWorks) to the video. Editing can also be accomplished by cutting and pasting on the time line. A button in the toolbar chooses whether the edit process will be in insert or replace mode.

The edit example in the figure starts out with a still image—this is indicated by the padlock icon in the first segment of the video track. During this still, the overlay track plays a titling animation that was created with Flying Fonts. After the animation, the video and audio start playing.

CineWorks also supports a number of video transition effects, such as dissolves, wipes, or fades. The effects are put in place of any cut transition in the time line, and their duration can be specified in frames. Effects are actually built as a separate .AVS file that is inserted into the EDL. This file is built automatically when you specify an effect and its duration. Once that has been done (it takes a few seconds), the EDL can be played and the effects are automatically in-line.

When editing is completed, you save the EDL for future use. Then you can go to the Complete item on the main menu where you can choose either to Build a Movie, Build SuperRTV, or Print to Tape.

The Build a Movie selection offers the choice of export file types shown in Figure 9.15. Three styles of RTV formats offer tradeoffs between data rate and

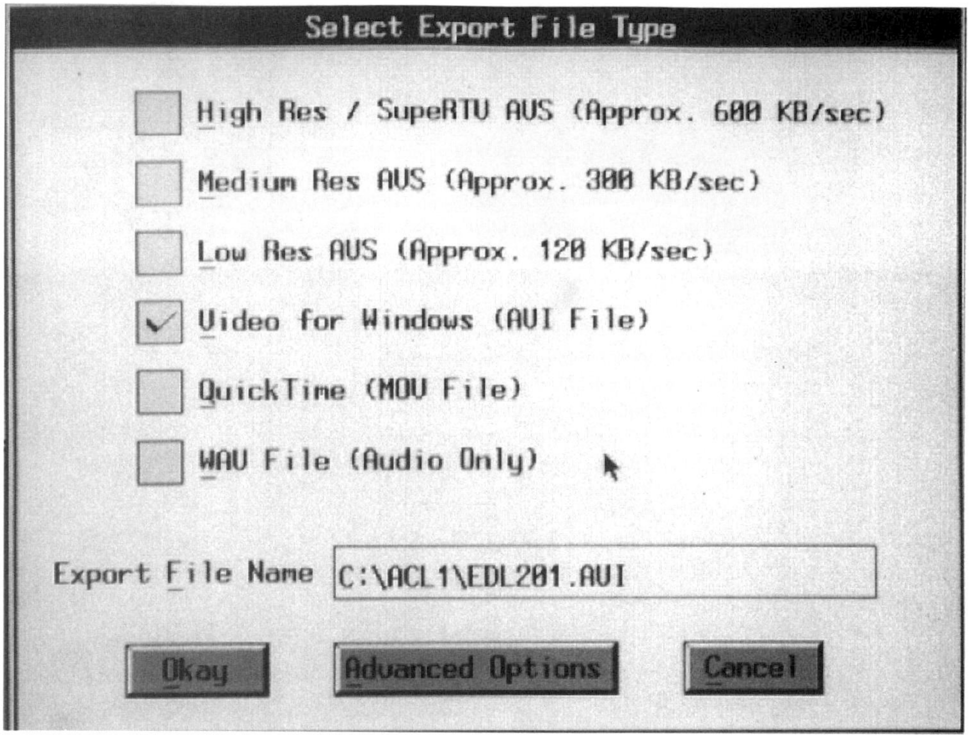

```
┌─────────────────────────────────────────────────────────────────┐
│                    Select Export File Type                      │
├─────────────────────────────────────────────────────────────────┤
│                                                                 │
│     □  High Res / SuperRTV AVS (Approx. 600 KB/sec)            │
│                                                                 │
│     □  Medium Res AVS (Approx. 300 KB/sec)                     │
│                                                                 │
│     □  Low Res AVS (Approx. 120 KB/sec)                        │
│                                                                 │
│     ✓  Video for Windows (AVI File)                            │
│                                                                 │
│     □  QuickTime (MOV File)                                     │
│                                                                 │
│     □  WAV File (Audio Only)                                    │
│                                                                 │
│  Export File Name  C:\ACL1\EDL201.AVI                          │
│                                                                 │
│     ┌───────┐   ┌──────────────────┐   ┌────────┐            │
│     │ Okay  │   │ Advanced Options │   │ Cancel │            │
│     └───────┘   └──────────────────┘   └────────┘            │
└─────────────────────────────────────────────────────────────────┘
```

Figure 9.15 The CineWorks Build a Movie dialog

picture quality. These are .AVS files that can play on most DVI-equipped systems. The Video for Windows selection creates an .AVI file that will play in a Windows environment. The QuickTime selection makes an Apple QuickTime format file. The last choice is to make an audio-only file in the Windows .WAV format. This is needed because Video for Windows does not support audio-only files in the .AVI format.

Once you have made a format selection, you can also choose from the Advanced Options dialog, shown (for the Video for Windows format) in Figure 9.16. Here you can choose the audio parameters and video parameters for image size, frame rate, and in the Video Config subdialog, reference frame parameters. When you have completed all the choices, click Okay and the export file is created automatically.

CineWorks is a very capable nonlinear editor that has minimal system requirements and is easy to learn and use. Its output formatting capability makes it suitable for building videos for PC display. It also is usable for outputting to videotape, but you need to have a high-end system with fast SCSI hard disks and

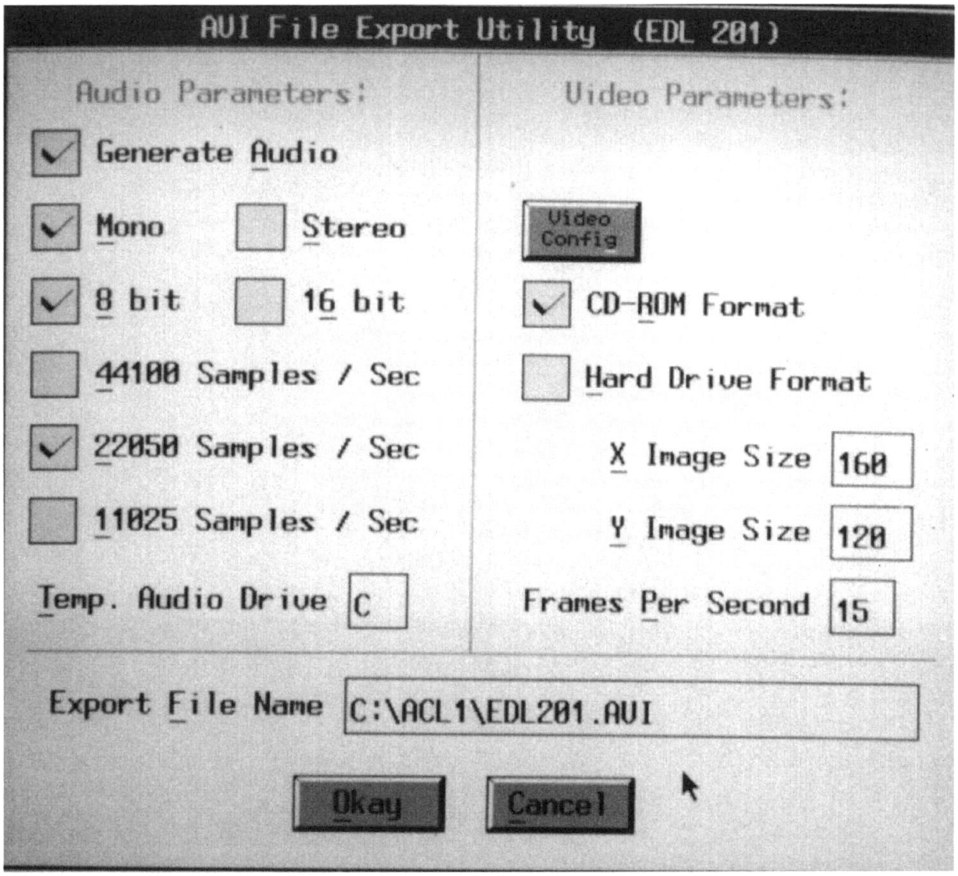

Figure 9.16 CineWorks advanced export options dialog

time code so you can use the SuperRTV output capability. Otherwise, the picture quality of the normal RTV is somewhat limiting for videotape use.

SUMMARY

Although postproduction of audio and video can be done entirely with analog equipment so that you can simply digitize the finished video clip, the equipment is expensive. You can see from the software tools just described that digital postproduction is very viable and calls for no equipment other than your PC. The flexibility of digital postproduction is so attractive that it is also being widely used in the professional and broadcast fields. There, it is more expensive because of the need for the highest possible picture and sound quality, but that trend pretty much proves that digital is better. If you don't already have analog postproduction equipment, don't get it—do everything digitally.

10

Still Images with Audio

Although the thrust of this book is digital motion video as the way to tell a story, motion video is not the only dynamic way to deliver a message by computer. It is not always the best medium. Alternative or augmenting approaches include the use of still images or graphics with audio, which I will discuss in this chapter, and animation with audio, which is the subject of the next chapter. There are numerous aspects to the use of stills in the areas of scripting, capturing, assembling them with audio, etc. that are different from the video considerations I have discussed so far. Proper consideration of these can make still/audio production easy to do and often just as effective as motion video in delivering part or all of your message.

WHY USE STILL IMAGES?

This question wouldn't need to be asked if digital motion video could always be presented at full-screen and full-resolution, mass storage capacities were unlimited, and it was always simple to produce motion video. Unfortunately, none of those things is true; there are tradeoffs in all categories. If the application calls for *both* high resolution images and motion, you are not going to be able to fully satisfy the needs with only motion video.

Figure 10.1 is an example of a high-resolution subject displayed at 640 × 480 full-screen VGA and the same subject displayed in the typical 160 × 120 software-only motion video window. You can see that the motion video window does not display the detail required to properly present the subject. In the large image you can really look into the scene and even beyond it, whereas the small image leaves you wondering what the scene is all about.

But how do the two windows in Figure 10.1 compare for data rate? With everything else being equal, the smaller window contains 1/16th the data per

Figure 10.1 The same scene shown at 640 x 480 pixels compared to 160 x 120 pixels (below)

frame because that's the ratio of the number of pixels in each. Another way of saying it is that the larger window has the same data as approximately 1 second of motion in the smaller window at 15 frames per second. These ratios can be modified by using compression, especially *delta-frame* compression in the motion stream. However, you can see that you can get several high-resolution still images for the data equivalent of a few seconds of small-window motion video.

Another form of still is a graphic drawing. A graphic is valuable when it is difficult to obtain a photograph of the idea you want to convey. You can draw *anything*, but you can photograph only things that are real. Incidentally, graphics usually take less storage than images, so that's another advantage.

I like to address the question of when to use stills vs. when to use motion video by starting with the use of stills and going to motion video only when stills do not do the job. This might seem backward for someone who is pushing the use of video, but it is reasonable when you consider that a video approach will almost always be more expensive than a still-image approach. Thus, you should try to solve each problem with the lowest cost approach and go to more expensive approaches only where actually needed. The list of reasons for using motion video given in Table 5.1 will help you decide. In the rest of this chapter, I will assume that you have been through all the considerations and you have decided to use stills.

SCRIPTING FOR STILLS

In most scripting that involves audio, it's usually best to script the audio first, without too much consideration of what the pictures will be. The audio tells the story, and it forms a baseline for thinking about what visuals to use. Of course, you may already have ideas about what visuals you want to do, but I still recommend audio first. Then you can see where your visual ideas fit into the audio script. Just because you write an audio script first doesn't mean you can't change it. As you develop the visuals, you may well see places where the audio can be improved or made to fit better. You're the boss, so change it.

To plan the visuals, begin by thinking about the one or two still shots that would best support the story. Expand on that by adding additional detail shots to enhance the presentations. These may be closeups at specific points or additional information not in the initial establishing shots. This process may bring you to places where still pictures just doesn't do it and you really need motion. These are the places where you must consider motion video.

Of course, if you have already decided that your presentation *has* to include motion video, then maybe you would approach this process the other way around—starting with video as a given and then asking where is the best place to put it? This is a more emotional approach to design; in general, it is better to build up the needs first and then plug in motion video where you find that you really need it.

An Example

Listing 10.1 is a script for a 3-minute presentation that teaches a woodworker how to use an electric router to round the edges of a table top. Since I did not want to print the full script more than once here, the listing shows it with the

Listing 10.1 Script for a woodworking presentation

Let me show you how I used an electric router to round over the edges on this table top.

After the top has been cut to shape and sanded, you are ready for the routing. The first step is to select an appropriate round-over bit for the router. Here, I have chosen a 3/8" radius carbide bit with a ball-bearing guide. This type of bit is designed precisely for the job that we have to do here.

After installing the bit in the router, you have to adjust the cutting depth so it will cut a full radius without the edge of the bit cutting at all. You can sight across the base of the router with a piece of wood to do this adjustment. When you are finished, you should make a trial cut on a scrap of wood to be sure it is correct.

Clamp down a scrap piece for the trial cut and make a short cut starting from one end. You should cut in a direction so that the bit rotation presents the cutting edge of the bit to the work. With most routers, whose shafts rotate counterclockwise, this means that you cut left to right when you are facing the work piece and cutting on its top. While making the sample cut, be sure the router base is flat on the top of the workpiece and the ball-bearing guide is running against the side of the piece.

This sample piece shows a cut that is too shallow on the left, just right in the center, and too deep on the right.

Once the bit is adjusted, you are ready to make the actual cuts. First, clear a work area large enough for you to move comfortably around the workpiece while making the cuts. Clamp the workpiece down to the bench with at least two edges slightly over the bench top. Be sure to use something under the workpiece and under the clamps to protect the wood. If you are going to round over both top and botton edges, it is usually best to do the bottom first—if you make any little goofs, they will be less likely to show, and you can make sure the same thing does not happen when you do the top.

Listing 10.1 (continued)

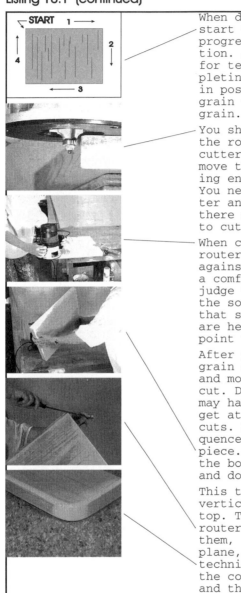

When doing the cuts, it is best to start with an end grain cut and then progress around the work piece in rotation. Since there may be some tendency for tear-out to occur when you are completing an end-grain cut, you will be in position for the next cut on side-grain to clean up the torn-out end grain.

You should start the router motor while the router base is on the work but the cutter is not touching the piece. Then move the cutter in until the ball-bearing engages the work and begin cutting. You need to be careful to smoothly enter and leave the work. At the ends there may be a tendency for the router to cut too deeply.

When cutting, be sure to keep the router base and ball-bearing guide against the work, and move steadily at a comfortable speed. You can usually judge the cutting speed by listening to the sound of the router—cut at a rate that slows the router slightly as you are hearing now, [pause] but not to the point that it appears to be laboring.

After you have completed the first end-grain cut, move the router off the work and move it back on to start the next cut. Depending on your work setup, you may have to re-clamp the work piece to get at all the edges for subsequent cuts. Be sure that you continue the sequence of cuts going around the work piece. After you have completed cutting the bottom of the piece, turn it over and do the top edge the same way.

This technique does not round over the vertical edges on the corners of the top. Those are too short to do with the router. If you want the same radius on them, it is best done by hand, using a plane, file, and sandpaper. Another technique is to cut a large radius on the corners before doing the routing and then run the router around the corners. This works well if the corner radius can be several inches or more.

complete set of visuals that were produced for it as a slide, graphics, and audio show. However, I will discuss later how the visuals evolved.

As recommended previously, the text script was written first, based on an outline prepared after actually doing the task in the workshop. Many of the visuals are suggested directly by the script, because I am talking about things I want to show. For example, in the first sentence where I say: "this table top," I am calling for a visual that shows the finished top. In other cases, I describe a procedure that I obviously need to show with a visual (sighting across the router base to adjust the depth of cut.)

There is one place in this presentation where the subject cannot effectively be illustrated with stills: that is where I am describing the handling of the router during the actual cutting. Here, it would help to use motion video or animation to show how you should move the router. I didn't include that, but I did add the router sound to the audio track so the viewer could hear how it should sound when cutting properly.

In describing how you should move around the sides of the top in sequence, I used a graphic drawing to point out the correct method. I also used a graphic overlay to show the correct relationship between router bit rotation and direction of cut. This example shows how multimedia techniques can make a presentation more effective.

This presentation runs for 190 seconds. If it had been done entirely with motion video compressed to 150 kB/second, it would take 28.5 MB of data and a fairly complex production would have been required to deal with the relatively low-resolution reproduction. With the 13 640×480 full-screen stills that were produced with photography and scanned into the PC and with 22 kHz 8-bit mono audio, it is 7 MB without any compression. Using ADPCM audio and JPEG image compression could probably get it under 2 MB.

CAPTURING STILLS

There are two ways to capture still images into your PC: capture live from a video camera or use an image scanner to capture from photographic prints. The live camera method is quick and easy, but the scanned photograph method produces substantially better picture quality. This is because of the picture-quality limitations of all but the most expensive video cameras that I discussed in Chapter 6. If you are using stills because of their higher resolution, you should use a scanner or a broadcast-quality camera. If you are making stills at higher than 640×480 resolution, then you *must* use a scanner because no presently available TV camera is a match for more than 640×480 resolution.

Hardware for Live Image Capture

Still images can be captured by the same add-in board that you use for motion video capture. However, it is important that the board support the higher resolutions you will need (some motion video capture boards do not support more than 320 × 240 resolution.) Also frame-grabber boards are available for displaying analog video and capturing at even higher resolutions.

If your video source is a camera, you need the highest quality one you can get. For best results in still capture, get a camera with an RGB output. RGB outputs are available only on professional cameras, which can become quite expensive. At a lower cost level, you can use S-VHS or Hi-8 cameras, which will also give good results. The last resort is an NTSC camera output—this is not a good choice for stills because the NTSC encoding causes a significant loss of resolution. Of course, whatever camera signal format you choose, you must make sure that you capture board supports it.

With regard to number of colors, it is desirable to capture at the highest bpp that your hardware can support so that your images will display at the highest quality on all systems. For example, if your capture hardware does 24 bpp, you should capture with that even if your display hardware cannot show that many colors. Most image software automatically takes care of displaying a 24-bpp image on 8-bpp or 16-bpp hardware. Saving at 24 bpp will create more image data, but it ensures that your images will look as good as any displaying hardware can show.

Although you can capture from photographs by placing them in front of a camera, you will get much better picture quality using an image scanner (see Figure 10.2.) These units are available now for substantially less than $1,000 and they can capture an 8 × 10 or larger photo with 300 dots-per-inch (dpi) or higher resolution at 24 bpp. Note that this can produce massive amounts of data (8 × 10 at 300 dpi and 24 bpp generates 21.6 MB of data). Because of that, scanner software allows you to reduce the scanned size and the dpi resolution. A typical computer display screen has only 70 – 80 pixels/inch, so it is reasonable to reduce the scanner dpi if you are scanning something that will be displayed 1:1 on the computer. Of course, if the reproduction on the computer will be enlarged compared to the original hard copy, then you must proportionately increase the scanning dpi or you will lose resolution.

Another way to look at the scanning dpi is that the scanning should produce the same number of pixels as the computer screen where the image will be displayed. For example, if you will display your images on a 1024 × 768 screen, and you are scanning originals that are 6 inches wide, you should scan at $1024/6 = 170$ dpi.

Figure 10.2 A flatbed color image scanner (courtesy of Microtek, Inc.)

Software for Image Capture

Some of the motion video capture software also supports high-resolution stills and some does not. For example, Microsoft VidCap does stills at up to 640 × 480 resolution.

Still Capture from Analog Video Using VidCap

To use VidCap for still images, you must choose an uncompressed format and the appropriate resolution from the Video Format dialog shown in Figure 10.3. The figure shows the dialog for the Intel Smart Video Recorder board. With other boards this dialog may be different. The Intel board uses the YVU9 format internally, which is a special format derived from color TV technology. It compresses only the color information to effectively give you 9-bpp. With most natural images, the effect of this compression is not visible. When you save a captured still, the copy that goes to disk is expanded to 24-bpp.

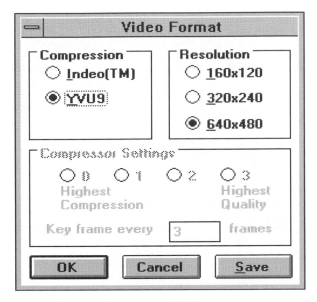

Figure 10.3 The Video Format dialog from VidCap

To perform the actual capture, you must click the Still Frame item in the Capture menu, as shown in Figure 10.4. Capture occurs instantly when you click the menu. Note that you could also use the optional keystrokes for the menu, in this case that is Alt-C,S. Once you have captured an image, you must separately save it using one of the Save items from the File menu.

Scanner Software for Capture from Photographs—Twain

Most color image scanners use an industry standard software architecture called Twain. This is a software interface that allows most image processing or editing tools to access any scanner installed with a Twain driver. This is usually available from a menu item called Acquire on the File menu of the image tool. The Twain dialog for the Microtek Scanmaker IIxe is shown in Figure 10.5. This dialog allows you to set up the scan area and resolution of the scanner and to perform a number of other processes on the scanned image.

You begin by placing the copy to be scanned on the scanner platen and selecting the Prescan button, which does a fast gray-scale scan and displays the result in the same dialog, as shown. A crop rectangle appears on that image; you can adjust it to specify the exact area of the image you want to scan. The image statistics are displayed at the right in the same dialog and they change dynamically as you adjust the scanned area or dot-per-inch resolution. Other buttons let you select further adjustments such as *gamma correction* (which is gray-scale adjustment

Figure 10.4 The main window of VidCap set up for 640 x 480 still capture

to enhance one range of grays vs. another) or color tuning. When you have made all the selections, click the Scan button and the rest is automatic. When the scanner has finished, it displays the resulting image in the workspace of the tool from which you called the Twain driver.

Image Conversion Tools

It's unfortunate that the industry has not been able to do much in standardizing of image data formats. Over 100 image formats are in use, both compressed and uncompressed. I won't go into them here, but some are discussed in Appendix A. Not all programs that deal with images can handle all the formats, so there is a place for tools that focus on image conversion. One of these is Hijaak Pro, by Inset Systems. It can import or export in more than 50 image file formats, it does several types of image compression, and it can do simple image processing such as resizing, cropping, rotating, or color correction. Everyone who works with a lot of images should have an image conversion tool.

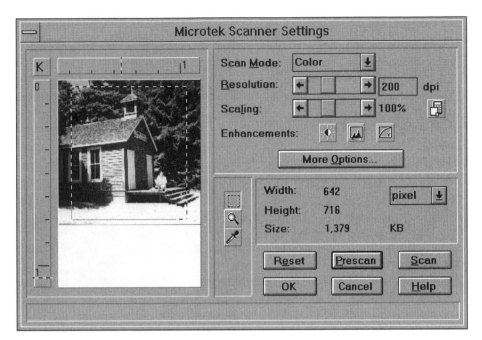

Figure 10.5 The scan dialog for the Microtek Twain interface

ASSEMBLING YOUR AUDIO AND STILLS

You will need presentation software to show your audio and stills presentation. There are programs specifically for that purpose, which are very easy to use. Examples are Microsoft PowerPoint, Lotus FreeLance, and Software Publishing's Harvard Graphics. If your presentation is part of a larger interactive multimedia project, you will probably want to get one of the more powerful multimedia *authoring assembly* programs such as Asymetrix ToolBook, Macromedia Authorware Professional, or one of the versions of Network Technology MEDIAscript. Because of their greater breadth and power, these programs are more complex and require a significant investment in learning how to use them. However, they do not require a high degree of programming skill. Authoring assembly programs are discussed in Chapter 13. If you are a programmer, you can also consider one of the programming-language products such as Microsoft Visual Basic.

An important factor in the effectiveness of an audio/stills presentation is precise timing. This gets more important the more stills you use in a given time. A presentation that has crisp timing where every still displays precisely when it is required will make its points much better than one where the audience is

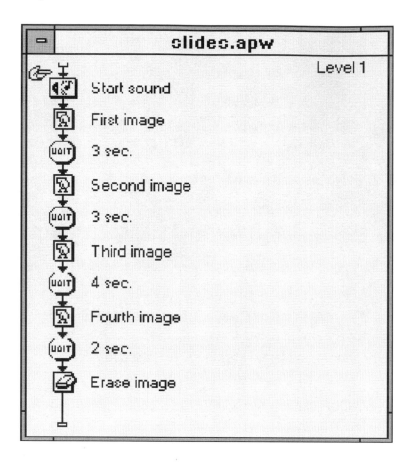

Figure 10.6 An Authorware Professional script for an image/audio presentation

constantly distracted by wondering why the screen being discussed in not the one being displayed. Different tools handle this timing in different ways and they vary in how difficult it is to obtain the timing you want. They also vary in how consistent they will maintain the timing on different systems with different hardware.

One factor that contributes to timing difficulties is that it takes a nontrivial amount of time to retrieve an image from hard disk and display it. This time can vary depending on the speed of the system and whether the image has to be decompressed or not. To minimize this problem, it is desirable that the reading from hard disk and decompression of images be done ahead of time, placing the image in an off-screen area of memory. Then, on the exact cue, the image can simply be moved in memory from off-screen to on-screen, which is a fast process that does not have any inherent delays. Not all presentation software lets you do this.

Figure 10.6 shows an example of a script in Authorware Professional that plays audio and displays four slides concurrently. The timing of the slides is determined by the Wait icons, which create delays from the preceding object. This works OK, but it is difficult to set up because the timing of a later object is determined by the accumulation of all previous objects. This becomes very awkward for a long presentation. When using this method, you should break your audio up into short segments that play one after another (you can tell Authorware to do that), so that you don't accumulate too many cascaded Wait objects. The accumulated time delay also includes the time it takes to load each image. That can vary on different systems and will cause the cueing to change somewhat.

MEDIAscript OS/2 uses a different approach that is much easier to manage with long presentations. An audio file's playing time is divided up into frames, just as with video, and an image event (or any other kind of event that is concurrent with the audio) is specified to occur on a specific frame number measured from the beginning of the audio. Thus, all concurrent events are independent of the others and you can adjust them very easily.

Figure 10.7 shows a MEDIAscript script that does the same thing as Figure 10.6. The first icon is a Window object that creates an off-screen window that will hold preloaded images. The second icon creates the display window for the screen, but it is hidden. After that, an Audio object starts the audio playing. Then a Message object tells the hidden window to show itself. Following that, another Image object preloads the next image. Then an Input object is created to wait for the exact frame number in the audio where the next image should be shown. A subscript that is inside the Input object shows the image on cue by transitioning it from the off-screen window to the on-screen window. This transition can be selected from a list of different effects. Once the Input object does the transition, the main script loads the next image off-screen and starts another Input object to wait for the next frame cue. The main script goes to two more Input objects that process showing and preloading on frame number cues as before. A final Input object makes sure the display of the last image continues until the end of the audio. The last two objects in the script are Message objects that tell both windows to destroy themselves, ending the presentation.

As you see in this example, with MEDIAscript you can set up so that each image is loaded into memory just after the preceding image is displayed. On cue, you simply show the new image that is already in memory. This eliminates the loading delay from the cue timing.

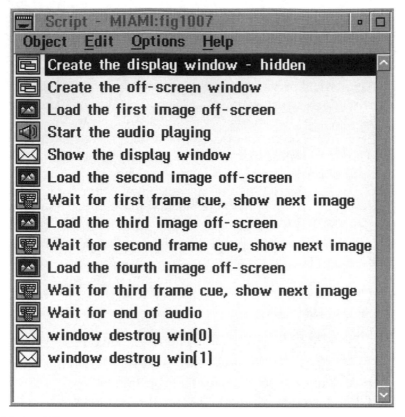

Figure 10.7 A MEDIAscript script that displays four images on exact audio frame cues

---

SUMMARY

Audio with still images is often a viable alternative to motion video that will be easier to produce and will use less data storage. In cases where you need the highest resolution presentation, it is the best choice. The same hardware you use for motion video will also do still images, although you need different software to work most effectively with them.

11

Animation

An alternative to capturing your motion video from live or tape sources is to have the computer *generate* it for you. That is called *animation*, and it is another way to reduce the data requirement of motion video. The most valuable use for animation is to present moving objects that don't exist in nature and couldn't be captured live anyway. In applications requiring simulation or display of things that you cannot capture with a camera, animation is the only approach. This chapter will describe the fundamentals of computer animation and then show some of the software products that will do it for you.

ARCHITECTURE OF ANIMATION

The same as motion video, an animation consists of a series of *frames* that are presented rapidly to convey smooth motion. Frame rates are typically 15 to 30 per second, the same as video. However, the frames themselves are different in that the computer knows a lot about what is in each frame. This is because frames are constructed by the computer. It assembles a set of different *objects* according to instructions from the designer of the animation (the *animator*.)

This process of assembly, called *rendering*, can take place at the time of display, or it can be done ahead of time and the rendered frames stored as frames. The latter approach is just like video where the stored format is in the form of frames, but the difference is the storage format for animated frames can be much more efficient (compressed) because the computer knows *exactly* what is the content of each frame. It knows what parts of one frame are like the previous frame and it knows what changes, how it changes, and what does not change—these are things that compression algorithms have a very difficult time figuring out about live video. It is why a good live compression algorithm takes so much processing. In

Figure 11.1 An example of a multi-cel actor moving along a path (multiple-exposure view) done with cels from Animation Works Interactive

animation, this information is already available, so efficient compression is easier to accomplish.

The objects in an animation are called *cels* (a name that is a contraction of *celluloid*, which is the medium used in the traditional animation process used in the movies), and they can either move or be stationary (in which case they are called *props*.) Cels move in successive frames according to a *path*, which can go anywhere in the display space or out of it. They can behave according to other rules, such as *scale*, which defines how the cel changes size as it moves along its path.

A more advanced concept is that of the *animated cel*, sometimes called an *actor*. An actor consists of a sequence of cels that represent movement of the same object. It is displayed sequentially in successive frames. For example, an actor might consist of eight cels that showed a person walking. If these cels are presented sequentially as they also move along a path, a very effective representation of a person walking is shown. Figure 11.1 is a multiple-exposure picture of such an action.

ANIMATION SKILLS

In the early days of cartoon animation for the movies, skilled animators drew each cel by hand. A feature film required tens of thousands of cels, so it was extremely tedious and the result depended directly on the skills of the animators. This skill is clearly evident when you watch one of the early Disney films—the animators deserved every bit of credit they could get!

With the advent of the computer into animation, some of the skills can be replaced by the precision of the computer. Things such as following paths, changing scale, or other primarily mechanical tasks can be completely taken over by the computer. However, the computer cannot do the original creation of cels, nor can it build the actors that give expression to cels—this still calls for a lot of artistry on the part of the animator. Even with the best computer animation tools, truly exciting animations are still created by artists.

If you intend to create original animations, you or someone working for you must have some artistic drawing skills. The modern tools have a lot of features that help you make the most of whatever artistic resources are available. For example, you can build a library of cels that can be used over and over, and you can even make simple modifications when reusing a cel. Some animation tools come with a professionally designed cel library that will get you started. Complete animations or any piece of an animation can also be modified and reused; the computer makes this very easy to do.

ANIMATION AUTHORING

Different tools for authoring (creating) animation use different approaches or metaphors. Two of those have already been mentioned—the path and the actor. A lot of animation can be built with just these two concepts, and it is easy for anyone to do it. A product that takes that approach is Animation Works Interactive (AWI) by Gold Disk. AWI provides tools to build cels, actors, and backgrounds. It also has a Movie Editor tool that lets you assemble animations with these parts and build paths for their movement. A library is included with a wide range of interesting cels and actors. This is a good tool for starting out with animation.

Gold Disk Animation Works Interactive

Figure 11.2 shows the main window of the AWI Movie Editor. The background of the animation is shown, and the actors are shown with their positions for frame

Figure 11.2 Main screen of Gold Disk's Animation Works Interactive

41 of a 100-frame animation. The path for the airplane actor to the left of center is selected for editing. The dots show the location of that object in each frame of the animation.

A control panel is at the lower right of the screen. This shows the current position in the animation (frame 41) and allows the frame position to be changed or all or part of the animation to be played or single-stepped. To the far left is a toolbar for movie editing operations and just to the right of that is a window that allows the actors in the animation to be viewed by themselves or new actors to be added to the current animation. Actors are stored in their own files having the extension .act.

Paths for the actors are drawn with the mouse, and several different draw modes are available to produce straight-line paths, polygons, or curves. The speed and duration of movement is specified in dialog boxes for each actor. Once a path has been created, its position can be edited by dragging with the mouse, and the dialog boxes can be called up to make changes in other parameters.

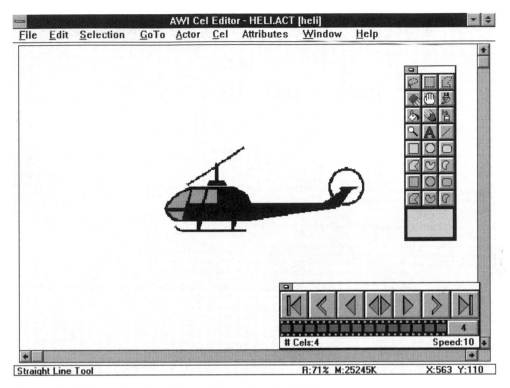

Figure 11.3 The Animation Works Interactive Cel Editor screen

Actors and cels are created or edited using the Cel Editor, shown in Figure 11.3. The Cel Editor is a separate tool from the Movie Editor, but it is well integrated so you switch between the tools by making menu selections, and the current item being worked on appears in each tool. Actors and cels are bitmaps, so the Cel Editor is a bitmap editor. A toolbox menu for the draw tools is at the right, and other editing tools are available through the menu bar.

You can create a cel by drawing it directly in the Cel Editor or by importing a bitmap from another draw tool. For example, it may be convenient to initially draw cels in a vector drawing tool such as CorelDraw, and export bitmaps from that tool to the Cel Editor. Having a vector original for cels will allow modifications and manipulations to be done more easily. However, to create a multiple-cel actor, you must use the Cel Editor.

The Cel Editor has several features to facilitate building of actors from cels. You can duplicate cels to create actors and then use the editing tools to modify each cel to show the desired motion. If the desired action is rotation, the Cel Editor will do that automatically for you, rotating the original cel and creating any number of rotated cels in your actor. The dialog box that controls rotation

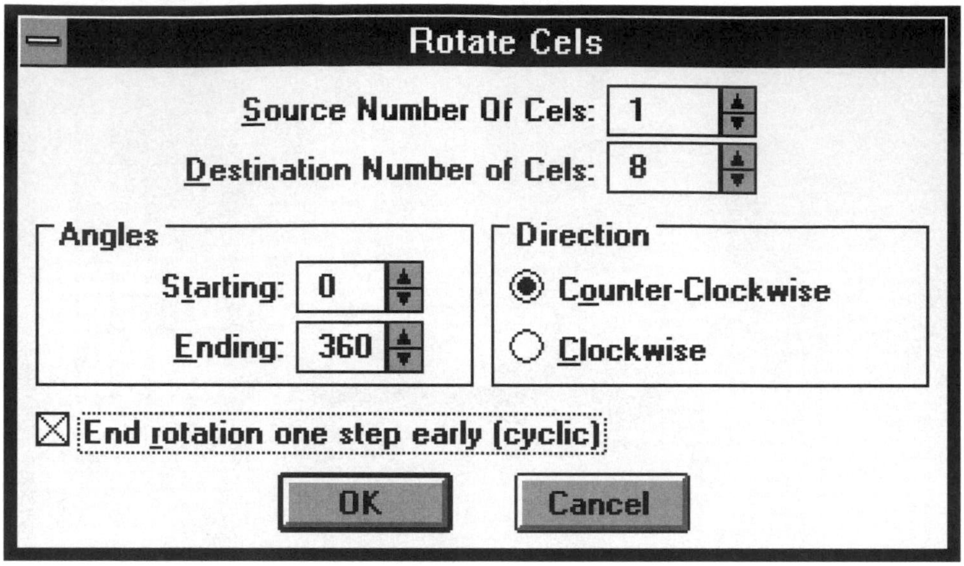

Figure 11.4 The rotation dialog of the Cel Editor

is shown in Figure 11.4. The figure shows how you set up for one source cel to create an eight-cel actor that provides 360-degree rotation. Clicking the box labeled *End rotation one step early* ensures that smooth cyclic rotation will be produced when the actor is displayed over and over.

Another nice feature of the Cel Editor is the ability to establish a reference point in each cel of an actor and have the Editor align those points. This is important if you have individually drawn or imported a series of cells and need to precisely align them.

Autodesk Animator Pro

Professional animators need powerful tools as well as plenty of skill to produce the impressive animations we see on television and in the movies. Animator Pro is a tool for them. It emphasizes power rather than ease of learning, but once it is learned there are features to work in nearly all animation metaphors. Output files from Animator Pro (which itself runs under DOS) are playable in DOS, Windows, or OS/2 and can be included in many different kinds of applications.

The main screen of Animator Pro is shown in Figure 11.5. There is a menu bar at the top of the screen and a floating menu, shown at the bottom in the figure. Depending on what is being done, there is a different floating menu. The one shown is the Home menu, which is the top-level menu. One frame of the

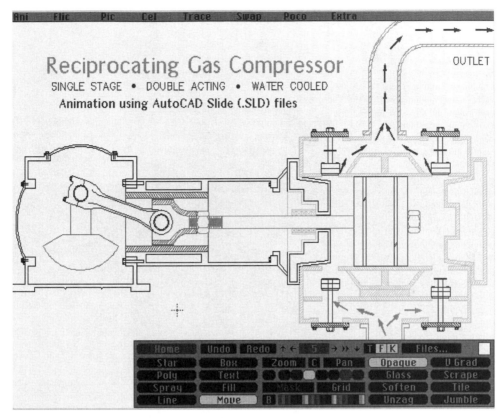

Figure 11.5 The main screen of Animator Pro

currently loaded animation appears behind the menu and menu bar. In this case, it is one of the sample animations provided with Animator Pro. This one is at 640×480 resolution. You can make an animation smaller than full screen, which will make a smaller animation file and play faster. In the case of a smaller animation (320×240, for example) you can reduce the screen resolution also if you want to view it larger.

I won't describe everything in the Animator Pro menus, that would take a book in itself. I also lack the room to describe all the different ways you can create animations with this tool. However, we can explore some of the more interesting features.

Polymorphic Tweening

In the days of hand-drawn animation, the master animator drew only the key frames of the animation, leaving many intermediate frames to be drawn by lesser

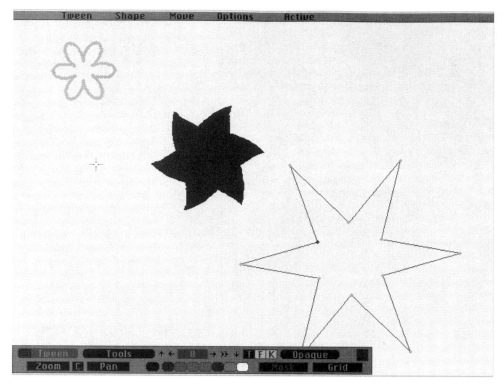

Figure 11.6 Tweening in Animator Pro

animators, using his key frames as a guide. This process was called *tweening*. Animator Pro can perform tweening automatically using a mathematical technique called *polymorphism*. To create a tweened sequence, you create the first frame of your animation and the last frame, using any of the "tweenable" drawing tools in Animator Pro, which include ovals, petals, polygons, stars, or custom shapes drawn freehand. If there are certain points on the starting image that should transform to specific points in the ending image, you can link them. Then, you tell Animator Pro to create inbetween frames to smooth out the animation. Figure 11.6 shows the tweening screen of Animator Pro with a petal shape being tweened into a star shape. The object at the center of the screen is one frame from the center of the tween.

Animator Pro provides a large array of different drawing tools; 8 out of a total of 22 are listed in the Tools panel shown in Figure 11.7. If that isn't enough, it also offers a selection of *inks* for drawing. An ink defines the process that Animator Pro uses to draw on top of the pixels that are already in the frame. The Inks selector panel is shown in Figure 11.8. It lists 8 of the 33 available inks. Any drawing operation can be directed to the current frame, a range of frames, or

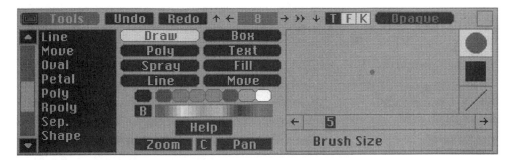

Figure 11.7 The Tools panel from Animator Pro

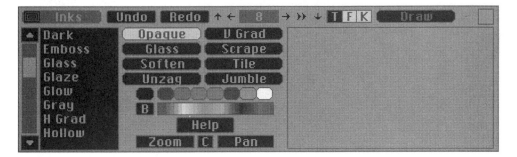

Figure 11.8 The Inks panel from Animator Pro

the entire animation. For hand drawing in between frames, there is a *blueing* feature that displays an outline of the contents of the previous and/or the next frame to serve as guidelines for drawing the current frame. Once the current frame is complete, the blueing lines can be deleted. There is a full set of tools for drawing text and animating text (titling). In total, Animator Pro is a mind-boggling set of tools for creating high-quality computer animation.

Autodesk 3D Studio

A different kind of program is needed to do three-dimensional animation where objects are solid and they can move in 3-D space. Autodesk 3D Studio is a professional-level program for this. It supports the creation of 3-D models (mathematical representations of objects that can be viewed from any angle), design of 3-D paths, and rendering of final frames from the models and paths.

There are four major modules in 3D Studio, the 2D Shaper, the 3D Lofter, the 3D Editor, and the Keyframer. In addition, there are tools for working with

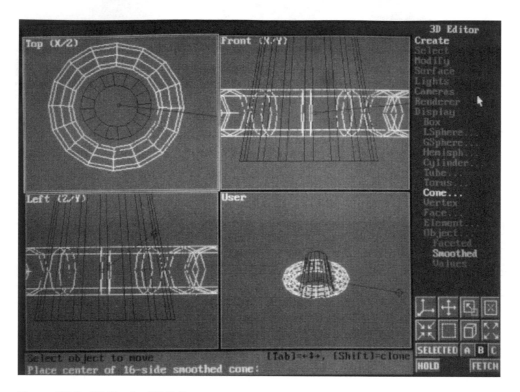

Figure 11.9 3D Studio 3D Editor screen

materials, textures, and backgrounds. When using the program, you move seamlessly between modules as you work, simply by making menu selections. The purpose of each module is as follows:

- **2D Shaper**—this is a powerful 2-D drawing program, in the style of Autodesk's AutoCad. You create shapes here that can be converted to 3-D using the tools of the 3D Lofter module.
- **3D Lofter**—this module contains various tools for making 3-D objects from 2D shapes: extrusion, lathe-style rotation, sweeping, and more sophisticated processes involving several shapes working together.
- **3D Editor**—in this module, you combine objects into screens and define rendering parameters such as texturing, shading, or lighting. You can also do still-image rendering from the 3D Editor.
- **Keyframer**—this module adds the animation to your screens by specifying paths, morphing, blurring, tweening, and so on.

Figure 11.9 shows the 3D Editor screen of 3D Studio.

Figure 11.10 3D Studio rendering screen

Rendering of 3-D is too slow to do during playback, so the usual approach is to render fully during development and save completed frames in the final sequence. At play time, the frames are merely displayed according to the animation's time scale. Because repeated rendering during development also takes too much time, most development work in 3-D is done with *wireframe* objects, which are drawn with lines only, as in Figure 11.9. Figure 11.10 shows the same model rendered as it will appear in the final animation. You can see that 3D Studio is an extremely powerful program for someone who has a lot of animation to do and is prepared to spend some months mastering the program.

Crystal Graphics Flying Fonts

Flying Fonts is an inexpensive animation tool for text and limited graphics objects. Within that limitation and a further limitation on the kinds of motion that are possible (you can select from a fixed palette of canned motion scripts for each object), this program produces very professional-looking animations that

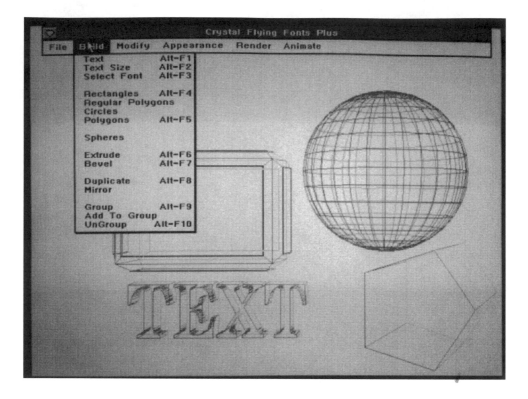

Figure 11.11 The main screen of Crystal Graphics Flying Fonts showing the Build menu

are easy to create. Flying Fonts is a DOS program, but it produces standard .FLC animations that can be played under Windows or OS/2 with an appropriate .FLI or .FLC player. It also can work at any screen resolution supported by your system.

Figure 11.11 shows the main screen of Flying Fonts. You create the model for your animation by using the Build menu items, shown in Figure 11.11. Using this menu, you can draw graphic objects such as rectangles, polygons, circles, or spheres. You can also draw text, with a full selection of fonts and sizes. Any drawn object can be extruded or bevelled also. The screen of Figure 11.11 shows a number of possibilities, all in wireframe view.

Once you have drawn objects, their attributes can be set using the tools in the Appearance menu. Here you can set the color or the material (metals, stone, etc.) of any object. You also can add texture maps or reflection maps to objects. When Flying Fonts renders your animation, it also can respond to the lighting of your

Figure 11.12 A Flying Fonts rendering of the objects shown in Figure 11.11

scene. You set that by positioning lights on the scene, also selected from the Appearance menu.

So far, you haven't animated anything. You do that from the Animate menu, where you can assign an action to each object in your model. You can select from a large number of actions, most of which follow some path and behavior as an object is moved on-screen or off-screen. However, there is a fixed portfolio of actions and you cannot create anything new. The available actions are quite diverse, including moving along curves, spirals, rotations, flipping, etc. Each action type has choices for where the action begins, but they all end where you have placed the objects on the screen. Thus, Flying Fonts is good for animations that build something on the screen or for exploding a screen object.

When you have built a model and assigned actions to it, there are several ways that you can preview the result. These choices are in the Animate menu, shown in Figure 11.12. For example, you can choose Make Preview, which will quickly render your animation to a black-and-white wireframe view and run it for you.

You can also do a full rendering with the Make Movie item, but that can take a very long time—minutes to hours, depending on the complexity of the animation and the speed of your machine. You will probably choose to get it pretty well fine-tuned using the Preview mode before investing the time in a full rendering.

The Animation menu Render Frames item will automatically output the animation to a group of separate frame files, which is used by several programs such as CineWorks or VidEdit to convert the animation to video.

Flying Fonts is an easy-to-learn program that can produce some impressive animations in its field of application.

INTEGRATION OF ANIMATION WITH VIDEO

One way of packaging an animation for delivery is to convert it to a motion video format that can be played by Video for Windows or another motion video player. To do this, you tell the animation package to output its frames as a sequence of individual image files. Most professional animation tools can do that and they will automatically set up a file numbering system where each frame file's name has the same prefix with a sequential number on the end. This sequence of files is identified to a video editor that can compress and convert them into an .avi motion video file.

VidEdit is a typical tool that can convert a sequence of images into a motion video file. It can take either a sequence of image files in the Microsoft DIB (device-independent bitmap) format, or it can import Autodesk animation files directly in the .fli and .flc formats. Figure 11.13 shows the VidEdit screen in this latter mode. The animation is one of the Autodesk Animator samples.

Some interesting statistics arise from this example. The sample animation is an eight-frame sequence that uses 16,594 bytes in its native animation format. If it is simply converted to .avi format without any compression, it would grow to 526,588 bytes. This is because VidEdit simply renders all the frames in 8-bpp format and places them in the .avi file with its required headers. In this form, the video plays at nearly the same quality level as the animation. The reason one might do this is that the animation is now in a video format and could be edited into other video clips.

If you apply compression to the rendered animation file using one of the algorithms in VidEdit, some data can be saved, but at the expense of lower quality. For example, Indeo compression reduces the file size to 84,220 bytes. It plays the same, but there is a slight softening of the image.

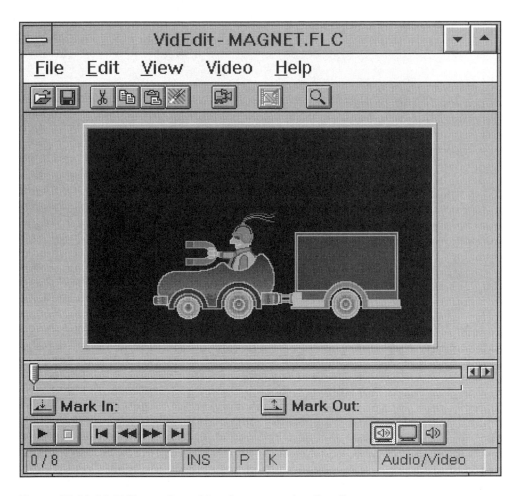

Figure 11.13 VidEdit creating video from an animation file

SUMMARY

Animation is a powerful technique for creating motion effects when you cannot capture what you need as natural video. Simple animations will save data compared to real video of the same size, but complex rendered animations will use the same or even more data. Producing a complex animation takes a lot of skill and it requires a commitment to learning the tools and techniques. However, it is the right answer when you need a motion effect that cannot be captured with a camera.

12

Integrating Audio and Video into Applications

Few applications use only audio and video. In general, applications are a combination of text, graphics, images, animation, *and* audio and video. These are the data types or the *media* of multimedia. There are many considerations about when to use what medium in your applications. Some of these have been discussed in previous chapters—mostly from a technical point of view, but in this chapter I will give an overview of the issues involved in choosing media types from the application's point of view.

Much of the discussion here has the flavor of large applications containing a lot of data. That's because large applications have the most problems with the limitations of the system and the user. If your prime concern is producing small presentations, some of these items will not be as important to you.

COMPARISON OF MEDIA

The following discussion of media types covers what the medium contributes to the objectives of the application and how it affects the user of the application.

Text

The principal use of text is to present information in the form of words. That is exactly the same as the purpose of printed text on paper, but the computer screen is a little different. Most people do not find it comfortable to read large amounts of text (more than a page or so) from the screen. That's probably because you have to hold your head up to look at the vertical screen whereas a printed paper or book can be held down so you can read with your head in a more relaxed position. It's also difficult to lean back in your chair and view a computer screen. If you have a lot of text to present in your application, it is desirable to offer the user an option to print it out for more comfortable and relaxed reading.

A second purpose of text is to provide a visual identification on a screen object such as a menu selection or a screen button. For this use, the text is usually very short, and the wording should be concise and clear.

Text has to be formatted for display purposes. That includes selection of fonts, sizes, styles, columns, justification, etc. The design of pleasing text screens is an art in itself, one that you should master if you produce text applications. I am not going to cover text design here, but there are many books on the subject. Probably the one most valuable guiding principle is that you select a set of text formatting rules for your application and apply them consistently throughout. Constant changing of the formatting is distracting and should be avoided. As in many things, simplicity is a good attribute.

Speech or Voice

Speech is another means of communication with words. Digitized speech can convey all the inflection and nuances of spoken words, which adds significantly to the impact of text compared to plain characters on the screen. It also has the advantage that the user does not even have to look at the screen to hear the speech or the screen can be used to display something entirely different such as a picture or graphic that illustrates what is being spoken about. This makes the presentation more powerful and effective.

Spoken text usually takes a little longer than the time you would need to read the same text off the screen. Also, it is not clear that the user will stand to listen to much more text than she will stand to read from the screen. Thus, large amounts of text are deadly traps to lose the user's interest or put her to sleep. As much as possible, you should break text or speech up into blocks and insert pictures, graphics, animations, or videos to liven up the presentation.

I have to point out that digitized speech is about 100 times less data efficient than plain text, and in most cases it is probably not 100 times more effective. However, if you have the data space, it will certainly help your application. Programs are available that can convert plain text into speech in real time. These are called text-to-speech converters, and they produce the typical strange-sounding computerized speech that is so often a part of the science fiction genre. This solves the data efficiency problem, but it introduces its own personality into your application, and you may not like that.

Graphics

The computer is very efficient at displaying or manipulating graphical drawings. This is a very good medium to illustrate points made in your text or speech that are hard to convey in words alone. A good diagram lives up to the old saw that a picture is worth 1,000 words. The flip side to this is that someone has to design and draw a graphic and it takes a degree of skill to make good drawings, so we have a better medium that is harder to apply.

Animation

A graphic that moves is an animation. Movement enhances the graphic because it can show things that are in motion. In presenting diagrams of moving objects, you should consider animation. Animation is not easy to create, however, so you should take that into account, too. You, or someone else, needs to supply the necessary skills.

Images

Images are pictures that have been captured from nature, as photographs, videotape, or with a video camera. For images to work well, you must have video display hardware that shows 16-bpp or 24-bpp images. Images are more realistic than a graphic drawing, and they are easier to produce because the scene is already sitting there—you just have to photograph it or shoot it with a video camera.

But images have a flip side, too: like digitized speech, they take a lot of data. However, when you need the realism, an image is usually worth its data. Images are another way to do the same thing you do with graphics—illustrate something. Graphics are hard to do and usually not realistic, but they use little data. Figure 12.1 shows a comparison between the same picture shown as a photograph on the left and a drawing on the right. (This was done using the tool CorelTrace to trace the photo to a drawing, which makes a drawing that has more detail than most artists would include.) You get what you pay for.

Motion Video

Motion video relates to animation the same way images relate to graphics. Video is easier to create than animation and it is more realistic, but you pay for it in data requirements. The data requirements of motion video are so great that you usually have to accept compromises in picture quality to have video at all. You

Figure 12.1 The same picture rendered as a photograph (left) and as a drawing (right)—drawing created by CorelTrace

also may need to have special hardware to get the motion video performance up to par. You must compare the needs of the application against the costs to decide when to use motion video.

Other Audio

I mentioned speech or dialog earlier, but audio can also be music, sound effects, or ambient (background) sound. Each of these contributes its own features to the application.

Music

Almost every dramatic production, whether film, stage, or television, uses music as part of its presentation environment. Custom scored music provides the mood for the production, it highlights key scenes, and it helps the audience absorb the message of the production. Music is such an integral part of many productions that, once you have seen the production, you can re-create whole scenes in your mind just by listening to the music. I'm sure you have learned how the music prepares the audience for what is about to happen; it probably prevents many heart attacks!

This kind of effect is created by composers who are skilled in the art of scoring for dramatic production. It is a high art that is unlikely to be available to you in your own production work. Unless you are lucky enough to have musical composing resources available, you will probably be making use mostly of "canned" music from a clip library. That can still serve to set mood and in some cases to highlight actions.

Sound Effects

An animation of a person walking is greatly enhanced by adding footstep sounds. That is a simple example of what you can do with sound effects. Even when you have recorded sound along with your video, you can make the video more powerful by enhancing the effects or adding sounds that the microphone did not capture.

Ambient Audio

Appropriate ambient or background sounds add a lot to the presentation. For example, we associate birds and crickets chirping with a forest setting, even when the picture doesn't show the forest. As with effects, these sounds can either be recorded live or taken from sound libraries. This may be an easier way to establish a setting than by trying to do it with realistic pictures. Since it ends up being merged in with the rest of your audio, it doesn't really add any more data. Your video can have a simple background, with the complexity added by the audio.

DECIDING WHAT TO USE

As you can see, the choice of medium or media is complex, embracing

- The platform for delivery of your application
- The characteristics of your users
- The media types you already may have
- How much data you want to present
- How much work you want to do
- What skills are available to you
- How much money you have to spend
- Matters of artistic style
- Data capacities of your storage media

And the list could probably go on. How do you get a handle on such a complex problem? I don't think a single logic path will carry you through all these questions and generate an automatic decision. However, there are some key things that you can do, which should help you figure it out.

First, the technical issues of target delivery platform, storage capacity, and delivery medium capacity will place definite bounds on the scope of the work, both in terms of total data and system performance. For example, consider a delivery platform that has a 386-33 CPU with an SVGA display and a sound board, and a single-speed CD-ROM for the medium but no other special hardware. This will give you the data capacity for a lot of audio and video, but the CPU and data rate limitations would put bounds on the performance. Video windows would have to be small, and there would be limits on the amount of things that could be concurrent. The point is, you cannot logically design an application until you know everything about the target environment that will run it.

The same thing can be said about your end users—you cannot design an application until you can precisely define who will be using it. How skilled is the user in the use of computers and in the subject of the application? How much time will she have to spend with the application? Does she have any particular preferences for type of presentation? What is the user's objective for the application? These questions all should be thought through before attempting any application design.

The proposed content of your application should be related to the list of platform capabilities to make sure that your delivery platform will be able to present your application. For example, if you are planning for a limited platform like the one used as an example and you have a lot of video that has to be shown full-screen, it's not going to work. You either will have to add video decompression hardware to the platform or face up to changing the video.

The Leading Medium

Most applications have one medium that carries the main thread throughout the application, and it is the one the user looks for to find out or choose what is next. I call this the *leading* medium. For example, in an encyclopedia application, text would usually be the leading medium. It would be present on all screens and the other media (audio, graphics, images, or video) are there to support what is said in the text. In many applications, especially those designed for a general-public audience, the leading medium is the audio. All messages are conveyed by voice audio and everything else supports that.

Choice of the leading medium for your application would depend on what will suit your audience and what kind of material you have available or can produce for this purpose. Whatever choice you do make, it is best to use it consistently throughout so as not to confuse the user.

Another possible leading medium is a video or animation talking head. This could be available at all times in a small video window with audio. Using this or another form of anthropomorphic character is especially effective when your users are children. Such characters are sometimes referred to as *agents*, which is an even further enhancement of the human guide character who takes you through the application.

The User Interface

If your application requires any response from the user, you have to think about what type of controls you will present to the user and how she will operate them. This is the *user interface*, which involves both hardware and software. All PCs have a keyboard interface and most have a mouse or trackball. Your user interface can use these, but if the user is not computer literate, you should consider a touch screen. A touch screen requires either a special monitor with the device built-in or it is an overlay that you place over a standard monitor. Either way, it is an additional hardware expense. In spite of that, it is the best interface device for information kiosks to be used by the general public because of its ease of use and ruggedness. Touch screens also require special software and you must be sure that your authoring assembly program (see next chapter) will support touch.

In the early days of personal computing, the keyboard was the only user input device and most programs required the user to learn certain keystrokes or command words that activated all the program's functions. This made it difficult to learn to use a computer, especially when you realize that every program had a different set of commands and keystrokes. As personal computing has matured (it is not there yet) and as graphical interfaces like Windows and OS/2 have been introduced, a concerted effort has been made to standardize user interface objects and actions.

Today, because of these standardizing efforts, most computer users already know how to operate a mouse and how to manipulate windows, buttons, check boxes, scroll bars, and other GUI controls. Unfortunately, from a program designer's point of view, it is still more difficult to create an interface using the standard controls than it is to have a magic set of keystrokes. Thus, you often will find that there are some "secret" keystrokes in many programs, especially for less-used functions. At least, if you have to use keystrokes, put a prompt on the screen that tells the user what keys to use so that she doesn't have to remember anything.

Most authoring assembly programs that run under GUIs have special features to make it easy to create and use standard GUI controls. They usually also support keystrokes, but you should make the effort to do everything your application needs with the GUI controls and resort to keystrokes only as a backup.

The most important thing about user interfaces is to choose an approach that is intuitive to the user and then stick with the same approach throughout the application. If the user might need help in mastering the interface, provide an opportunity for help or a tutorial at the start of the application. It is also valuable to have a help button on all menus or selectors so the user can refer to the help at any point in the application.

By the way, help screens are another place where special tools are available, and it takes special skills to design them. You have to work with only a few software products before you learn how wide a range there can be in the usefulness of on-line help. Many programs that I have used have built-in help, but often it never seems to be able to answer any real questions that I have. If you plan to include help in your application, also plan to expend enough effort on it to learn what kinds of questions the typical user will have and make sure the answers are in your help screens.

SUMMARY

Deciding where and when to use audio and video is an important step in designing your applications. There are many considerations, both technical and non-technical, and the task is complex. The actual job of integrating audio and video is part of the authoring process, which is discussed in the next chapter.

13

Multimedia Authoring

The term *multimedia* is used today to describe computer programs that make use of animation, audio, and video as well as the more familiar computer metaphors of text and graphics. The process of creating a multimedia application is called *authoring*. It includes many tasks, from the initial acquisition or creation of materials to their assembly into the sequence and the logic of the application. Software tools are available to assist all steps of this process. Authoring tools fall into these categories:

- Media creation, including drawing, painting, animation, and audio/video capture.
- Editing, including audio and video editors, and image processing.
- File management, including libraries, or organizers.
- Assembly, which is the process of building the complete application. Note that many writers equate the word *authoring* to this one step. I prefer a broader definition of *authoring* that includes all the tasks in this list.
- Distribution, including CD-ROM formatters and recorders, and installation tools.

This chapter discusses authoring tools and the process of authoring, a subject about which I have written an entire book. If you want more than is here about authoring, I recommend you look at that book, *Authoring Interactive Multimedia* (AP Professional, 1994).

REQUIREMENTS OF YOUR APPLICATION

Many requirements in authoring are dictated by your applications. For example, if you will be doing text-intensive multimedia database applications, you will probably want *hypertext*—the ability to link actions to certain words in the text.

Not many authoring tools support hypertext, so that is an important constraint. Obviously, you need to think about all the needs of your applications before beginning the quest for authoring tools.

Application Style

An important part of application requirements is the issue of *style*. By that, I mean what does the application look like to the end user? For example, many authoring tools create application screens that look just like any other computer screens. In Windows or OS/2, you get standard windows with borders, title bars, etc. This is the *computer style*. However, if your application is targeted for users who are not necessarily computer literate, such as the general public, they may actually be put off by the computer style. For these users, a better choice is the *television style*.

A television-style application does not look like a computer at all, it looks like a television screen. The application always uses the full screen, and there are no standard GUI windows or control objects; there may not even be a mouse cursor. Non-computer people don't know how to use a mouse. As I mentioned in the previous chapter, applications for general audiences should be driven by a touch screen. Even with that, you will probably need to prompt your user to touch the screen—it's not natural to go around touching TV screens!

Touch controls are areas of the screen that respond when touched; they are indicated by objects drawn or otherwise displayed on the screen. You might even display a photograph and make certain objects in the photo respond as touch controls. None of the computer-standard screen objects should show. If you are designing for television style, you must have authoring tools that support full-screen displays, touch control, and hiding all computer objects.

Another aspect of computer vs. television styles is the way screens and objects behave dynamically. On a computer, when you make a selection that starts something new, there is often a delay while files are loaded, memory is allocated, and other things are set up. Then, when things begin to happen on the screen, you often see objects getting built piece by piece: Windows appear first as blanks and the contents get filled in one piece at a time. As computer users, we accept that and simply tolerate the delay it represents. When we see a message box that says "Please wait," we wait. Maybe we even dream about buying a faster machine to speed up such things.

The television-style user will view all the computer delays and machinations as being clunky—that's not the way it happens on TV. Television screens change smoothly, often with a fancy transition effect, and as far as the viewer is concerned, things happen when required without any delays. Your television-style user will expect your application to look and behave the same way. This poses difficult requirements for your authoring, because you must use tools that are capable of the smooth, responsive operation that goes along with television style.

A computer is capable of operating in television style; it requires that screens and objects be built fully in memory before they are displayed and slow operations like file loading must be planned to occur ahead of time so the system can respond quickly when the user asks for the next thing. Many authoring tools are capable of the smooth display with fancy transitions, but few easily support preloading of objects to reduce delays. The delay problem is especially problematical for audio, video, or animation objects where large files often have to be loaded before playing.

The User Interface

In the last chapter, I discussed an application's user interface. This is another important part of the application requirements that affects authoring. You should make sure that your assembly tool supports the type of user controls you will need. For example, if you require list boxes or pull-down menus in your application, you have to get tools that can author them. Similarly, special hardware requirements, such as touch screens, must be supported.

Consistency is an important part of a good user interface—you should use the same approach throughout your application. Some tools can help you with this by providing globalized user interface features that are accessible on every screen. This will simplify the task of authoring the interface because it can be designed only once and then simply be called up everywhere you need it.

AN AUTHORING ENVIRONMENT

Effective authoring requires a powerful PC and a collection of special hardware and software. I call this an authoring *environment*. With a good authoring environment, you can author for many different delivery platforms. It is not necessary for the delivery systems to have the same hardware as you use for authoring. In most cases, the delivery platform is deliberately chosen to be a low-cost system because there will be more of them than there are authoring platforms. A powerful platform speeds authoring and provides the storage and software capabilities to support creating many different applications.

For authoring, I recommend a fast 486DX PC or better, with 8 MB or more of RAM, as much hard disk space as you can afford (500 MB for starters), and capture hardware for audio and video. Other features that are valuable include a drawing tablet, audio and video compression hardware, and a large-screen SVGA monitor.

Your authoring software will consist of a collection of tools for drawing, digitizing, editing, assembling, format converting, and many other tasks. You can easily fill up a 500-MB hard disk with authoring software alone, even before you start collecting any data. The selection of the hardware and software depends closely on the kind of work you will be doing, how much of it, and how much skill you have or will develop for the various tasks of authoring.

A valuable resource of authoring software is the IBM Ultimedia Tools Series. This is a marketing initiative by IBM that has brought together a set of authoring software products from the industry's leading vendors. The result is a collection of more than 90 tools covering all the categories of authoring and designed specifically to work effectively together. IBM also provides a Ultimedia Tools Series Sampler CD that presents all the programs in the tools series, demonstrates them, and in some cases has actual working models that you can try out yourself on your own kind of work. One of those CDs is included with the book I mentioned previously.

STEPS OF AUTHORING

Like most any complex task, authoring can be broken down into a number of steps:

- Concept development
- Application design
- Content collection
- Assembly
- Testing
- Distribution

The first three steps have already been discussed in preceding chapters. Authoring assembly is the task of bringing together all the content elements and connecting them with the logic of the application. Many people refer to this one task as authoring, but I prefer to think of authoring as the entire application-development process and call this task *assembly*. That terminology makes more sense when you come to talk about the tools because you can distinguish between tools that do assembly and tools than do not. I will cover assembly tools in this chapter, and distribution is the subject of the next chapter.

THE ASSEMBLY TASK

Assembly is the fun part of authoring because it's where you see all the parts of your application come together. What you are doing in assembly is creating a computer program that "plays" your application. You could do that by actual programming, using almost any of the widely available programming languages. Multimedia programming is complex and not for the faint of heart, but there's an easier way that doesn't require you to be a programmer—you use one of the many multimedia assembly tools on the market. These tools are specifically designed to make multimedia assembly easy.

More than 100 assembly tools are available, covering a wide range of application targets and author skill levels. Some tools really don't require any programming skill, although this limits their applicability. That is because a complex interactive multimedia application inherently involves a lot of programming concepts. If you have no programmer training, you will have trouble understanding the capabilities of your tool. Concepts such as loops, variables, Boolean logic, data formats, and mathematics are essential to working with complex multimedia applications, no matter how user-friendly your tools may be.

The list shows the assembly step occurring after all content has been collected. This does not have to be the case. A very useful approach is to initially do the assembly with dummy content and then plug in the real content as it is collected. This allows testing to begin much earlier in the process and provides more time to fine tune the application architecture. It also allows the content to be checked in the application before it has all been collected; if changes are indicated, less content development effort will be wasted.

AUTHORING METAPHORS

Since programming models for authoring assembly will be understood only by programmers, easy-to-use assembly tools generally choose some other simplified model to represent the structure of the application and the task of assembly. I call these *authoring metaphors*. Metaphors are the basis for the tool's *authoring interface*, which is the way the author interacts with the tool. There are many authoring metaphors, nearly as many as there are assembly tools, but I'll cover only the most widely used ones here. Those are

- The slide show metaphor
- The book metaphor
- The windowing metaphor

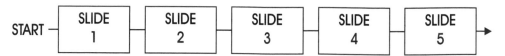

Figure 13.1 Diagram of a slide show presentation

- The time line metaphor
- The flowchart metaphor
- The network metaphor

These metaphors simplify the task of authoring assembly because they provide an easy model for the author to use in thinking about and working with his application. Once you relate your application to a particular metaphor, you probably already know the nomenclature, and you almost intuitively know the things you will be able to do with the application.

The Slide Show Metaphor

A presentation using 35-mm slides or overhead transparencies consists of a linear sequence of slides, one after another, as shown in Figure 13.1. The idea of a linear sequence of separate presentation objects is the *slide show* metaphor. With this metaphor, you author slides one at a time and then arrange them in sequence. The arranging is usually done with a *slide sorter* screen, as shown in Figure 13.2 from Microsoft PowerPoint. All the slides in the current presentation are shown and arranging is done by dragging slide images around with the mouse, much the same as you would do with 35-mm slides on a light table.

Because the basic architecture of the slide show metaphor is a straight line, this metaphor is capable of only limited interactivity. You can provide user controls that allow jumping from one place to another in the sequence—that's all. However, that is all you need in many applications, such as business presentations and small applications that are just presenting data.

Very good tools are available for creating slide show applications, supported largely by the business presentation market. Tools such as Lotus FreeLance, Microsoft PowerPoint, Asymetrix Compel, Software Publishing Harvard Graphics, and others make presentation-building extremely easy. Their general approach is to provide a collection of *templates* for the author to select a style for his presentation. Then the content is filled into each slide by typing into the blanks provided by the template.

Figure 13.3 shows a template screen from FreeLance. The screen shows a type-in field for the subtitle. That is what comes up when you click on each text object in the template. The screen also contains a palette of drawing tools at the

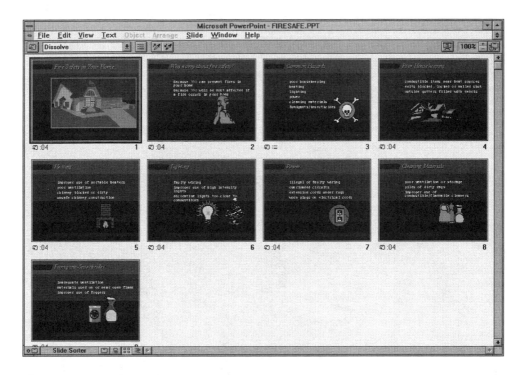

Figure 13.2 The slide sorter screen from Microsoft PowerPoint

left and a toolbar in addition to the menus at the top. These give access to all the many features of this program.Notice the menu at the bottom of the screen that offers a selection of formats. These are different classes of screens that all match the style of the basic template so you can vary the slide format within your presentation, but maintain the consistency of the overall style. At any time you can run your current presentation or view it in the slide sorter view.

An outline view in FreeLance lists the text content of the presentation in the order of the slides. You can enter or edit text in this view, and it will automatically be formatted according to the template you chose. Presentation programs provide for inserting additional objects such as drawings, images, and graphs into any slide. You can also create your own custom templates and add them to the list.

Most presentation programs support adding audio, video or animation objects to a slide. This can be set up so the object plays when the slide is first shown, or a button can be placed in the slide for the end user to choose when the object plays. The audio, video, or animation is part of the current slide and can be started only while that slide is displayed. Some tools allow audio to be started on one

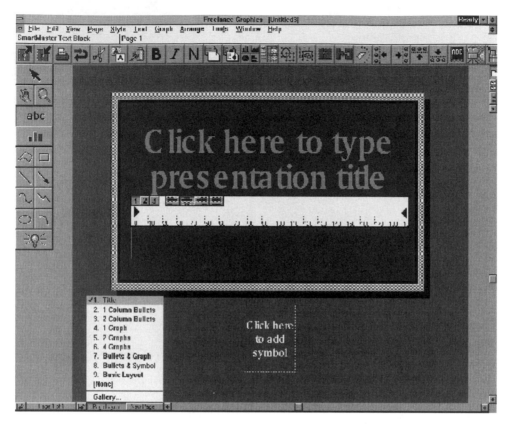

Figure 13.3 A template screen from FreeLance

slide and then play continuously while slides are changed on cue to create the kind of presentations described in Chapter 10.

Presentation authoring programs are quite mature and very effective for quickly authoring slick, professional presentations for on-screen viewing, 35-mm slides, overhead transparencies, or hard copy output. Their main limitation for broader multimedia use is the one-dimensional slide show metaphor, but the simplicity of that is also the reason that presentation authoring tools can be so easy to use.

The Book Metaphor—ToolBook

Closely related to the slide show metaphor is the book metaphor, for which the premier tool is Asymetrix ToolBook. In the book metaphor, an application is viewed as one or more *books*, containing any number of *pages*. In that respect,

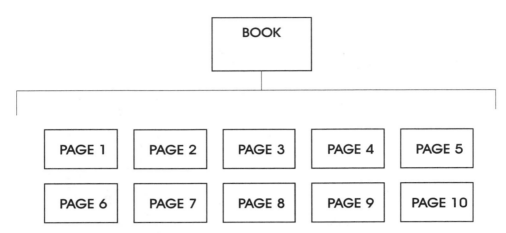

Figure 13.4 The book metaphor

pages are much like slides in the previous metaphor, but ToolBook provides much more capability in a page than the typical presentation program offers for a slide. Also, pages do not have to be presented in sequence; they are a collection of objects that can be presented in any order. This organization is shown in Figure 13.4. Within one page you can have interactive controls that affect what happens in the page, you can author a sequence of actions in the page, or you can go to other pages.

ToolBook runs only one book at a time, and each book usually has only one window on the screen. However, the multitasking capability of Windows can be used to get multiple books and multiple windows at the same time by running more than one instance of ToolBook. That is not as awkward as it sounds because ToolBook loads quickly and does not use a lot of system resources. It does make authoring a little more complicated because you have to keep track of several different books that will work together.

ToolBook is a full-featured assembly package for almost any kind of application. It supports complex interactivity and multimedia objects such as images, audio, and video. You can graphically create screens, adding buttons or other kinds of controls, and importing text or multimedia objects. However, to specify any actions on the screen, you must do a little programming. That is because action is imparted to controls and objects by writing little programs called *handlers* in a special authoring language called OpenScript. This language is easy to learn but it is complex because of the number of features in ToolBook. If you expect to build complex multimedia applications without any programming at all, then ToolBook is not the assembly tool for you.

A very significant interactivity feature of ToolBook is its built-in support for hypertext. That allows you to assign actions to individual words or blocks of words

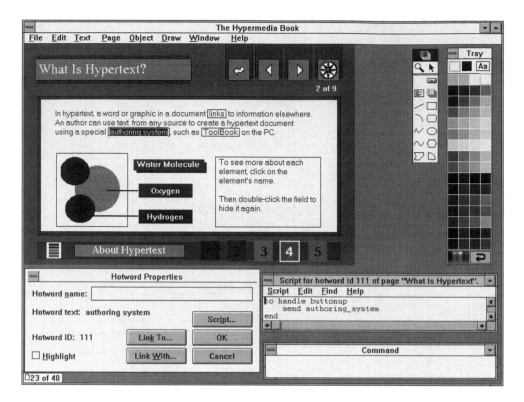

Figure 13.5 The authoring screen of Asymetrix ToolBook showing the authoring of hypertext

in your text (these are called *hotwords*.) You can, for example, go to another page, display other text or graphics, or assign almost any other action to a hotword. Hotwords are automatically highlighted on-screen, so the end user knows which words have actions attached to them. You are probably familiar with hypertext because it is used widely in the on-line help screens of Windows and OS/2.

Figure 13.5 shows the authoring of a screen from a ToolBook sample application that uses hypertext. The dialogs open at the bottom show how you assign a hotword and the handler script that specifies its action. In this example the handler calls a function that simply displays a message box containing the definition of *authoring system*.

The Windowing Metaphor—Visual Basic

Many types of applications need a multiplicity of windows on the screen at once—more than is reasonable with the approach used in ToolBook. An example

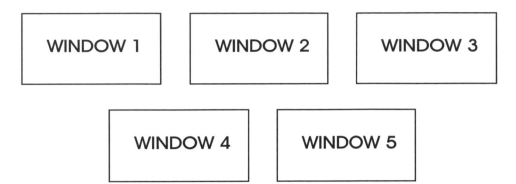

Figure 13.6 The windowing metaphor

of such an application is a multimedia database where you want to have separate windows for text, pictures, graphics, or video that might be presented simultaneously. An authoring approach that suits such applications is the *windowing* metaphor. In this architecture, the fundamental structure is a window, which may be on-screen or hidden. All presentation and actions occur within or between windows. A good example of this is Microsoft Visual Basic (VB).

VB is usually thought of as a programming language and it is that, but it also contains powerful tools for graphically creating windows without programming. However, like ToolBook custom program code is required to impart action to objects. Also like ToolBook, VB makes this as easy as possible by managing all the program structure and presenting the author only with the places where he has to write code. You do need to know programming, but it is easy.

Figure 13.6 shows the basic architecture of the windowing metaphor. The windows are all independent of each other, but they can communicate with each other and their existence, showing, and actions can be controlled from any window. Figure 13.7 shows the VB authoring screen with an authored window ("Profiles") containing a number of controls. A script is shown for the action that occurs when the highlighted button ("Include") is clicked. The screen also shows the VB tool palette at the top and the palette of objects that can be placed into windows at the left. Other windows list the properties of an object and list all the resources in the application.

Interactivity in VB can include any type of Windows control object or special types of controls that you author by custom programming. Any control object can show or hide windows or make changes to any window or object.

The windowing metaphor is good when you need a lot of windows. It may not be a good deal for television-style applications where you usually would have only a single full-screen window with no borders or controls. VB can make such a window, but many of its built-in features for window controls will not help you

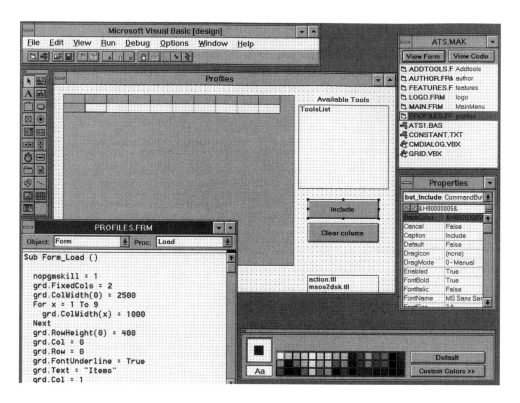

Figure 13.7 The authoring screen from Visual Basic

very much. That just means that it will take more programming on your part. However, VB is a full programming language, so you can theoretically use it to do anything, the result just depends on how good a programmer you are.

The Time Line Metaphor—Action!

Applications that have a lot of preplanned activity that must happen on cue are candidates for *time line* authoring assembly tools. A time line is a diagram that puts all the objects in the application onto a time scale that shows what happens when. You can add objects and move them around on the time line to build your application. An example of a time line authoring tool is MacroMedia Action!. It is a presentation-building tool that supports text, graphics, images, animation, and audio.

The authoring screen of Action! is shown in Figure 13.8. Action! divides an application into *scenes*, which are much like slides in other presentation programs.

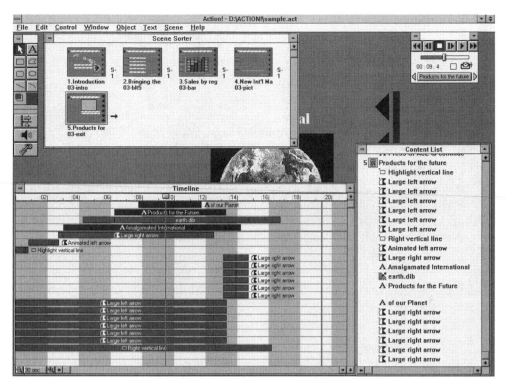

Figure 13.8 The authoring screen of Action!

The scene (slide) sorter window is shown at the upper left of the screen. Scene 5 is selected; it is displayed in the main window (behind the other windows); its time line is at the bottom of the screen and a list of its contents is in the window at the right. A tool palette is at the upper left and a control panel is at the upper right.

Action! allows an audio file to be played from one scene into the next, which means you can easily build a stills-with-audio presentation. Each still image can be cued by positioning it on the time line. However, Action! can display only one full-screen image at a time, and it cannot transition between them except by placing each image in a different scene. Although the timing of scenes is controllable, it is done by specifying the duration of each scene, which we have seen is an awkward way of cueing.

Interactivity in Action! is accomplished by assigning *link* action to any object in a scene. If the user clicks on a link object, program control can move to a specified other location in the application—another scene, another time position. This is the usual behavior for slide-show interactivity, but Action! goes a little further. A scene can have a *return* action when it finishes; such a scene can then become a subroutine. When it is linked from another location in the application, it will return to the linking location when finished. This significantly expands the interactive possibilities.

The Flowchart Metaphor—Authorware Professional

Flowcharts are familiar to programmers. They are two-dimensional diagrams of how the elements of a program are logically connected. MacroMedia Authorware Professional is an assembly tool based on flowcharts. It runs under Microsoft Windows. This metaphor is advantageous in that has no underlying structure of slides, scenes, or windows into which your application must be divided. An application consists of a master flowchart and any number of subordinate flowcharts or subroutines. The entire structure is managed graphically so that you never have to write code although you do have to understand programming logic to read the flowcharts.

Authorware was developed originally as a computer-based training authoring tool. Because of that heritage, it contains many features that support the kinds of interactivity used in CBT. However, that is a plus because CBT requires some of the most sophisticated interactivity, so you'll find that Authorware can probably support the needs of any other type of interactive application.

The icons used on Authorware flowcharts are shown in Figure 13.9. There are only 11 types (the two flag icons are used to mark start and stop points in a flowchart for testing purposes), which is a small number considering the power of this program. You author by dragging icons from the palette into a flowchart window and then you author the contents and properties of the icons using a number of dialogs that are opened by double-clicking on icons.

Figure 13.10 shows the main authoring screen of Authorware Professional. The example in the figure is a simple application consisting of a menu screen (shown in the presentation window) with three selections. The main flowchart is called demo.apw, which is the file name of the application. It has one interaction icon (the one with the question mark in it) and three "map" icons, which are essentially subroutines represented by other flowcharts. The flowchart for the "Slide Show" map icon is shown below—this is an audio/still image presentation containing three slides that are shown at fixed times while the audio plays. As you can see, the times are set up by a sequence of Wait icons, which I have described before as a workable but not very convenient technique.

You probably are wondering where are the icons that draw the menu screen. Those actions are actually contained within the Decision icon and they are accessed by double-clicking on the decision icon. When you do that, a draw tool

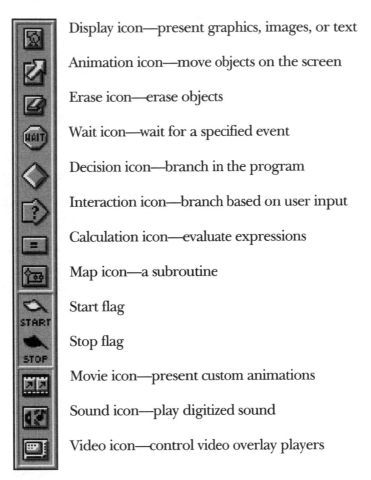

Display icon—present graphics, images, or text

Animation icon—move objects on the screen

Erase icon—erase objects

Wait icon—wait for a specified event

Decision icon—branch in the program

Interaction icon—branch based on user input

Calculation icon—evaluate expressions

Map icon—a subroutine

Start flag

Stop flag

Movie icon—present custom animations

Sound icon—play digitized sound

Video icon—control video overlay players

Figure 13.9 The icon palette of Authorware Professional

palette is displayed for you to draw or edit on the screen, and while this palette is open you can also import graphics or images into the screen.

Authorware uses only one window at a time. If you need other windows, you have to draw them manually and manage them with part of your program.

Another assembly program that uses the flowchart metaphor is AimTech's IconAuthor. This is also a prime CBT tool that is readily applicable to all classes of application.

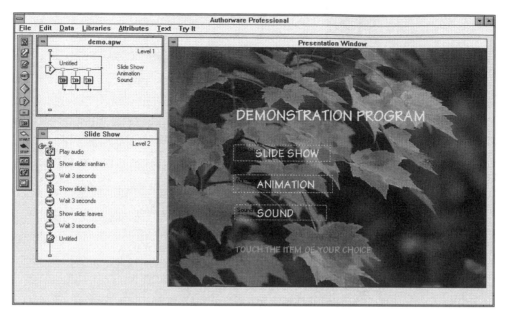

Figure 13.10 The authoring screen of Authorware Professional

The Network Metaphor—MEDIAscript OS/2

Another way to expand the possibilities for interactive structure is the *network* metaphor used by Network Technology Corporation's MEDIAscript OS/2. This is a comprehensive authoring tool that includes audio, video, and image capture; drawing; and application assembly. It runs under OS/2 and supports the DVI ActionMedia II board. It provides an authored application full access to other computer resources such as printers, communication ports, interprocess communication, and various custom peripherals.

The network metaphor has nothing to do with computer networks—it simply means that an application structure is a network of active pieces, where any piece can be connected to any other piece. The connections can be dynamically changed as the application runs. The building blocks of MEDIAscript OS/2 networks are *scripts*, which are executable and reusable program modules. Scripts are built from a palette of iconized *objects* (shown in Figure 13.11), and they are connected using a built-in tool called the *Organizer*.

The authoring interface of MEDIAscript OS/2 is shown in Figure 13.12. The main window is at the upper left; it shows icons for all the applications that are currently being authored (they are called *projects*.) When you double-click on a project icon in the main window, a Scripts window opens showing all the scripts in that project. Similarly, double-clicking on a script icon opens it in another

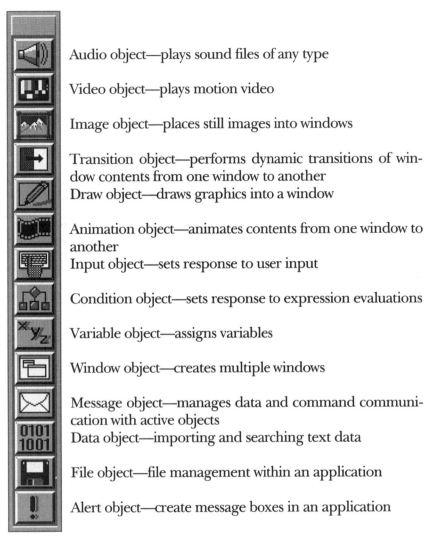

Audio object—plays sound files of any type

Video object—plays motion video

Image object—places still images into windows

Transition object—performs dynamic transitions of window contents from one window to another
Draw object—draws graphics into a window

Animation object—animates contents from one window to another
Input object—sets response to user input

Condition object—sets response to expression evaluations

Variable object—assigns variables

Window object—creates multiple windows

Message object—manages data and command communication with active objects
Data object—importing and searching text data

File object—file management within an application

Alert object—create message boxes in an application

Figure 13.11 The object palette of MEDIAscript OS/2

window to show its contents. The object palette appears whenever a script is open; this is used to add objects to a script. When you double-click an object icon that is already in a script, a dialog opens to show its contents. For example, Figure 13.13 shows the contents of the video object that is highlighted in the script window of Figure 13.12. You can see that there are many options for how video is played; in fact, there is another dialog for advanced options, also shown in Figure 13.13. This is typical of all the MEDIAscript objects, each one is very rich

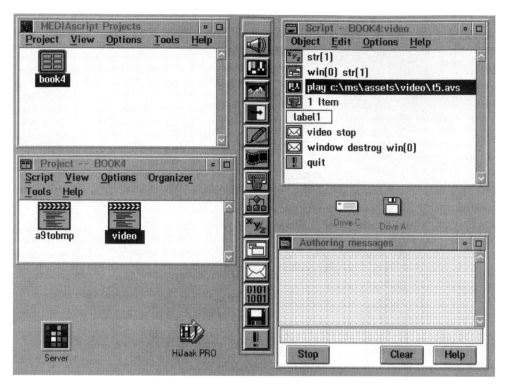

Figure 13.12 The authoring interface of MEDIAscript OS/2

with options. That is how the power of this program gets encapsulated into only 14 authorable objects.

Another window in the lower right corner in Figure 13.12 is called "Authoring messages." It shows error messages during testing of a script. It also shows messages from MEDIAscript about the program status and confirmations of important tasks such as saving of scripts or projects. You can also deliberately add objects into your script to display variable values or other things by using the query option of the Variable object.

Figure 13.12 shows an icon in the lower-left corner with the name *Server*. The Server is the MEDIAscript OS/2 runtime module; it is a separate application that remains resident on the OS/2 desktop and provides multimedia services when sent commands via DDE. Authoring is done by a separate program, called the *AUI* (authoring user interface); it creates the authoring windows shown in Figure 13.12 and it communicates with the Server via DDE. When you distribute an application to other users, you must make sure they have copies of the Server because it is needed to run any MEDIAscript application. This architecture makes optimum use of the OS/2 multitasking capabilities.

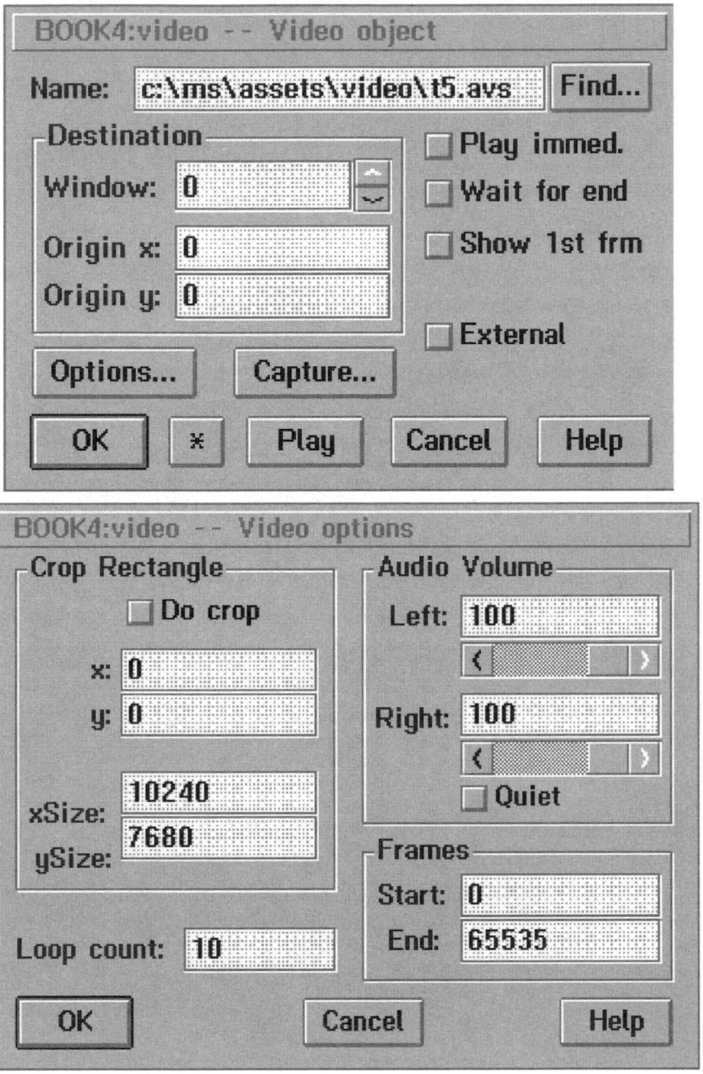

Figure 13.13 The dialogs for authoring of the highlighted Video object shown in Figure 13.12

Although MEDIAscript OS/2 has a graphical author interface, it also has an authoring language. Scripts that you author graphically are stored in the MEDIAscript authoring language. With the MEDIAscript OS/2 Professional Edition (PE) an author has access to that language and can view and edit scripts directly in the language. This allows authoring features not available through the GUI authoring. Of course, it takes more skill to work with the language directly, but that option is available for authors who want to get the ultimate out of the system.

Interactivity in MEDIAscript OS/2 occurs primarily through the Input object, which can manage an application's responses to keyboard, mouse, touch, frame number events in video or audio, timer events, or incoming DDE messages. Potential responses can be jumping to another script, going to another place in the same script, calling another script and returning to this object, executing a subroutine contained in this script, or quitting this script (which gives control to the MEDIAscript Organizer to determine what happens next.)

In Figure 13.13 you will notice that the coordinate values seem strange—the size of the crop rectangle is shown as 10240×7680. That's an extremely large image! In fact, these numbers refer to an *abstract coordinate system* that supports MEDIAscript's unique *scaling* system. The numbers 10240×7680 represent the full-screen of any system, regardless of what the screen resolution actually is. Thus, if you author a full-screen application at 10240×7680 resolution, you can run the same application with no changes on a 640×480 screen and everything will automatically scale down to fit. This is the normal behavior of MEDIAscript. You can modify that to cause your application to be scaled to a less than full-screen window. This is particularly useful during authoring because you can show a test version of your application in a smaller window, leaving the rest of the screen for your authoring dialogs or other tools. When authoring is finished, you can turn off the special scaling feature and your application will automatically grow to full-screen.

MEDIAscript OS/2 is the premier multimedia authoring tool for OS/2. It supports the full multitasking features of OS/2 and gives an author access to all the features of the OS/2 Presentation Manager, MMPM/2, and DVI Technology, if you have that.

TESTING

Before an application can be put into use, it must be thoroughly tested to confirm that it does what you expect of it and it does not hang up or crash the system under any circumstances. Most authoring assembly tools have built-in safeguards against the latter problems, but they cannot protect you from your own programming or logic errors. Thus you must test your work.

Assembly tools all have means to run your application or part of it while you are authoring. They usually have other mechanisms to observe what is going on while the application runs, such as single-stepping, error windows, or other kinds of debugging tools. These allow you to confirm that the application does what *you* expect. They also help you figure out what is wrong when it doesn't perform correctly.

If your application has any user interactivity, it is important to test your application on the intended users or someone like them. The users may very well do things that you never thought of or they may not understand your user interface and become stumped. The only way to find these things out is to perform user testing. Part of your planning and scheduling task should be to figure out how you will accomplish user testing—who will be the testers and when (in your schedule) will you give them preliminary copies of the application (usually called *beta copies)* for testing.

SUMMARY

Multimedia authoring requires powerful hardware and a suite of software tools. These together constitute an authoring environment. No single software package is likely to provide everything required for your authoring, so you face the task of selecting the tools you need.

The key authoring tool is the program that does assembly, the task of putting together all the pieces of an application. There are numerous assembly tools, using different approaches, and you have to choose one that matches both your needs for capability and your preferences for how you want to work.

14

Distributing Digital Video Applications

Few applications play on the machine where they were authored. Unless you are your one and only end user, you will have to transport your applications to other machines. That means recording the application and its content data on some kind of removable medium that can be sent to other machines. Another possibility is to communicate directly with other systems by wire or wireless transmission. These are some of the options for *distribution* of your application. This chapter discusses the means of distribution, their characteristics, and their selection.

END USERS

Whatever applications you create, you will have a specific audience of users in mind. It may be your colleagues in your company, your bosses, a school class, or even the general public. To choose appropriate distribution means, you must know the following things about your proposed target audience of users:

- How many users will there be? The number of copies to be distributed is important because some media are suited only for small quantity distribution while other media are practical only for large quantities.
- What type of system(s) do they have? Obviously your users must have the hardware and software capability to utilize whatever medium you select. If your users' systems are already in place, you probably have to choose a medium that they already are able to use.
- Do the users already have any of the software required to run your application? Authored applications require that the authoring system or its

runtime module be installed to run the application. Sometimes this is free software, sometimes it is not.

- Will they do their own installation of your application? Most applications require that at least part of the application software be installed on the user's hard disk. This question refers to how automatic that process should be.
- Will your applications need regular updating? Some applications require that the content data be regularly updated. This may call for a special kind of distribution that occurs repeatedly. It may actually be a different medium than is used for the initial distribution.

The significance of this list of user questions depends on the degree to which you can control your users and their equipment. If you can dictate the distribution requirements to your users, the problem is simpler than if you have to work with what they already have. The following discussion assumes that you have some control over the situation.

DATA SIZE

Another important determinant of distribution methods is the amount of data and programs in your application. To get this, you simply add up all the bytes of data in the application program itself, the content files, and any executables, libraries, or drivers needed to run the application. Of course, if you expect that some of the latter files will already be on the users' machines, they need not be included with every distribution. If, as I recommend, you are figuring this before the application has been completed, it will have to be an estimate.

With the profile of your audience determined and the knowledge of your application (including its size) that you already have, you can consider the applicability of the different media for distribution. It is desirable to choose the distribution means before completing the design and authoring of the application because that choice may place its own requirements on the application design. For example, if you have to use floppy disk distribution, the data size limitation is so severe that it will restrict the design of any but the simplest application.

DISTRIBUTION MEDIA

The possibilities for digital distribution media include removable mass storage media and communications media. They are

Table 14.1 Comparison of distribution media

Distribution Medium	Data (MB) per unit	Data Rate (MB/second)	Access Time (seconds)	Medium Cost/MB	Drive Cost
3½" Floppy	1.44	0.03	0.5	$0.7	$50
Hard Disk	100–1,000	0.5–5.0	0.01–0.03	$1.0	$1.0/MB
CD-ROM	680	0.15–0.6	0.2–0.3	$0.002	$100–500
Tape	120–4,000	0.05–1.0	(minutes)	$0.2	$150–1000
Network	N. A.	1.0–16.0	0.1–1.0	N. A.	$200–500 ^
Modem	N. A.	0.001	30 *	$5.0 **	$100 ^ ^

* Dial-up and connect time
** Long distance charges at 9600 Baud
^ Network interface hardware and software
^ ^ 9600 Baud modem cost

- Floppy diskette
- Hard disk
- Compact disc (CD)
- Magnetic tape
- Computer network
- Modem communication

I discuss each of these in the following sections. Table 14.1 is a summary comparison of the different digital media. In certain instances, it may be desirable to distribute an application by analog means, such as videotape or videodisc. I'll discuss that further, too.

Floppy Diskette

Floppy diskettes are small, convenient, and low in cost. However, they are severely limited in storage capacity compared to the sizes of most multimedia applications. The 3½" high-density (HD) diskette is standard on nearly all machines being built today—its data capacity is 1.44 MB. That will only hold about 10 seconds of motion video. To support a video application of any size, a number of floppies have to be used. That's not too bad up to maybe five or six diskettes, but it poses an awkward and inconvenient installation problem. Because the floppy disk data rate is only about 30 KB/second, installation takes about a minute per disk and all disks have to be copied onto the user's hard disk. That data rate is 5 to 10 times too slow to consider running an application directly from floppies. Except for very small applications, floppy diskette distribution is not practical.

Higher capacity floppy diskette systems have been developed, from 2.88 MB (double) up to the range of 20 MB. However, none of these is very widely used so they remain expensive. Unless you have complete control over the user's hardware, higher capacity floppies are not a choice, either.

Hard Disk

Hard disks are usually an internal part of a system. For distribution purposes, you would exchange or replace an entire hard drive. A few drives on the market have removable platters, but they are not widely used. However, for distribution of data in situations where the end user's hardware is uniform and under your control, replacing internal hard drives can be a viable distribution method. The data capacity of this method depends on the size of the hard drive used for distribution. Hundreds of megabytes of data capacity is very reasonable and the cost is now less than a dollar per megabyte. Since replacing a hard drive requires opening up the system, this is not something that you would want to do every day. Opening up the system can be avoided with an external hard drive. This is a very practical alternative, especially if you use a SCSI interface.

One example where the hard drive method is often used is where you are supporting a number of interactive kiosks, such as in a shopping mall. This might involve a two-stage process of distribution—for major updates, the systems' hard drives are replaced, and more frequent updates are done by floppy disk or a communications method. Such kiosks usually require frequent updating because they are displaying sales information that changes fairly often. That is accomplished by floppy disk, network, or other form of communication. Updates are prepared on a master system located somewhere in the mall office area or at a local vendor who is supplying the service. For installation or major updates, one or more spare hard drives of the type used in the system are kept to support exchange in the kiosks out in the mall.

Hard drive exchange is a very workable approach when the distribution is local and all the hardware is under your control. It will also work over larger distances as long as the appropriate precautions are taken in packing and shipping the hard drives, since they are somewhat fragile. Of course, the hardware still has to be under your control to insure that all systems use the same type of drives and the same type of interface.

CD-ROM

Mass-produced CD-ROMs offer the lowest cost per megabyte of any distribution medium. You can't beat 680 MB for less than $2 per unit. However, this low cost is available only if you need to make hundreds of copies or more. At smaller quantities, the costs go up significantly because of the one-time mastering cost, which is $1,000 or more. But low cost is only one of the reasons for using CD-ROM distribution.

The small 12-cm (4¾") CD is durable, lightweight, and easy to ship. Because it is a read-only medium, you don't have to worry about your data becoming corrupted by an inadvertent write to the disc. The data transfer rate of late-model drives is fast enough at 300 kB/second that playing motion video directly from the disc is very satisfactory. Even faster transfer rates are becoming available, with triple-speed (450 kB/second) and quad-speed (600 kB/second) drives. Although the faster drives are more expensive, prices are coming down rapidly.

However, the access time performance of CD-ROM drives seems to be stuck in the 200 to 300 millisecond range, which is 20 times slower than current hard drives. If your application requires a lot of accesses to different files on the CD while running, the CD-ROM access time will slow things down substantially. You can help this by properly designing your application, taking account of caching capabilities that are in many systems, and planning so that CD accesses will occur ahead of time to move important data into memory or onto hard drive. However, this seriously complicates the authoring and usually requires an assembly tool that has a full programming language.

A simpler approach to deal with CD-ROM's slow access is to provide an installation capability for your CD that moves the application's executable code and key data items to the delivery system's hard drive. This also may take some programming (to write the install program), but it is something that can be done once and in a way that it will apply to any CD-ROM that you produce.

Returning to the creation of a CD-ROM, there are two ways to go. If you will need more than maybe 10 copies of each CD product, it makes sense to send your data to a CD mastering house and have the CDs pressed. This takes maybe a week and costs about $1,000 plus a per-unit charge. You can get faster service by paying more, but you can't get faster than one-day service, not counting any transportation time that may be involved.

Writeable CDs

For small quantities, you can now buy writeable CD drives that connect to your authoring PC. These are in the $5,000 range, but prices are still coming down. With such a drive, you can create CDs that will play on any standard drive. The cost of blank discs for this is $50 or more and writing a full disc will take from 30 minutes to 1 hour, depending on the speed of the drive. However, this is far cheaper and faster than mastering for the first 1–10 discs. Even if you plan to go to mastering for full distribution, it is a good idea to create a one-off disc for full testing of your product, and the one-off disc can be the medium that you send to the mastering house.

Obviously, if you are going to author 680 MB of data for a CD-ROM, you need room on your system's hard drives to store that data. Furthermore, if you are going to use a writeable drive, you also will need the capability to read that data out to the writeable drive at the proper data rate without interruption. This requires special features in both your hard drive and its software. Many hard drives will periodically interrupt their operation for a few hundred milliseconds to perform a calibration routine. You cannot allow that to happen during a CD writing session, so you need a special hard drive that does not calibrate that way (these are called *A/V drives*). Also, you must map the data on the hard drive in exactly the way it will be on the final CD (this is called a *CD image*) so that it can be read out during recording without the hard drive having to do any seeks. Special software is needed to do that. When purchasing a writeable drive, you should consider buying from a vendor that can deliver a package of hardware and software that will do it all for you. This is important because the software for CD-ROM emulation can become expensive when purchased separately.

Magnetic Tape

Another large-capacity low-cost storage medium is magnetic tape. It is used widely to backup hard drives and is available in storage capacities up to 4 gigabytes (4,000 MB.) Tape media costs in the range of $20.00 per unit. In the higher capacities, it is almost competitive with CD-ROM. However, the fact that tape is a linear medium creates some major disadvantages that result in it seldom being used for mass distribution.

Access of an individual data item on a tape requires fast-forwarding the tape up to the linear location of the data, and then accessing it. Access times can be measured in *minutes*, so an application could never be played directly from a tape. The end user always must copy the entire tape to hard disk, even the motion video files. For hundreds of megabytes or more, this can take up to an hour, and of course, there must be enough hard disk storage in the user's system to handle it. For this reason alone, I think tape distribution is applicable only for data capacities below about 100 MB.

But there's a second problem with tape; it is caused by the lack of standards for tape equipment and tape formats. You and your users must all have the same type of tape drives. You have to be working in a situation where you can control the hardware used by your users.

The third problem about tape is that there is no such thing as high-speed mastering. Each tape has to be individually recorded at normal running speed. Thus, the process of recording tapes is expensive in terms of the time it takes. The more data you have, the more time for recording. Again, this limits the practicality to much less data than the theoretical capacity of the medium. I see tape distribution being practical only in special, controlled, small-scale situations.

Computer Networks

Many business groups have all their systems connected by a computer network, which provides for data transfer, e-mail, and many other communication features. This an ideal medium of distribution of video or other multimedia data. It is a compelling idea to have a networked digital video server that contains all the video files of the organization, accessible to everyone. However, actually using such a capability will bring most present networks to their knees. Motion video is simply too much data that has to be delivered too fast. Most networks just cannot handle it. In recognition of this problem, new server and network architectures are being developed to support the needs of motion video. If you are planning a network for motion video, you should look into these new designs.

Networks are designed to service multiple users by interleaving packets of data moving between different servers and users. That means a particular user cannot expect to receive a large block of data without interruption and the number of interruptions will increase as more users access the network. For most computer uses this is not a big problem—the user just waits a fraction of a second more for her data. When you are on a network, you get used to this. But with audio or video, that fraction of a second interruption can break up the video or put a gap in the audio. It is intolerable.

Audio and video players for network use can buffer their incoming data locally so that short interruptions in the incoming data are hidden by playing from the buffer during the interruption. However, to make this work over a long playing period, the network must be capable of delivering a specified minimum data rate to the audio/video user. New network software is being developed to do that, and audio/video use of networks will surely grow in the future. Also, higher speed network systems are being cost-reduced in anticipation of greater multimedia use.

The preceding discussion assumes that you are playing audio or video in real time from data received from the network. Of course, you can receive the data over the network ahead of time, store it on your hard disk, and then (later) play it from there. When you are finished with it, you delete it from your hard disk to make room for something else. This is completely practical today with existing networks because it does not depend at all on the network's ability to deliver a specified data rate. If you make the large data transfers at off-hours when others are not using the network, it's even better.

A look at some numbers will help you appreciate this. For example, if you have a network with a theoretical data rate of 10 megabits (Mb) per second, and you need to transfer a 50 MB motion video file (which might be 5 minutes of video), it will take 80 seconds if you can get 50% of the network capacity for the transfer. That's a very reasonable time for moving that amount of data, especially if you set up to do it on off-hours when both the network and your machine are idle. This is a good distribution approach if your need is to distribute to users who are all on your company's network.

Network hardware and software designers are now facing up to the requirements of audio and video data. New system designs will solve these problems and networked motion video and audio will be widely used in the future.

Modem Communication

Everyone has a telephone, and its use for data communication between computers using modems is well established. It is much like a computer network except that it extends anywhere in the world, and you can connect to anyone simply by dialing her number. However, there's a large mismatch between the speed of the dial-up telephone network and the needs of digital video or even audio. The standard modem speed today is 9600 bits per second, which works out to about 1 kB per second or 1 MB in 16.6 minutes. You can see what that means to the multimegabyte audio or video file. Considering the cost of a telephone call, that is impractical even if you have the time to make the transfer.

Faster modems are available, but they get expensive and they may not be reliable over all telephone lines. Digital telephone lines are also available, at data rates up to 1.2 Mb/second. These require bringing in a special line and terminal equipment. They are reasonable only when you can justify committing to the significant monthly cost of such facilities. As the telephone systems improve their capacity with fiber optic lines, etc., these costs will come down, and the "information superhighway" thinkers envision the time when such connections will be in every home. That's surely true, but we are many years from it.

There is one situation where modem communication is a practical part of an audio/video environment. In the case where you have a number of users at a distance and regular updating is required, a telephone connection may do the job. An example is the maintenance of data in information kiosks along an interstate highway, or maybe maintaining the content in a series of corporate training stations located in plants around the world. Here, the main updating would be done by periodic distribution of CD-ROM discs, maybe on a quarterly basis. More frequent updates would be done by telephone. Of necessity, these would be limited to update of text content, programming details, or other things that don't take great masses of data. This can work if the application is designed for it. Update of actual audio or video content would wait for the next CD-ROM to come out.

ANALOG DISTRIBUTION

In some cases your application may need to be converted to an analog medium for distribution; for example, where digital facilities do not exist. This sounds ridiculous, but it's not if the only local means of viewing recorded material is analog video. Two analog media can be considered—videotape and videodisc. Both store and play in standard NTSC or PAL television formats.

In any transfer of digital images to television, you must consider the limitations of the television system and design your application to deal with them. Two aspects are significant: interlaced scanning and resolution. As explained in Appendix A, interlacing is not very suitable for display of digital images, text, or graphics, because digital screens often display high-contrast, horizontally oriented features that are a single pixel wide. This happens especially in text and graphics and causes unacceptable flickering of the image. You must design your application to avoid single-pixel lines because TV systems are always interlaced.

The second limitation is that television resolution is typically less than even the 640 × 480 standard VGA resolution, particularly in the horizontal direction. This means that fine detail in your screens will not be visible when converted to TV. Text is not very readable if you use more than 40 or 50 characters per line. This is also consistent with TVs viewing ratios, which are at least twice those for computer viewing. Therefore, you must design to have a lot less information on your screens at once. Another part of the TV resolution limitation is that color information has even less resolution than monochrome on a TV screen. Bright reds or blues will smear substantially when compared to the computer screen. You should avoid using these colors in fine detail, especially in text.

Videotape vs. Videodisc

Videotape has a long playing time—up to 6 hours in the VHS format. It is inexpensive and you can easily make your own recordings with readily available equipment. However, it has essentially no random-access capability so it is not practical to produce an interactive application on tape. It can be used only for linear presentations. The second problem with tape is that the low-cost formats like VHS and 8-mm have horizontal resolution values that are about half what the TV system itself can achieve. Thus, the consideration of resolution become more binding if you are going to output onto tape.

The optical videodisc, on the other hand, does not limit resolution compared to the TV system and it has random-access and is interactive. However, it has limited playing time (30 minutes per side) and the recording process can be done only with special, expensive facilities. Videodisc players are inexpensive, but they are not as widely available as VCRs. You need to make more of a commitment to use this medium.

Using the interactivity of a videodisc requires some special programming for your application to control the disc player. Some disc players have computer interfaces built-in, and others are only manually controllable. If you plan on interactivity, be sure to select players that can handle your needs.

Outputting to Video

There are also special hardware considerations for outputting to video, because most computers do not have NTSC or PAL video outputs. You need either an external box to convert VGA to video or an add-in card. Since there is a lot of usage of computers to create materials that are intended for showing on video, such as animation and video postproduction, there is a wide range of add-in hardware that does deliver a TV signal from a computer. These range from a few hundred dollars to many thousands—it depends on the features you need. You can find out a lot more about this from the video production magazines or from audio/video dealers who specialize in computers.

RUNTIME SOFTWARE

In addition to the data files for your application, your end users need the proper executable program to run your application. Approaches for this vary in different authoring assembly tools. Some tools create a special executable module for your application that contains the complete application except for the data files. This is called *compilation* and it is the usual approach if you are using a programming language such as Visual Basic or C++. With compilation, the one program is all that you need.

The most common approach for assembly tools is a *runtime module*. This is an executable program that can run any application created with its parent tool. The structure of your application is contained in a separate file or files that are *interpreted* by the runtime module to present your application. The separate files are called *command files* or *scripts*. They contain only the structure and logic of your application, encapsulated in the special format of the assembly tool.

Generally, script files are viewable or editable only by the assembly tool itself, but some are in plain text format that could be modified by anyone who knew the format details. You probably don't want your users to mess around with your scripts, so check for the security approach of any assembly tool you are considering.

Each of your end users requires a runtime module, which means that you must distribute a copy of that module to all users. Some assembly tools let you do that for free (unlimited copies), but others require that you pay a small runtime royalty for each copy you distribute. Check the license documentation for your assembly tool to find out.

Some of the lower priced assembly tools require that the tool itself be present to run any application. This means that each of your users must have the assembly tool even though they are not going to be doing any authoring. This is OK if the tool is inexpensive and it offers a simple way for scripts to be played in a run-only mode.

PATHS AND INSTALLATION

Unless you are in control of all users' systems, you cannot expect that the hard disk layout on your user's systems will be the same as your authoring system. The drive letters may not be the same and the directory structure may be different. Your application must be able to run and find all its data regardless of the setup of each user's system. This does not happen by itself, and there are several approaches taken by different assembly tools.

The simplest case is when your application is on CD-ROM and it runs directly from there. The user's hard disk is not involved at all. The user makes the CD drive the default drive and enters the name of the executable module (or she sets up Windows or OS/2 to do that). That program runs and can find everything on the CD because it is the default drive and the CD directory structure is obviously known to your program. Unfortunately, this is seldom satisfactory because of the CD's slow access time. It is much better to move the executable modules and certain critical data modules to the user's hard disk to speed up execution. Of course, that approach is mandatory if your application is distributed on floppy diskettes.

Now, you have to provide an installation routine that will copy the appropriate modules from CD or diskette to hard drive and then set up a way to tell the system where everything is whenever your application runs. Specialized tools are available for building installation routines. They take care of most of the details and are recommended as the best method. If you have installed very many commercial applications, you have probably noticed that many of them seem to use the same style of install program even though they are from different vendors. They are examples of the work of the install-building tools that you also can use.

Some installations copy their files into generic directories that they know will exist on the user's machine, such as the Windows directory or its subdirectories. This is a very bad practice because it clutters up the user's machine with files that she will not know about if or when she chooses to remove your application. It is much better and friendlier to the user to create a special directory for *all* your files and face up to the path problem discussed next.

Returning to the matter of paths in the case where you have copied the executables to the user's hard drive, the user needs to know where the executables are located, and the executable needs to know where the data is. If you copy everything to hard disk, the easiest way is to have the user set the default directory to this location before running the executable. Then, your application need not worry about paths at all—everything is local.

However, if some of the data will be on CD-ROM or elsewhere on the user's hard disk, the application must be specifically told where that is. One way to do that is to specify an operating system *environment variable*. That can be done by adding a line to the system's startup file (autoexec.bat for DOS, or config.sys for OS/2.) This requires that your installation program either modify the users's startup file or ask the user to do it (a good installation program will give the user the choice of which way to get it done.) Another way to accomplish setting of an environment variable without messing with the user's startup files is to make an operating system *batch file* that sets the environment and then runs the application's executable. Batch files have the extension .bat in DOS and .cmd in OS/2. A batch file is run just like any other program by entering its name at a command prompt or in a settings window for a GUI icon.

If you will need any of these approaches for locating files, make sure that the assembly tool you are considering will support one of the methods for passing file locations. All will work when everything is in the default directory, but not all support environment variables or changing directories within an application.

SUMMARY

As you can see, distribution of an application is not a simple matter. You must choose the appropriate medium for your users and your application and you must decide how the application will run on the user's system. These decisions can well affect your choice of authoring tools and also the design of your application. You also may need to buy a separate tool to create an installation program to set up your application on the user's system.

15

Future Developments

Technology and markets do not stand still. Problems today become opportunities tomorrow and today's newest products are tomorrow's baseline. After having written chapters like this in four other books since 1988, I have given my forecasting abililties a pretty good test. The result is that, like every other forecast I have read, you can't hope for complete accuracy. In fact, maybe you can't hope for any accuracy. But what you can do is expose your readers to the possibilities and let them make their own forecasts. That is what I will do in this chapter.

TECHNOLOGY

One way to characterize the forces acting on a marketplace is to group them into technology forces and market forces. Both types are always present and either kind seldom dominates for very long. Let's begin by looking at what is happening in technology that will affect the future of digital video.

Solid-state Technology

Essentially all modern electronic units are based on integrated circuit chips. Gordon Moore of Intel Corporation made a projection in the late 1960s that said "the number of devices on a integrated circuit chip will double every two years." For more than 20 years he has been right, and his curve, now called *Moore's Law*, shows no sign of changing its slope. The implications of that growth have been massive—in fact, the entire existence of today's electronics industry has resulted from it.

In computers, Moore's Law is manifested in the ever more powerful CPU chips; current chips have surpassed 100 MIPS (million instructions per second, a measure of CPU speed) and by the year 2000 they may be pushing 1,000 MIPS! Similarly, the steady increase in memory chip capacity derives from the same law. Today, there's no reason not to have at least 8 MB of RAM in your PC, and the future "standard" RAM size can also be expected to increase. Don't doubt for a minute the ability of software designers to find ways to use this massive power (see later).

Mass Storage Technology

As you have seen from the preceding chapters, there is never enough mass storage capacity for digital video applications. Fortunately, mass storage technologies are not standing still either. Advances in capacity, speed, and reliability are continuing. Magnetic storage technology, which is the basis for floppy and hard disks, shows no signs of having reached its limits. Improvements in storage capacity, access times and data rates, cost/megabyte, and reliability continue to come. These trends will continue, although on not as steep a curve as solid-state electronics.

Optical storage technology is just coming into its own. The CD-ROM, which has been around for more than 10 years, has now come down the learning curve and is available at prices that match its parent, the audio Compact Disc. Writeable optical drives are now available around $1,000—only a few years ago that was $10,000, and before that it didn't exist at all outside the laboratory. You can even buy drives that will write your own CD-ROMs for under $5,000. This is a moving target, and major price reductions and performance improvements are coming.

Television Technology

Much of the production equipment and production techniques for digital video originated in the television industry. Now, the reverse is happening—television is going digital! TV recording and postproduction are already digital, and the HDTV broadcasting standards are expected to be digital. That represents large additional markets for digital technologies, which will finance even greater rates of advancement.

Digital television equipment for broadcast stations has tended to be custom designed, rather than programmable PC based. This happened because the broadcast industry is used to having its own custom equipment, at high prices, and until very recently, PCs lacked the power to process broadcast-quality digital video. Current top-of-the-line PCs, with add-in video boards, can reach broadcast quality levels. Because of the large and fast mass storage needs of high-quality digital video, these systems are still quite expensive, although they cost less than custom broadcast equipment for the same purpose. The trends in CPU power, memory, and mass storage mentioned previously will bring costs down over time, and you will see more and more PC-based digital video equipment in broadcast stations.

The impact of digital television on PC digital video is to cause improvements in video picture quality to happen faster than might have otherwise occurred. Broadcasters will not tolerate loss of picture quality for any reason, not even for a lower price tag. A digital video product must meet some minimum quality standards to get their attention at all. However, in the PC market, digital video is a new capability and many users accept it at quite low quality levels just because it is new and different from anything else on their PC. Obviously, they would like higher picture quality, but they won't pay much for it. Let the broadcasters pay for the development of high picture quality; the PC users will buy that when the price comes down.

Display Technology

The VGA display (640 × 480, 16 colors) has been the standard for some time, but now most machines are shipped with SVGA adaptors having at least 1 MB of video RAM. That means most machines can support 1024 × 768 resolution at 256 colors. This requires larger than the standard 14" display to be fully effective.

Except for portables, all PCs have CRT displays. The color CRT is a mature technology, having been used in TV for 40 years. However, a PC display is different than a TV display because it will be viewed close up at viewing ratios as low as 1:1, whereas TVs are viewed at ratios of 4:1 or greater. That means a computer CRT must have substantially higher resolution to look sharp at such close viewing, which is the reason the CRT dot pitch specification is so important to computers. The result is that a PC display costs at least twice as much as the same size TV receiver. The 14" VGA display manufacturing quantities are aready in the millions and have been there for at least five years, so there will not be much further improvement in price.

However, the situation is different for the larger PC displays in the range of 17" and up. These are new to the market and manufacturing quantities are still low and prices are high. With the wider use of SVGA in new PCs, sales of large monitors will grow and prices should drop to be more in line with twice TV prices at the same size.

Software Technology

It takes time for software developers to learn how to utilize new hardware capabilities and integrate them into their products. Therefore, hardware generally leads software into the market by one to two years. For example, PC sound boards were on the market for several years before sound capability was added to Windows, and there was a further one to two years before applications running under Windows added built-in sound capabilities. We are now in the stage where users are learning how to use sound in their projects. All of this is the natural process of market acceptance; it has to happen in series in several levels.

A similar process is under way for motion video. In this case, there are two thrusts—hardware based and software based. In the hardware case, powerful video processing add-in boards have been introduced, such as ActionMedia II or RealMagic. However, each of these boards requires its own proprietary software, which makes them difficult for application developers to integrate into their products. This is the reason why Microsoft and IBM introduced the MCI capability into Windows and OS/2. MCI provides a generic interface to any hardware whose manufacturer provides an MCI driver.

This works, but even with today's fastest PCs, the MCI approach is a little slow. It takes several seconds to begin playing video, and commands issued during video play are equally slow to respond. Correcting this requires tighter integration of the video capability into authoring software. For example, MEDIAscript OS/2, which has DVI Technology tightly built-in, can provide fractional-second response times for playing video. The solution to this is either substantially faster PCs, which will come in time, or getting more of the available hardware to be directly accessed by authoring programs. That also will come as the motion video hardware reaches greater penetration of the market.

On the software motion video side, the issues are different. In this case, the software is ahead of the hardware. Present software-only video plays too slowly in too-small windows—that is because the software is expecting too much from the machine. Over time, as faster machines come out and people buy them, this will be overcome. However, the cost to the end user will very likely be much higher than if he simply bought some digital motion video hardware, and it will take several years before fast enough PCs are available.

Unfortunately, I'm afraid that the PC market will not broadly choose the digital video hardware approach simply because it's too difficult to decide which hardware to buy. It's easier to wait until you can buy a super-fast PC that will do a good job with software motion video. Besides, for many other reasons, people will buy those super-fast machines anyway.

Regarding the subject of hardware platforms, many systems that are different from standard PCs are being introduced for other markets, especially the consumer market. These include the Philips CD-I and the 3DO player, both of which have motion video hardware. Because of this hardware proliferation, professional multimedia software developers are embracing the concept of *cross-platform development*, where applications are developed in a format that can be easily ported to other platforms. That way an investment in content and programming can be distributed to more users, even ones using a future new hardware platform. This is a software development strategy that recognizes the lack of a single-platform hardware standard and solves the problem in software. It is another example of the flexibility that is possible with well-conceived software approaches.

Digital Network Technology

Digital networks are widely used in large business organizations and universities. They facilitate sharing data among many users and give them access to centralized data as well. Subject to the limitations discussed in Chapter 14, this also applies to motion video and audio data. However, recognizing the needs of video and audio, network developers are addressing the limitations of speed and protocol to make improvements that will give better support to video and audio on the network. Expensive solutions are already available, and in the future we will see these features available at steadily reducing prices.

The *information superhighway* concept envisions the extension of digital networks into homes across the country. Telephone and cable TV companies are vying for the right to bring this service to every home. However, the economics are very complex, and the current media hype has extrapolated the possibilities way beyond what can actually happen in the next five years. It will happen, but not until the cost vs. performance of networking is advanced by several orders of magnitude.

MARKETS

Technology developments do not become valuable until they find a market. Markets are always looking for improvements and they will embrace the right new developments, but these are not necessarily the same as what the technologists are doing. If such a mismatch exists, technical developments will fail. Thus, we must study markets and what they want to see where things may go in the future.

The PC Market

With well over 100 million PCs in use worldwide, the PC market is definitely a force to be reckoned with. Those PCs are in industry, government, education, the military, and homes. Most of them are not powerful enough to use motion video and few are even equipped to use digital audio. So the market for video- and audio-capable PCs has barely been tapped. This is a vast opportunity for video and audio hardware and software, but its successful capture depends on several factors.

No one will buy video and audio add-ins or an entirely new PC for video and audio unless he knows what he will use those capabilities for. Since digital video and audio are recent arrivals in the market, most users have not even thought about their use in their own work or play—until now it was not even a choice. It takes high-visibility "flagship" applications to get people thinking about a new capability and how they might use it.

One very large example is the rapid introduction of thousands of CD-ROM titles that are runable only on audio/video equipped PCs. These fall mostly into two categories: games and information delivery. Both are valuable applications to certain people and even justify buying new equipment. However, they do not provide the same incentive for the mass of PC users who use their machines for word processing, graphics, databases, or other productivity applications.

In the business world, the flagship use of audio and video is in presentations—internal meetings, sales presentations, and corporate image presentations. However, these uses are specialized in terms of the majority of PCs used in business, and they do not justify wholesale replacement of equipment. For the special groups who are doing presentations that will be enhanced by audio and video, the appropriate hardware and software is being purchased as fast as budgets will allow.

The broader promulgation of audio/video capability in business PCs is coming in a different way. It comes because the capabilities are becoming so inexpensive that PC manufacturers are building them into all their new PCs. Thus, new PCs going into businesses very likely have CD-ROM, SVGA, and audio already installed. Over time, this will provide increasing numbers of platforms that businesses can use for various kinds of corporate communication purposes. It will make sense for general corporate information to be distributed on CD-ROM or via the company's digital network. Operations manuals, training programs, sales promotional information, and product documentation will all be digital and will use audio and video where applicable.

Another major market segment for PCs is education. Here, the value of audio and video in teaching has been well established, and presenting it by computer is recognized as the way of the future. However, it has not happened as fast as technology would support because of financial and managerial limitations in schools and, to a lesser degree, universities. By and large, the proof of the CBT approach has been made in industrial training, where training departments are buying equipment and building courseware as fast as they can afford to. In schools the acceptance has been slower, but it will continue to grow as cost reductions make the technology more and more irresistible.

The Consumer Market

As already mentioned, the consumer market (the home) is part of the PC market. However, it is much more than that because digital video and audio are becoming part of television or, saying it the other way, television is becoming digital and up until now, television has dominated the consumer market.

TV Broadcasting on the present channels will remain analog until past the turn of the century because of the vast infrastructure of transmitters and receivers in existence. However, HDTV will very likely be broadcast digitally and that will become a massive user of digital video technology. Because HDTV is a replacement technology that offers incremental improvements to users who already have TV, its acceptance will probably be slower than its developers would like, much as the acceptance of color TV took more than 10 years. But as HDTV is in the acceptance phase, there will be increased development of digital video technology, which should have a much quicker payoff to the PC market. This will just add to the digital video momentum on PCs.

Television is a passive technology as far as the user is concerned—he simply sits there and watches, with the only interactivity possible being to change channels. This is consistent with the widest use of television, which is entertainment, but it also works with classes of information delivery such as news. The normal viewing situation for TV is that the user sits some distance away, in comfortable seating. The large viewing ratio (4 or more) also allows multiple viewers to see the screen, which facilitates an entire family watching TV together.

Because of the wide acceptance of interactivity with personal computers, there have been proposals to make television interactive. The user would interact with the TV much as one does when playing a video game. Although the technology could support this, it is a mismatch to the viewing situation of normal TV because high interactivity requires that each viewer have his own display and that he sit close to it so that he can read text or see finely detailed images and graphics. I believe that consumers will accept interactivity, but they will not give up their normal TV viewing situation to get it. Therefore, I think interactive TV will not be a large success because personal computers can do it so much better and PCs will be in the home, too. Interactive services in the home will be PC-based.

The Information Superhighway

Further, as digital networking becomes available to homes, there will be new sources of digital video and audio to be viewed. There are many possibilities for the equipment that will fill this need. A grand view of digital networking to homes, schools, and businesses has been named the *information superhighway* by the Clinton administration in the United States. The media has picked up on this and made it appear that such a capability is just around the corner, pointing to the jockeying for position between cable TV companies, telephone companies, PC manufacturers, and TV manufacturers as proof. However, from the technological point of view, it's not just around the corner—unless you think 10 years is just around the corner! But it is coming, and it's not too soon to begin planning. In any case, as I said, I think the interactive viewing device will be a PC, regardless of who is delivering the service.

Standards

Designers generally view a standard as an impediment to creativity and marketeers generally view it as an advantage. Although I am an engineer, I side with the marketeers on this one. A standard is an opportunity for all vendors to address a larger market while competing within the framework set by the standard. There is no better example of this than the original IBM PC, which was condemned by designers everywhere as a backward step that would hold back the industry. In fact, exactly the opposite happened—the industry grew faster than anyone dreamed! IBM established the PC architecture and published it to everyone so that a much larger market developed than would have been possible with just one vendor, even IBM.

Standards are difficult to establish. When competing vendors are already in ther market with product, choosing a standard can give one vendor an unfair advantage, or it will hurt everyone equally. Usually the latter approach is taken, and the hurt is temporary because the total market eventually grows faster, but it can be fatal to a small start-up company that has few financial resources to survive even a temporary setback.

A better approach is to try to standardize before products come out. However, this is also difficult because it usually means that vendors must reveal the details of what they have in development; after all, there has to be some input of technical information before the standardizing process can even begin. There also has to be a forum for the standards discussion, where company representatives can talk freely and publically so there will be no anti-trust repercussions. This generally happens within some existing industry organization. What such groups usually do is try to agree on a standard that will apply some time in the future, by which time the vendors would come out with new products or updates. That way, current product is not obsoleted overnight.

Digital video is at the stage where multiple vendors are entering the market and widely accepted standards have not been settled. The MPEG initiative has completed the MPEG-1 standard, but that is very compute-intensive and requires dedicated hardware support, so it does not apply to the part of the market that wants software-only video. Individual manufacturers have come out with various algorithms, often more than one per company, indicating that even within a single company they could not agree on one standard.

Since we are talking about software, it is a possibility to use the flexibility of software to make a system that can accomodate multiple standards. That is what has been done in both Windows and OS/2—those systems are designed to accomodate installable algorithms. Anyone who puts his algorithm into the installable format can run it on any system. If you have all the algorithms installed in you system, you do not need a "standard."

I think the situation will stay that way for the PC software-only video market. However, the consumer market has a greater need for standards, and this is where MPEG will be important. As low-cost MPEG hardware is developed for consumer use, it will also be adapted for PC use. Of course, there also will be the HDTV standard and that definitely has to be a single one to allow the lowest cost receivers to be built. Eventually, though, everything will be programmable anyway (even in the consumer market), and the PC installable algorithm approach seems to be a satisfactory solution that allows for continued product improvement.

CONCLUSION

The preceding discussion presents many of the issues about how (not if) digital motion video capability will grow in the future. No matter how you look at it, we are embarked on a course that leads to more and better computer motion video and audio. The opportunity is there for those who begin now to utilize this exciting capability.

Appendix A
Video and Audio Technical Data

This appendix gives additional technical details on some subjects that I covered lightly in the text. It is intended for those readers with technical backgrounds who want more technical information.

DISPLAY SCANNING

As explained in Chapter 2, computer displays usually use progressive scanning while television employs interlaced scanning. This difference exists because of the need to make a tradeoff between the visual flicker effect and bandwidth in television systems. A scanned display relies on the *persistence of vision* effect in the human eye to prevent the movement of the scanning spot being seen. However, if the vertical refresh rate is too low, the eye will see flicker in the display. The visibility of flicker also depends on the image brightness (it is easier to see flicker when a display is brighter) but for normal computer displays that are progressively scanned, flicker will show if the vertical refresh rate is below about 60 Hz.

The designers of television systems also faced this problem and wanted to keep the refresh rate at 60 Hz or higher. However, because television is transmitted over the air, the availability of frequency spectrum space for a number of TV channels posed another limitation. With television's 525 or 625 scanning lines, using progressive scanning at 60 Hz vertical rate would require video bandwidths of 8 to 10 MHz. That would have limited the number of channels for broadcasting to a number that was judged to be too low. (Today's proliferation of TV stations and cable channels proves how true that judgment was.)

Then the TV designers came up with the idea of interlaced scanning, where each vertical refresh scanned only half of the total lines. It would then take two scans (called *fields*) to display all the lines in a frame. One field scanned the odd-numbered lines in the frame and the next scan did the even-numbered lines. If the vertical refresh rate is kept at 60 Hz, going to interlacing cuts the horizontal scanning rate in half, which means half the bandwidth. In a sense, it is a video compression technique. Interlacing allows a TV signal to be broadcast in a 6 MHz total channel, including the sound.

The interlaced TV display does not show flicker because adjacent lines in a TV image are often similar and at normal TV viewing distances (with viewing ratios of 4:1 or higher), the eye does not see that each line is actually being displayed at 30 per second. So interlacing works because TV images usually don't have a lot of vertical detail and we sit too far away from the screen to see it anyway.

In a computer display, the viewing ratio is much smaller (2:1 or less), and there is often a lot of fine detail in text and graphics. Since all pixels in a computer display are independently controllable by the CPU, fine horizontal (or nearly horizontal) lines and sharp horizontal edges are common. The user sits close enough to the display that she can see them, too. Thus the compromises that let interlacing work in TV break down for computer displays. Although some computers have interlaced scanning modes, they are unsatisfactory for most purposes and you should avoid them.

In fact, as TV image quality is being improved, the interlace flicker problem is getting worse. Therefore, some high-end receivers already are using digital memory to store the interlaced image being broadcast. That allows the actual display to be progressively scanned at 60 Hz or higher by reading out the memory at a different rate than it is being written. The result is that interlace flicker is eliminated.

The human eye is more sensitive to flicker effects when they occur in peripheral vision. A TV screen will be seen to flicker when viewed out of the corner of your eye. At the small viewing ratios for computer display, part of the screen may be in peripheral vision and will flicker unless the refresh rate is made higher than 60 Hz. For that reason, current practice in SVGA displays is to run the refresh rate up to 70 or 75 Hz.

THE NTSC COLOR SYSTEM

The developers of color television faced a video compression problem much like the one we have today on personal computers. They wanted to transmit color TV in the same channel that presently served only monochrome TV. Since color TV theoretically requires three monochrome channels (red, green, and blue), a 3:1 compression ratio was needed compared to monochrome TV, which is already slightly compressed via interlaced scanning. The necessary compression for color was obtained by combining two analog techniques: reduced color bandwidth and frequency interleaving.

Color theorists knew that the human eye could not discern as much detail in color as it could in monochrome. This fact could be used to reduce the bandwidth for transmitting the color information (only), thereby reducing the total bandwidth required. But first, the color and monochrome information in the RGB color signals had to be separated. That was accomplished by creating a luminance signal by adding up the correct proportions of the R, G, and B signals, which are

```
Y = 0.30 R + 0.59 G + 0.11 B
```

This luminance signal, called the *Y* signal, contains only the *brightness* values perceived by the eye.

The color information could then be isolated by subtracting the luminance value from the original color signals to obtain *color difference signals*. These signals then represent the color information alone (*chrominance*). Note that only two color difference signals are required since the original RGB signals can be represented by the correct combination of only three signals (the luminance being one of them). The exact color difference signals used in NTSC television were selected by taking into account that the eye also has different perception capability for different colors. One signal was chosen to contain the colors of maximum perception and the other was chosen for the colors of least perception. The exact equations for the NTSC color difference signals are

```
I = 0.60 R - 0.28 G - 0.32 B
Q = 0.21 R - 0.52 G + 0.31 B
```

These signals are called *I* and *Q,* respectively. (The meanings of those letters will come later.)

Because the eye does not perceive high resolution in color, the bandwidths of both I and Q signals can be reduced to 1.5 MHz and 0.5 MHz respectively, without the viewer seeing much loss of resolution. The Y signal remains at full bandwidth and it provides the sharpness content of the picture.

The second technique used by NTSC television is called *frequency interleaving*, which is based on the spectral characteristics of a typical monochrome TV signal. The horizontal lines of the scanning raster are a form of sampling for picture components in the vertical direction. This causes the frequency content of a video signal to be clustered around the harmonics (multiples) of the line scanning frequency. Halfway between the line scanning harmonics are gaps in spectral energy, leaving places where another similarly sampled signal could be interleaved with minimum interference. This is where the color components are placed.

To obtain correct interleaving, the I and Q color components are modulated on a *color subcarrier* whose frequency is precisely set to accomplish the interleaving. In the NTSC standard, that frequency is exactly 455/2 times the line frequency of 15,734.26 Hz, giving 3,579,545 Hz. *Suppressed-carrier* modulation is used so that if there is no color information present, there will be no subcarrier energy. As a region of the picture becomes more highly colored, the subcarrier energy increases in that region. The I and Q signals are both modulated on the same carrier, but at different phases of the carrier; they are separated in the receiver by phase detection. Hence, *I* stands for *in-phase* and *Q* stands for *quadrature*.

Because of the interleaving and also because the subcarrier frequency is near the high end of the monochrome spectrum, the subcarrier components are actually not very visible in monochrome pictures. Thus, we have a color system that transmits all its information in one monochrome TV channel yet the signal still works on monochrome receivers—it is *compatible*. For more information about the NTSC system, refer to the Bibliography.

The NTSC color television system was a brilliant development for its time, as attested by it still being the world's most widely used color TV system—over 40 years later! Some of the principles of NTSC are applicable to digital video compression; for example, color bandwidth reduction, which is now called *color subsampling*. We can only hope that the HDTV system now being developed will be as successful as NTSC.

THE PAL COLOR SYSTEM

The European countries developed their color TV system some years after NTSC was designed, and they had the benefit of the early operating experience with NTSC to create an improved design in some ways. Their system, PAL, embodies the same principles discussed for NTSC, but it goes farther to reduce some important operational problems with NTSC. One problem is that analog circuits transmitting the NTSC composite signal can introduce phase and amplitude distortions into the color subcarrier components. This causes undesired changes in the color tint and color saturation of NTSC color pictures. All NTSC receivers have controls to adjust these parameters (usually called *tint* and *color* controls.) However, constant need for adjustment of these controls is not practical—broadcast stations must carefully control distortions to maintain consistent signal performance. In the early days, that was extremely difficult to do.

The PAL system utilizes the *phase-alternating line* principle to cancel first-order phase and amplitude distortions of the color components. The acronym *PAL* comes from this technique. The result is that PAL receivers do not need tint and color controls, and it is somewhat easier to maintain color quality in a PAL broadcasting system. Note, however, in the 30 years since PAL was designed, the difficulties with maintaining color quality in NTSC systems have been overcome with good engineering, and it is no longer a problem.

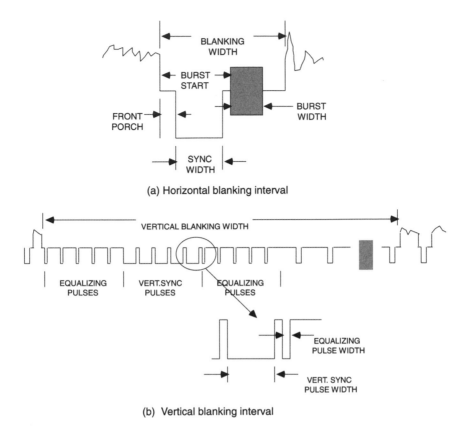

(a) Horizontal blanking interval

(b) Vertical blanking interval

Figure A.1 Typical NTSC television signal waveforms

BLANKING INTERVALS

Video signals allow a period of time at the end of each line and field scan so that the scanning spot can be returned to the starting position for the next line or field. These periods are called horizontal and vertical *blanking intervals*. In existing television systems, the blanking intervals represent a significant portion of the time: 18% for horizontal blanking and 6% for vertical blanking. This is necessary for retrace of analog scanning devices, but it is also utilized for transmission of synchronizing information and other auxiliary classes of data, such as time codes and test signals. Figure A.1 shows the waveform parameters of NTSC television signals; this is typical of all TV systems. The enlargement of horizontal blanking shows the horizontal sync pulse for synchronizing the horizontal scan and the color burst for synchronizing the color subcarrier in a receiver. Similarly, the vertical blanking interval contains vertical sync pulses, which are chopped up at twice the horizontal rate to maintain horizontal synchronization throughout the vertical sync on both fields of interlaced scanning. The vertical blanking interval is 20 lines long, and some of the lines after the sync pulses can be used to transmit test signals, time codes, or other forms of data.

Digital video transmission systems do not need such long blanking intervals because the necessary retrace times for physical display can be obtained by appropriately reading the data from memory during display. Typically a digital system includes a description of the data structure in a header at the start of the file or data stream and then the data is packed as tightly as possible.

CAMERA RESOLUTION

Resolution is expressed either in *pixels* or in *TV lines per picture height* depending on the type of camera pickup device, and it relates to how well the camera can see closely spaced objects or sharp edges. In general, resolution behavior differs for objects that are closely spaced horizontally (horizontal resolution) compared to objects that are closely spaced vertically (vertical resolution). This is because of the multiple-line scanning pattern usually used. In standard TV cameras, scanning follows a horizontal line pattern starting at the top of the image plane and continues with repeated lines that are placed below the previous line until the pattern reaches the bottom of the image plane. Then the scanning jumps (*retraces*) to the top of the image and starts over. The multiple line pattern introduces a sampling process into reproduction of vertically spaced objects; this does not exist for horizontally spaced objects. Sampling means that the reproduction occurs as an equally spaced series of discrete values rather than as a continuously varying analog signal. All cameras are sampled in the direction perpendicular to the line scans, but they can be either analog or sampled along a scanning line. The following discussion applies to the resolution behavior along a scanning line.

Camera pickup devices are either electron beam-scanned vacuum tubes or solid-state sensor arrays. These behave quite differently for many of the aspects of measurement, so they will be covered separately in much of this discussion.

Because solid-state camera resolution is a little easier to understand, let's take that first. A solid-state camera contains an array of equally spaced individual sensing spots or pixels in its image plane. For example, a particular camera may have an array of 400 pixels horizontally by 300 pixels vertically—this would be called a 400 × 300 array. When the camera is scanned, each pixel along each horizontal line delivers its output in sequence, creating a video signal. The output from each pixel is an analog voltage that represents the accumulated amount of light that has fallen on that pixel since the last time it was scanned. Therefore, we get a video signal that is analog in amplitude, but it is sampled in time.

A solid-state camera cannot distinguish more than one value for each pixel. Thus, a small point of light will be reproduced in the video signal as a whole pixel in size, so the width (or height) of a single pixel is the smallest feature that a sampled camera can distinguish. The camera mentioned earlier that has 400 pixels horizontally will have an ultimate precision of 1/400th of the image plane width, or 0.25%. This is the maximum performance, a practical camera will also be affected by many of the other effects that will be mentioned, reducing its performance from the maximum. Today, solid-state image sensors are available with array dimensions ranging from 300 pixels to about 2,000 pixels. The smaller sizes are most prevalent and are low cost because they are used for high-volume television cameras. Larger array sizes above about 700 pixels are made for professional cameras and can become very expensive.

Tube cameras use an electron-beam scanned photoelectric surface in a vacuum tube, such as a vidicon or one of its many relatives. The resolution in these devices is limited by the size of the scanning electron-beam spot and the tendency of the charge pattern to spread on the photoelectric surface. Resolution performance is often specified by quoting TV lines per picture height (TVL), which is the maximum number of equally spaced black and white lines that can be distinguished across a distance corresponding to the height of the image plane. Typical numbers range from 300 to 800 TVL. However, you cannot directly compare TVL numbers to the pixel count numbers in a solid-state camera, because the TVL number is a *limiting* resolution number, representing a line pattern that you can barely see in the reproduction. The limiting resolution is reproduced with a very low contrast, often less than 10%, whereas a solid-state camera will theoretically reproduce adjacent black and white pixels at 100% contrast. Thus, a 400-TVL tube camera will not produce as sharp a picture as a 400-pixel solid-state camera.

But another difference between tube and solid-state cameras somewhat offsets the apparent differences in sharpness. If you take a small point of light and move it slowly across the image field, the solid-state camera will reproduce the spot as jumping from one pixel to the next. As I've already said, it cannot tell the position of a spot more closely than the width of one pixel. This is most clearly seen when reproducing a near-vertical line. The reproduction will show a jagged line as the horizontal position jumps from one discrete pixel position to the next while the line scanning moves down the screen. This effect is called *aliasing*, and it is an inherent result of the sampled nature of the solid-state camera. Aliasing can be reduced or even removed by partially defocusing the optical image presented to the sensor array and appropriately controlling the bandwidth in the video circuits (called *filtering*); however, this is difficult to do well and it may worsen the effect of noise.

Performing the same moving spot or near-vertical line test on a tube camera will show the spot or line reproduced wider than it really is, but it will move smoothly in position and show no aliasing. This is because the tube camera has no discrete pixel pattern that limits the precision with which it can represent position.

All cameras show aliasing on horizontal or near-horizontal lines because of the sampling caused by line scanning. This can also be reduced by filtering before scanning, but that is difficult to accomplish. Older tube cameras did not have this problem because the electron-beam scanning spot was wider than one line—this introduced the necessary filtering.

VIDEO SIGNAL BANDWIDTH

The theoretical resolution limits in the sensor devices was explained already. However, practical cameras also include video amplifiers and processing circuits to bring out the video signal so it can be passed to other devices. Any video circuit has a bandwidth specification, which is the highest frequency that the circuit can pass without loss. Typical bandwidth numbers for TV-scan cameras are between 4 MHz and 10 MHz. For standard TV scanning, there is a fixed relationship between the TVL resolution and the required bandwidth: each 80 TVL require 1 MHz of bandwidth. Therefore, a camera with a resolution of 480 TVL needs a bandwidth of *at least* 480/80 = 6 MHz. It usually will not hurt to have more bandwidth than the minimum.

IMAGE FILE FORMATS

Image files have been around almost since the start of personal computing. During that time many formats have been developed, and quite a few are still in use. This causes a significant problem when moving files between different programs, giving rise to a market for file conversion utilities. The most important image file formats are described here:

Tagged image file format (.tif)—TIFF is one of the most popular and most flexible bitmapped image file formats. Nearly all applications support it. However, it has many variations, and few applications support them all. For this reason many programs ask you to specify the target application when saving an image, to make sure you will get a variation that the target application can handle.

Targa format (.tga, .win)—This bitmapped format was originally developed by Truevision, Inc. for use with its TARGA true color family of boards. Because it was one of the first true color formats for the PC, it is still widely used for 16-bpp, 24-bpp, and 32-bpp bitmapped images.

Bitmap formats (.bmp)—Both OS/2 and Windows have .bmp formats, but they are not the same. For either 4-bpp or 8-bpp formats, the image can be compressed or uncompressed; it also handles up to 24-bpp images uncompressed only.

PC Paintbrush format (.pcx)—This bitmapped format was developed by Z-Soft Corporation for their PC paint programs (PC Paintbrush, etc.). It is widely used and supports most bpp values, with or without palettes.

Windows metafile format (.wmf)—A *metafile* format combines both vector and bitmapped components in an image. WMF is used by many Windows draw programs.

Encapsulated PostScript format (.eps)—The PostScript language was originally developed for use with laser printers. It is a metafile format, having both bitmapped and vector components.

Graphics Interchange Format (.gif)—This format is CompuServe's standard for bitmapped images. It supports 4-bpp and 8-bpp images with palettes.

Device-Independent Bitmap (.dib)—This is a format developed by Microsoft for display on a variety of display systems (devices).

Computer Graphics Metafile (.cgm)—This is a metafile standard supported by the American National Standards Institute (ANSI). It is widely used in the publishing, CAD, and graphics markets.

DVI formats (.a9, .a16, .avs)—DVI Technology has several formats that embody its unique compression methods. The a9 format (sometimes called *im9* or *cm9*) is for images that are in DVI Technology's unique "9-bpp" compressed format. Similarly, a16 (or c16 and i16) is for 16-bpp images, compressed or uncompressed. The .avs format is a general format for DVI video data that can contain any combination of still images, motion video, and audio in any of the DVI formats.

Nearly all tools that are involved with graphics or images support several image file formats. This is usually handled in menu items called *Export* and *Import*, although in some cases it will be in the Save As and Open menus. It will be most convenient for you if the image tools you select support the file types you have to deal with. (The other side of this is to try to control the image file types to match the tools you have.) However, the standards for image files are not very good, and there are sometimes small differences between the same standard implemented by two different tools.

Appendix B

Sources of Hardware and Software

This appendix lists some sources of digital video and audio hardware and software.

THE ULTIMEDIA TOOLS SERIES

The IBM Ultimedia Tools Series is a comprehensive source for multimedia authoring software. Managed by IBM, it is a competitive mail order marketing operation with several different twists—it specializes in multimedia authoring tools only, and it has a vision of an authoring environment where all the tools work smoothly together. All the tools it markets have been qualified against a set of specifications for that vision. More than 90 tools are in the series, from over 30 vendors (including IBM). In addition, it sells the IBM multimedia hardware, including ActionMedia II, CD-ROM drives, and audio and video add-in boards.

Buying software is a risky business because you often cannot try out software before you buy it. The Ultimedia Tools Series has attacked that problem by offering a Sampler CD-ROM disc that contains product information, demonstrations, and *working models* for most of the products. Of course the working models are limited in some ways, but they provide an excellent means for you to try out the product before you commit to buying it. In the list that follows, I will not repeat references to the companies whose products are in the Tools Series, but I will list other companies whose products have been mentioned in the book.

You may contact the IBM Ultimedia Tools Series at

IBM Ultimedia Tools Series
1055 Joaquin Road
Mountain View, CA 94043
1 800 887-7771 (Voice)
1 800 887-7772 (Fax)

OTHER SOURCES OF DIGITAL VIDEO TOOLS

The following list includes hardware and software vendors whose products are mentioned in this book. Contact information is given for each company along with a list of the relevant products.

Intel Corporation
DVI Technology, *ActionMedia II*, *Smart Video Recorder*, *Indeo*
1-800-548-4725

Aldus Corporation
PhotoStyler
411 First Avenue South
Seattle, WA 98104-2871
1-800-685-3569
1-206-622-5500

Corel Systems
CorelDRAW
1-800-772-6735 x23

Creative Labs, Inc.
Sound Blaster products
1-800-998-5227
1-408-428-6600

Media Vision, Inc.
Pro Audio Spectrum 16, *Pocket Recorder*
3185 Laurelview Court
Fremont, CA 94538
1-800-845-5870

Microsoft
Windows 3.1, *Windows NT*, *Windows for Workgroups*, *PowerPoint*, *Video for Windows*, *Visual Basic*
1-800-426-9400

Software Publishing Corp.
Harvard Graphics
1-800-336-8360

Lotus Development Corp.
FreeLance Graphics
55 Cambridge Parkway
Cambridge, MA 02142

Inset Systems
Hijaak PRO
1-800-374-6738

CrystalGraphics, Inc.
Flying Fonts
Santa Clara, CA 95054

Touchvision Systems, Inc.
CineWorks, D/Vision PRO
1800 Winnemac Ave.
Chicago, IL 60640
1-800-838-4746

Autodesk, Inc.
3D Studio, Animator Pro
1-800-879-4233

Panasonic Broadcast & Television Systems
Camera, VCR, and editing equipment
One Panasonic Way
Secaucus, NJ 07094
1-800-524-0864

Asymetrix Corporation
ToolBook, Multimedia ToolBook
1-800-671-3951

AimTech Corporation
IconAuthor
20 Trafalgar Square
Nashua, NH 03063
1-800-289-2884

Network Technology Corp.
MEDIAscript, MEDIAscript OS/2
Dobbs Ferry, NY 10522-0240
1-914-478-4500

Yamaha Corporation
Music and audio equipment
1-800-932-0001

Midisoft Corporation
Studio for Windows
PO Box 1000
Bellevue, WA 98009
1-206-881-7176

Turtle Beach Systems
Wave for Windows
PO Box 5074
York, PA 17405
1-800-645-5640

Microtek Lab, Inc.
Scanmaker image scanners
3715 Doolittle Dr.
Redondo Beach, CA 90278-1226
1-310-297-5000

Appendix C

Using the Reference CD-ROM

This appendix gives you instructions for setting up the Reference CD-ROM on your Windows or OS/2 system. In either case, all you have to do is copy a few files to your hard drive and set up a program object on your desktop. This will enable an information presentation application that displays the appropriate one of the GUIDEWIN.INF or the GUIDEOS2.INF files. These files contain detailed information about the contents of the disc and how to use it. The application that displays them looks similar to the help windows in your other OS/2 or Windows programs. Before proceeding with installation, you should look at the README.TXT file in the root directory of the CD, which may contain additional information. This file can be read with any text editor.

SETTING UP UNDER WINDOWS

Windows should be Version 3.1 or later. You can do the necessary file copy operation from a DOS prompt, from a DOS screen in Windows, or from the Windows File Manager. You have to create a directory for the files somewhere on your hard disk; you can call it \REFCD or any other name that suits you. Then access your CD drive and copy the contents of the \GUIDEWIN directory to \REFCD on your hard drive. For example, if your CD drive is E: and your hard drive is C:, the command line under DOS would be

```
COPY E:\GUIDEWIN\*.* C:\REFCD
```

The rest of the process must be done from the Windows Program Manager. Pull down the File menu and select the New item. In the resulting dialog box, select Program Item and click on OK. This will bring up the Program Items Properties dialog shown in Figure C-1. Fill in that dialog as shown in the figure, substituting drive letters and your directory name as necessary for your situation. The complete command line does not show in the figure. It is

```
C:\REFCD\XVIEW.EXE C:\REFCD\GUIDEWIN.INF
```

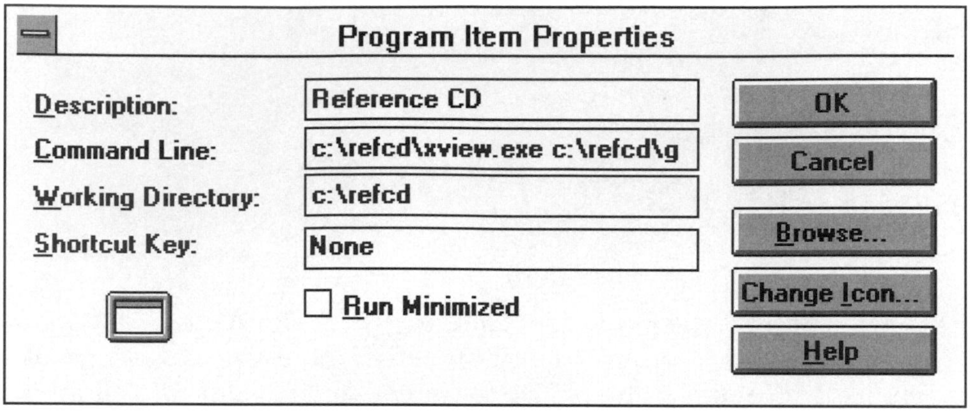

```
┌─────────────────────────────────────────────────────────────┐
│ [─]            Program Item Properties                        │
├─────────────────────────────────────────────────────────────┤
│ Description:      [Reference CD              ]      [  OK  ]  │
│ Command Line:     [c:\refcd\xview.exe c:\refcd\g]  [Cancel]  │
│ Working Directory: [c:\refcd                 ]               │
│ Shortcut Key:     [None                      ]     [Browse...]│
│                                                               │
│        [  ]       ☐ Run Minimized               [Change Icon...]│
│                                                    [ Help ]   │
└─────────────────────────────────────────────────────────────┘
```

Figure C-1 The Window Program Properties dialog for the Reference CD item.

When you click on OK, a new program object will be placed in the program group that was open when you started this process. All you have to do now is double-click on the new icon and the information file will appear.

You can explore the information file to get a feel for what is on the CD and how to use it. Thumbnail pictures of many of the items are there. The information file also describes the tool programs on the disc, which are mostly shareware applications, and explains their installation procedures. You can examine many of the data items in more detail using audio, video, or animation players that are already in your operating system.

SETTING UP UNDER OS/2

OS/2 should be Version 2.1 with MMPM/2 or later. The OS/2 installation procedure is a little simpler because the program files for viewing are already in the OS/2 directories. You just have to set up a directory on your hard drive and copy the file \GUIDEOS2\GUIDEOS2.INF from the CD to that directory. You can do that from an OS/2 window with the commands

```
MD C:\REFCD
COPY E:\GUIDEOS2\GUIDEOS2.INF C:\REFCD
```

Then you create a new program object on the OS/2 desktop by dragging a Program template from the Templates folder in the OS/2 System folder. The Settings notebook for the new object will automatically open as shown in Figure C-2. Fill in the path, file name, and the parameters as shown. You can also go to the General page of the notebook and enter the name that will appear for the

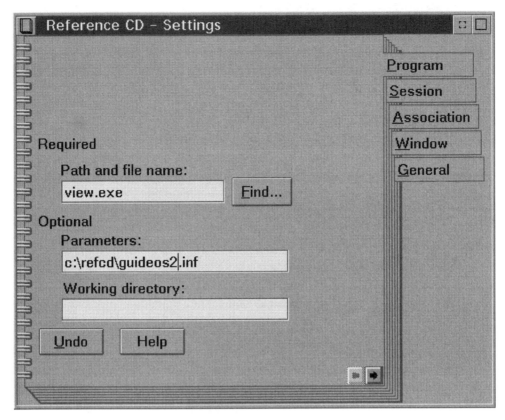

Figure C-2 The OS/2 Settings notebook for the program object that displays the Reference CD information file.

object on the desktop. Then close the settings notebook by double-clicking on the upper left corner of the window.

The contents of the OS/2 information document are exactly the same as the Windows one. You can explore it to view the contents of the disc and how to use them.

Glossary

A/B roll In audio or video editing, a process where two separate tapes (A and B) are made that contain alternate segments of the final sequence. These are run simultaneously and a final edit is made by electronically switching between them and recording the result onto a third tape.

accelerator A hardware unit that assists the CPU to speed up a particular process. For example, a graphics accelerator speeds up the processing and display of graphics.

access time in digital storage devices, the time it takes to retrieve the first bytes of the desired segment.

active line in television or other video display systems, the portion of a horizontal line scanning interval that is visible on the displayed screen.

actor (in animation) *See* animated cel

adaptive differential PCM (ADPCM) A compression technique that depends on the incoming data not changing too much from one sample to the next. As a result, fewer bits can be used to represent the changes between samples than it would take to code the samples themselves. ADPCM is used for audio compression, where it can deliver up to 4:1 compression.

ADC *See* analog to digital converter

additive color system A color reproduction system in which an image is displayed by mixing appropriate amounts of red, green, and blue lights. It is the color system used by color television and computer displays.

ADPCM *See* adaptive differential PCM

ADR *See* automatic dialog replacement

algorithm A group of processing steps that perform a particular operation, such as drawing a line or compressing a digital image.

aliasing An effect caused by the visibility of individual pixels on sharply defined edges in a digital picture. It shows as jagged edges that are particularly troublesome on diagonal lines or text characters.

ambience track In audio production, a track that contains background or surrounding sounds for the location; for example, wind and animal noises in a forest or the crowd noise at a baseball game.

amplitude In electrical signals, the parameter of signal strength. For example, in audio, amplitude equates to loudness; in video, it equates to brightness.

analog Pertains to a system in which values are represented by continuous scales.

analog production Production (audio and/or video) where analog recording devices are used.

analog to digital conversion (ADC) The process of creating a digital representation of an analog signal (also called *digitization*).

animated cel A cel that contains multiple frames to be played sequentially when the cel is displayed in an animation. For example, a man walking is shown by a sequence of frames that depict the motion of one complete step; repeating this sequence while moving the cel produces the effect of walking.

animation A process for creating artificial video where the computer calculates or assembles the content of each frame for display.

anti-aliasing A process that reduces the visibility of the aliasing effect on edges by modifying pixels around the edge with intermediate colors between the light and dark colors making up the edge.

API *See* application programming interface

application A computer program written for a specific purpose.

application programming interface (API) The means whereby an application communicates with the system software. An API is usually specified in terms of one or more computer languages, such as C or Pascal.

artifact An unnatural element in the reproduction of a natural image or sound. It is a distortion that interferes with the proper reproduction of the original.

assembly In multimedia authoring, the process of bringing together all the content elements and the user interface to create a complete application or presentation.

audio–video interleaving (AVI) In digital video files, the practice of placing together the audio and video data for each block of time, such as a video frame—1/30th second.

authoring The process of creating a multimedia application program, including planning, media creation, assembly, testing, and distribution.

automatic dialog replacement (ADR) The process of producing a dialog track in a studio by having the actor repeat his dialog while watching video of the scene. ADR is used when satisfactory audio cannot be captured while the scene is being shot, usually because of ambient noises or inaccessibility of microphones to the actors.

AVI *See* audio–video interleaving

balanced audio cables Balanced cables (for audio) use two signal conductors and one shield. The signal conductors carry the same signal, but of opposite polarity; the two are combined at the receiving end. The result is that many types of interference picked up by the cables get cancelled out when the signals are combined, giving higher quality transmission.

bandwidth Refers to the range of frequencies contained in a signal or to the frequency-handling range of a transmission circuit.

basic input/output system (BIOS) A software module built into the computer hardware (usually as ROM). It provides the first level of software interface between the hardware and an operating system.

BIOS *See* basic input/output system

bit The fundamental unit of digital data. Its value can be either 0 or 1.

bitmap A region of memory or storage that contains the pixels representing an image arranged in the sequence in which they are scanned to display the image.

bits per pixel (bpp) The number of bits used to represent the color value of each pixel in a digitized image.

bits per sample (bps) In a sampling process, the number of bits used to represent the value of each sample.

blanking interval In a television signal or other video signal, the time interval between individual line scans or frame scans. Blanking intervals allow time for the scanning retrace in cameras or display devices, and they are also used for transmission of synchronizing information in composite signals.

bpp *See* bits per pixel

bps *See* bits per sample

bus In a computer system, the means for interconnecting the various units of hardware, such as the CPU, RAM, mass storage, etc.

byte A digital value represented by eight bits. A byte can represent integer values between 0 and 255.

cache A region of memory in a computer that is used to temporarily store a block of data retrieved from mass storage. In case the CPU needs to access the same area of mass storage again, it first looks in the cache because that will be accessed much faster than another access to mass storage.

camcorder A unit that combines a video camera and a video recorder.

capture The process of bringing video or audio signals into a digital system. It normally requires conversion to a digital format and storing in the mass storage of the digital system.

cathode-ray tube (CRT) The electron beam-scanned display tube commonly used for television and computer displays.

CBT *See* computer-based training

CCD *See* charge-coupled device

CD-ROM *See* compact disc read-only memory

cel In animation, a single object that moves in the animation. Cels originally were hand-drawn on transparent celluloids that were placed in front of a background for filming one frame at a time. In computer animation, cels are bitmap objects that are used the same way.

central processing unit (CPU) The unit that performs system control and computing in a personal computer. The CPU is usually a single microprocessor chip.

channel In television broadcasting or cable TV, the path of transmission for a single TV signal.

charge-coupled device (CCD) A solid-state video camera pickup device for converting optical images to electrical signals. CCDs are very popular for their high performance, stability, and reliability.

chroma keying In television production, the process of placing one image over a second (background) image by making areas of the first image be transparent in the combining process. A specific color (often blue) is used to define the transparent areas.

chrominance In color video systems, signal components that convey the color information; usually in the form of color-difference signals.

clapboard A device used in video production that combines a slate displaying information about each shot along with a mechanical device that makes an audio sound (a clap). The clapboard is held in front of the camera and clapped during the initial recording run-in for each shot. It provides a synchronized aural and video identification of the shot.

clip art library A collection of vector drawings or bitmapped images that can be selected, modified, and combined to create screens for an application or presentation. The same library approach is often also used with audio, video, or animations.

clip media A clip library for any type of medium, such as audio, video, images, animation, or artwork.

clock frequency In a microprocessor, the frequency at which the internal circuits run. For microprocessors of the same type, a higher clock frequency will give faster performance.

CLUT *See* color lookup table

color difference signals In a color video system, signals that contain only color information. This is achieved by subtracting their luminance values.

color lookup table (CLUT) In color display systems, a technique that stores a table of color values, which is read out to display each pixel using the pixel value as an index. The table may be loaded with color values in up to 24-bpp format, while the index value (and thus the pixels) may be only 8 bpp.

compact disc read-only memory (CD-ROM) A digital data version of the audio CD (Compact Disc). The CD-ROM can be inexpensively replicated and holds up to 680 megabytes of data. Because it is read-only, the data cannot be changed by the user.

compiler A computer program that converts a program written in a high-level language into the microprocessor instructions that will perform the tasks represented by the language statements.

component video A color video signal system that uses more than one signal to describe a color image. Typical component systems are RGB or S-video.

composite video A color video signal system that contains all of the color information encoded into one signal. Typical composite television systems are NTSC, PAL, and SECAM.

compression A digital process that allows data to be stored or transmitted using fewer than the normal number of bits. For example, *video compression* refers to techniques that reduce the number of bits required to store or transmit images or motion video.

computer-based training (CBT) The use of a computer to deliver programmed one-on-one personal training.

contouring In digital video systems that cannot display enough colors, an artifact called *contouring* becomes visible as the system abruptly switches from one color to the next when it tries to reproduce smooth color shading.

control track In a video recorder, a special recording track that helps the playback heads synchronize with the video tracks on the tape.

coprocessor A microprocessor that assists the main CPU for a specific task, such as floating-point math or video compression or decompression.

CPU *See* central processing unit

cropping In an image, the process of selecting and cutting out a partial area of the image.

cross-platform development In creating computer programs, the process of authoring a program on one platform, but in a form that will run on one or more different platforms.

CRT *See* cathode-ray tube

DAC *See* digital to analog converter

data transfer rate In a digital transmission or bus system, the rate at which data moves—usually expressed in megabytes per second (MB/sec).

DDE *See* dynamic data exchange

decibel A parameter that expresses the ratio between two like quantities as a logarithmic value. It is widely used to describe audio signal levels, where it refers to the actual level compared to a reference or standard level. Decibel is abbreviated dB.

decompression The process of restoring compressed data into its original uncompressed form.

delta frame In video compression, a delta frame is a frame whose reconstruction will depend on the previous frame (or sometimes the next frame in bidirectional compression)

depth of field In optical imaging, the range of distance over which the image stays in focus.

difference frame *See* delta frame

digital A system in which values are represented by groups of bits.

digital effects In a video system such as television, the use of digital technology to achieve dynamic transition effects such as zooming, sliding, or rotation.

digital production A production process for video and/or audio where the scene is captured directly to a digital data format.

digital to analog converter (DAC) A device that converts digital signals to analog. A DAC is used to convert the data going from a computer to a display monitor.

digital signal processor (DSP) A special form of programmable microprocessor designed to be most efficient at doing data processing tasks such as compression or decompression.

digitize To convert to digital, as in an analog to digital converter (ADC).

display accelerator A special-purpose integrated circuit that assists the CPU in performing display functions. Display accelerators are usually located on a video display adaptor board.

display memory The memory that holds the screen image for monitor refresh. It is usually located on the video display adaptor.

dissolve A video or audio transition where one signal drops in amplitude while a new signal increases in amplitude to achieve the transition. The effect is a temporary overlap of the signals as the first signal dissolves into the second signal.

distortion When transmitting or processing electrical signals, any undesirable changes to the signal due to spurious effects in the circuit or transmission path.

dithering In video display systems that have a limited number of colors, the effect of more colors can be achieved by dithering, which is alternation of colors among adjacent pixels. It works to the extent that the viewer does not see individual pixels, but rather his eye averages the dithered pixels to a different color.

DOS The original operating system for the IBM-compatible family of PCs. The name stands for *disk operating system*, and it is distributed by Microsoft. A compatible system called PC-DOS is distributed by IBM.

dot pitch In a computer display monitor, the size of an individual dot of color on the physical screen. For proper reproduction of an image, the dot pitch must be smaller than the size of a single pixel in the image.

driver A software entity that provides an interface to a specific piece of hardware. For example, a video driver provides software access to the video board hardware.

DSP *See* digital signal processor

DVI Technology A hardware and software system developed by Intel and IBM to add audio and motion video capability to personal computers. The hardware is marketed under the name *ActionMedia II*.

dynamic data exchange In multitasking operating systems, a means for communicating between concurrently running applications.

edit decision list (EDL) In audio or video postproduction, a list of commands and values that defines a series of edits to be made to assemble a scene.

EDL *See* edit decision list

effects track In audio production and postproduction, a track that contains sound effects elements.

EISA *See* extended integrated system architecture

emulation In computer software, a software model of a different environment that allows programs for that environment to run on the current machine. For example, a PC emulator for the Macintosh allows PC programs to run on a Macintosh.

encode *See* compression

environment The collection of hardware and software that performs a specified set of tasks for the user; for example, an authoring environment.

enhanced integrated system architecture (EISA) This is a high-performance 32-bit system bus.

fade In audio or video postproduction, a transition where one signal fades out to blank or silence followed by a second signal fading up to normal levels.

field In interlaced television systems, a field is one vertical scan period, typically scanning alternate lines of the complete image (frame). Thus, it takes two fields to scan the complete frame.

floating-point A data representation for numbers that uses a mantissa and exponent format. It is capable of representing decimal numbers with extreme precision.

font A definition for drawing a set of text characters. It may be either in the form of a bitmap for each character or a mathematical description of how to draw each character in the specific style of the font (a vector font).

frame A complete scan of an image. In interlaced systems, a frame is two vertical scans (fields). In noninterlaced or progressive-scan systems a frame is completed in one vertical scan. A frame is one complete image of a motion video sequence. In motion video, images are presented typically at 30 frames per second to create the illusion of continuous motion.

frame grabber A hardware add-in board that is capable of capturing and digitizing a frame from a real-time analog video stream.

frequency The repetition rate of a periodic process. Frequency is normally expressed in cycles per second, for which the engineering term is *Hertz*, abbreviated Hz.

frequency response In electrical circuits, the response of the circuit to a range of frequencies, usually expressed as a graph of amplitude vs. frequency.

gamma correction In image processing, the altering of the gray-scale rendition (amplitude linearity) to enhance one region of gray values relative to another region. For example, the black region may be stretched while the white region is compressed; this will enhance the visibility of detail in the black regions.

generation In audio or video recording, a generation is the complete process of recording and replaying the signal once. Many editing techniques require re-recording the signal several times, leading to multiple generations. In analog recording systems, this leads to accumulated degradation of the signal quality.

graphical user interface (GUI) A computer-user interface that combines a graphical screen capable of displaying graphics and images with a pointing device such as a mouse, which allows the user to move a pointer object on the screen. The user makes selections and issues commands by clicking the mouse button(s) while the pointer is over a graphic icon representing the desired task.

gray-scale test pattern A video test pattern consisting of a series of successively brighter areas going from black to white (or reverse). This pattern is used to test the amplitude linearity of a system.

GUI *See* graphical user interface

hard disk A mass storage device based on read/write magnetic recording on one or more rigid rotating disks.

HDTV *See* high-definition TV

Hertz (Hz) The unit of frequency—one Hertz is one cycle per second.

Hi-8 A high-quality VCR tape format based on the 8-mm tape size.

high color An alternate name for a color display system using 16 bits per pixel. Such a system can reproduce up to 65,536 unique colors.

high-definition TV (HDTV) The name for the next-generation TV standard being developed in the United States and many other countries. It offers higher resolution and a wider aspect ratio and is expected to be a digital system.

hypertext A text display system that provides highlighting of specific text words or phrases to indicate to the user that he can click on that item for additional information.

icon In a graphical user interface, a graphic or image that visually represents an object in the environment.

IDE *See* integrated disk electronics

IEC *See* International Electrotechnical Commission

image processing Techniques which manipulate the pixel values of an image for some particular purpose. Examples are: brightness or contrast correction, color correction, or changing size (scaling).

industry standard architecture (ISA) The 16-bit system bus introduced in the IBM PC/AT and now used as the basis for most IBM-compatible PCs.

information delivery The process of using a computer to provide the user with specific information. For example, a kiosk at a travel site that provides hotel, restaurant, and entertainment information for the surrounding area.

information superhighway The popular name given to the long-range plan to interconnect all businesses and homes with high-speed digital communications.

integrated disk electronics (IDE) The most common hard disk interface standard for ISA-bus computers.

International Electrotechnical Commission (IEC) An international standardizing body that is very active in the fields of audio and video.

interactivity The ability of a user to control the presentation by a multimedia system, not only for material selection, but for the way in which material is presented.

interface In computer software, a connection between two entities; for example, an application programming interface (API) is the software connection between an application program and the system software of a PC. Similarly, a user interface is the way that a user sees, hears, and controls a computer.

interpreter A form of computer program that reads a high-level language and converts it to computer instructions that are immediately executed.

ISA *See* industry standard architecture

Joint Photographic Expert Group (JPEG) A working party of the ISO IEC Joint Technical Committee 1, that developed standards for compression of still images, called the *JPEG standard*.

JPEG *See* Joint Photographic Expert Group

key frame In animation, a frame of data that is drawn independent of any other frames. Additional frames can be created between key frames by a process called *tweening*. This smoothes out the motion.

kilobyte 1024 (2^{10}) bytes.

kiosk A free-standing interactive computer system used for public access or information delivery.

lip-sync Refers to the process of achieving good enough audio/video synchronization that a talking head image looks correct.

local bus In a PC, a special bus that connects directly between the CPU and another unit (such as a video display adaptor) without going through the main system bus.

lossless compression When the result of compression followed by decompression is exactly the same as the original.

lossy compression When the result of compression followed by decompression is not the same as the original. Normally a lossy compression system will throw away data that the end user will not easily see or hear.

luminance In color video systems, a signal component that represents only the monochrome brightness values of the image.

mass storage Nonvolatile (permanent) storage used in a PC. Typically the mass storage is a magnetic hard disk, although floppy disk drives and optical drives are also used.

MCA *See* microchannel architecture

MCI *See* media control interface

media control interface (MCI) In multimedia computers, a device-independent software standard for communicating control information between applications and the system.

megabyte 1,048,576 (2^{20}) bytes.

megahertz A unit of frequency. One megahertz means that something is happening 1 million times per second.

memory The part of a computer that stores data to be processed by the microprocessor. It is usually composed of random-access memory chips, and is called RAM.

microchannel architecture (MCA) The bus design used in IBM PS/2 computers. It is a high-performance 32-bit bus.

MIDI *See* musical instrument digital interface

mixing In audio postproduction, the process of combining several tracks into an output track.

monitor A video display device.

motion compensation In video compression, the process of determining what parts of the picture have moved from one frame to the next. Only the parts that move need to be included in the data stream.

morphing A technique where the computer generates a sequence of frames that smoothly transforms one image into another.

Motion Picture Expert Group (MPEG) A working party of the ISO-IEC Joint Technical Committee 1, working on algorithm standardization for compression of motion video for use in many industries.

MPC *See* multimedia personal computer

MPEG *See* Motion Picture Expert Group

MS-DOS *See* DOS

multimedia In computers, the presentation of information or training by using audio, motion video, realistic still images, and computer metaphors.

multimedia personal computer (MPC) A PC that contains equipment for multimedia, such as audio, video, and CD-ROM hardware. Standards for MPCs are published by the Multimedia PC Marketing Council, an organization of PC manufacturers.

multitasking In a computer, a technique that allows several processes (programs) to appear to run simultaneously even though the computer has only one CPU. Multitasking is accomplished by sequentially switching the CPU between the tasks, usually many times per second.

multithreading In a multitasking computer system, multiple concurrent activities (threads) within a single process (program).

musical instrument digital interface (MIDI) A serial digital bus standard for interfacing of digital musical instruments. MIDI is widely used in the music industry.

National Television Systems Committee (NTSC) The standardizing body that in 1953 created the color television standards for the United States. This system is called the NTSC color television system.

network A system that connects multiple PCs and allows data sharing between them.

noise In electrical signals (audio or video), noise is a random fluctuation of signal value that is inherent to some degree in all analog circuits. In video images, noise is usually referred to as *snow* and, in audio it is called *hiss*.

nonlinear editing In conventional (linear) audio or video editing, one must rerecord the edited sequence every time a change or addition is made. In nonlinear editing with a computer, the edited sequence is stored as an edit decision list (EDL) that can be played at any time by using the random-access capabilities of the computer's mass storage to instantly retrieve and present audio and video.

NTSC *See* National Television Systems Committee

object linking and embedding (OLE) In multitasking operating systems, a means for sharing data between applications such that the user can access or edit the data from either application.

OLE *See* object linking and embedding

operating system In a personal computer, the core program that provides an API to applications for access to all of the hardware resources of the system. Typical operating systems are DOS and OS/2.

OS/2 A multitasking and multithreading operating system supported by IBM.

PAL *See* phase-alternating line

palette The collection of colors that can be simultaneously displayed on the screen. Some systems that have a limited number of palette entries because of a low bpp (such as 4 or 8 bpp) use a palette that can be customized from a larger array of colors. This is called a *color lookup* table (*See*). However, a single image or single screen still cannot have more colors than will fit into a single palette.

pattern In a microphone, the way that sensitivity depends on angle.

PC-DOS *See* DOS

PCI *See* peripheral connect interface

PCM *See* pulse code modulation

PCMCIA *See* PC Memory Card International Association

PC Memory Card International Association (PCMCIA) An association that produced standards for a plug-in card interface, primarily intended for portable computers. The PCMCIA interface can be used for memory or mass storage expansion, a modem, or other hardware peripherals.

peripheral connect interface (PCI) A local bus specifically designed for use with the Intel Pentium processor.

phase-alternating line The name of the color system used in most of Europe and other parts of the world. It was designed later than the NTSC system used in the United States and is similar but with some improvements.

pixel A single point of an image, having a single color value.

pixellation The effect produced when there are too few pixels for the size of the image. Pixels become visible as small rectangles or squares of color.

platform In computers, the base architecture of a computer system. Typical hardware platforms are IBM PC-compatible or Macintosh. However, the definition of platform also include the operating system, so an IBM-compatible running DOS is a different platform from the same hardware running OS/2.

postproduction In video or audio, the process of merging original video and audio from tape or film into a finished program. Postproduction includes editing, special effects, dubbing, titling, and many other video and audio techniques. You can do digital postproduction with a computer.

preemptive multitasking A multitasking system is *preemptive* if it is capable of interrupting any application regardless of what the application may be doing. This prevents a single application from ever hogging all the system resources or hanging the system.

primary colors The three colors needed to reproduce color images. For additive color systems that combine colored light, such as video displays, the primaries are red, green, and blue. For subtractive color systems that use color filters or inks, such as photography or color printing, the primaries are magenta, cyan, and yellow.

process In a multitasking operating system, the name given to an executable entity (typically an application). In some systems, processes can contain subblocks, called *threads*.

production In video, refers to the process of creating programs. In more specific usage, production is the process of getting original video onto tape or film and ready for postproduction.

productivity In computer applications, refers to applications that assist the user in doing his job. Typical productivity applications are word processing, spreadsheets, and planning.

pulse code modulation (PCM) The system of sampling an analog waveform and quantizing the samples to produce a digital data stream representing the analog waveform.

quantization In digitization, the process of converting samples to digital values.

quantization noise The visual or aural effect caused by poor quantization (usually too few bits).

RAM *See* random-access memory

random-access memory (RAM) Memory that can be directly accessed at any location, for example, at every byte position. RAM usually refers to the main memory of a computer, which is solid-state read/write memory.

read-only memory (ROM) A special type of solid-state memory where the data is permanently written into the chips and cannot be changed after chip production. It is especially used for holding the BIOS software in PCs.

reference frame In video compression, a frame that contains all its own data and can be reproduced independent of previous or future frames.

render In computer graphics, the process of creating an image or screen from mathematical or computer-language descriptions.

resolution The ability of a video system to reproduce fine detail. In analog systems it is defined by the number of scanning lines and the bandwidth; in digital systems it is determined by the number of pixels in the horizontal and vertical directions.

retrace The returning of a scanning spot to a start position to begin a new line or a new field.

reverberation In audio systems, reverberation is the multiple echoes that occur in an enclosed space, such as a concert hall or church. The effect can be achieved electronically by the use of delays.

RGB Refers to red, green, blue, the additive color primaries. An RGB video system has three signal wires, one for each of the primary colors.

RLE *See* run-length encoding

ROM *See* read-only memory

run-length encoding (RLE) A data compression technique that exploits equality of adjacent data objects such as bytes or pixels.

runtime module A separate application that plays back the output of an authoring assembly tool. Runtime modules are distributed at low cost or sometimes even free.

S-video A two-channel component video format that handles the chroma and luminance components in two separate channels. It provides better performance than NTSC and is used to interface the latest VCRs, TVs, and monitors.

S/N *See* signal to noise ratio

sampling The process of reading the values of an analog signal at evenly spaced points in time.

sampling rate The clock frequency for sampling or the number of samples per second.

scaling A process for changing the size of an image.

scanner A device that converts hard copy images or photographs to a bitmapped digital image by moving an image sensing device across the image (scanning).

SCSI *See* small computer system interface

SECAM Acronym for *sequential coleur et memoire,* the color TV system developed in France and used there, in Russia, and in various other countries in Eastern Europe.

sensor A device for converting natural sources such as audio (microphone) or video (CCD chip) into electrical signals.

signal to noise ratio A measure of the amount of noise present in an analog system. It is usually expressed in dB.

small computer system interface (SCSI) A special bus for connecting devices to a PC. Most often used to connect CD-ROM or hard disk drives.

spectrum Refers to a display of the frequency content of a signal. It is normally displayed as a graph of energy content vs. frequency.

storyboard A method of planning the content of a presentation by drawing sketches of each screen with notes about what happens in that scene.

subsampling In video compression, the process of reducing the pixel count for the color components of an image, done by discarding samples in a regular pattern.

subtractive color Color reproduction by mixing appropriate amounts of color paints or dyes on white paper, used for color painting and printing. The color print primaries are "red," "blue," and yellow. Note that "red" as used in printing is technically a magenta color, and "blue" is technically a cyan color.

Super VGA (SVGA) An extension to the VGA specification that offers increased resolution and/or increased number of colors. The use of Super VGA requires increased video memory and higher-performance display monitors.

SVGA *See* Super VGA

sweetening In audio postproduction, the process of electronically manipulating audio to make it sound better.

system bus The main bus in a PC.

talking head In video and audio production, a close-up shot of someone speaking.

thread In some multitasking operating systems, one or more concurrently executing tasks may exist within a process—these are called *threads*.

time code In video or audio recording, a track that records an unique time or frame-count code for subsequent use to identify cuts for editing.

transducer Another word for *sensor*.

transparency In a digital image, the process of defining one or more color values that will not be reproduced when the image is copied over another image. Instead, pixels having the transparency values will still display the previous image. This is used to overlay objects over a background, such as the weathercaster standing in front of a weather map background.

treatment A written narrative that describes the proposed operation of a new application.

tristimulus The use of three *primary* signals to represent color information, such as red, green, and blue.

true color A digital display system that uses 24 bits per pixel, thus being capable of displaying 16,777,216 colors.

tweening In animation, the process of creating new frames between other frames to smooth out the motion displayed by the frames. The original frames are called *key frames*. In computer animation, tweening is often accomplished with a morphing algorithm.

user interface The means by which a user communicates with a computer. It includes not only the devices used (mouse, keyboard, touch), but also the objects on the screen and the sounds made by the computer in response to the user.

VCR *See* video cassette recorder

VGA *See* video graphics array

VHS-C A modification of the VHS VCR recording cassette in a smaller size for portable recording. VHS-C cassettes are playable on standard VHS VCRs by means of an adaptor.

video cassette recorder (VCR) Equipment that records and plays back video and audio from a videotape cassette. VCR standards are available for home, professional, and broadcast use.

video graphics array (VGA) This is the standard display type for most PCs. VGA provides many optional formats, but the most common one is 640 × 480 pixels with 16 colors.

video overlay Analog video that has been converted so it can be shown on a computer display along with the computer's own images and graphics.

VL bus This is one standard for a local bus that couples the video display adaptor directly with the CPU.

voice-over In audio postproduction, the technique of using a narration track instead of or in addition to natural sound from the scene.

WAVE A standard for digital audio based on PCM sampling of analog audio without compression.

wavetable In digital music synthesis, the storing of sampled segments of actual instrument sounds from which are assembled musical notes at any pitch.

wireframe In 2-D or 3-D rendering, the display of objects as outlines to speed rendering for testing purposes.

Bibliography

The following list is not meant to be an exhaustive bibliography of multimedia publications. It is a list of the books and periodicals that I reviewed before writing this book.

BOOKS

Benford, Tom, *Welcome to PC Sound, Music, and MIDI*, New York: MIS Press, 1993.

Bunzel, Mark J., and Morris, Sandra K., *Multimedia Applications Development*, second edition, New York: McGraw-Hill, 1993.

Desmarais, Norman, *Multimedia on the PC*, New York: McGraw-Hill, 1994

Fetterman, Roger L., and Gupta, Satish K., *Mainstream Multimedia*, New York: Van Nostrand Reinhold, 1993.

Koegel-Buford, John F., *Multimedia Systems*, New York: ACM Press, 1994.

Luther, Arch C., *Digital Video in the PC Environment*, second edition, New York: McGraw-Hill, 1991.

———, *Desiging Interactive Multimedia*, New York: Bantam Books, 1992.

———, *Authoring Interactive Multimedia*, Boston: AP Professional, 1994.

Microsoft Corporation, *Microsoft Windows Multimedia Authoring and Tools Guide*, Redmond, WA: Microsoft Press, 1991.

———, *Microsoft Windows Multimedia Programmer's Workbook*, Redmond, WA: Microsoft Press, 1991.

Parker, Dana J., and Starrett, Robert A., *A Guide to CD-ROM*, Carmel, IN: New Riders Publishing, 1992.

Radecki, Steven, *Multimedia with Quicktime*, Cambridge, MA: AP Professional, 1994.

von Wodtke, Mark, *Mind over Media*, New York: McGraw-Hill, 1993.

Wodaski, Ron, *PC Video Madness!*, Carmel, IN: Sams Publishing, 1993.

Yager, Tom, *The Multimedia Production Handbook*, Cambridge, MA: AP Professional, 1993.

PERIODICALS

Aldus Magazine, published by Aldus Corporation, 411 First Ave. S., Seattle, WA 98104-2871.

AV Video, published monthly by Montage Publishing, Inc., 701 Westchester Ave., White Plains, NY 10604.

Byte, published monthly by McGraw-Hill, Inc., 1 Phoenix Mill Lane, Peterborough, NH 03458.

Computer Pictures, published bimonthly by Montage Publishing, Inc., 701 Westchester Ave., White Plains, NY 10604.p

Keyboard, published monthly by Miller Freeman, Inc., 600 Harrison St., San Francisco, CA 94107.

OS/2 Magazine, published monthly by Miller Freeman, Inc., 600 Harrison St., San Francisco, CA 94107.

OS/2 Professional, published monthly by I. F. Computer Media, Inc., 172 Rollins Ave., Rockville, MD 20852.

PC World, published monthly by PC World Communications, Inc., 501 Second St. #600, San Francisco, CA 94107.

Videomaker, published monthly by Videomaker, Inc., PO Box 4591, Chich, CA 995927.

Windows Magazine, published monthly by CMP Publications, Inc., 600 Community Drive, Manhasset, NY 11030.

CD-ROM

Microsoft Developer Network CD, Disc Five, Microsoft Corporation: Seattle, WA, 1993.

Index